TEXAS ZYDECO

Brad and Michele Moore Roots Music Series

TEXAS ZYDECO

BY ROGER WOOD   PHOTOGRAPHY BY JAMES FRAHER

UNIVERSITY OF TEXAS PRESS *Austin*

Requests for permission to reproduce material from this work should be sent to:
Permissions   University of Texas Press   P.O. Box 7819   Austin, TX 78713-7819
www.utexas.edu/utpress/about/bpermission.html

♾ The paper used in this book meets the minimum requirements of
ANSI/NISO Z39.48-1992 (R1997) (Permanence of Paper).

LIBRARY OF CONGRESS CATALOGING-IN-PUBLICATION DATA

Wood, Charles Roger, 1956–
Texas zydeco / by Roger Wood ; photography by James Fraher.— 1st ed.
          p.   cm.
Includes bibliographical references (p.   ) and index.
ISBN-13: 978-0-292-71258-4 (cl. : alk. paper)
ISBN-10: 0-292-71258-8
1. Zydeco music—Texas—History and criticism. 2. Zydeco musicians—Texas.
I. Fraher, James. II. Title.
ML3560.C25W66 2006
781.62'410764—dc22   2005035649

To Mack McCormick

and

to the memory of
Doris Clifton McClendon,
the Continental Zydeco Ballroom,
and Frenchtown.

CONTENTS

ACKNOWLEDGMENTS

Roger Wood and James Fraher hereby express special gratitude to the following individuals and organizations:

Mack McCormick, Carl Lindahl and the University of Houston Folklore Archive, Tom McLendon and his Big Easy Social and Pleasure Club archive, Steve "Red" Delasbour and Across the Board Entertainment, Joe Norman and zydecoevents.com, Ed Berry, John Minton, Richard Allen Burns, Andrew Brown and his Texas music history archive, Chris Strachwitz, Pat Jasper, Alan Ainsworth, Edwin Gallaher, Ruben Duran, Gay Ann Gustafson, Thomas Randolph, Mary Thomas, Gerald Joseph, John Mayhon, Nancy Bless and Texas Folklife Resources, Brett Bonner and *Living Blues,* John Nova Lomax and the *Houston Press,* Reg Burns, Maria Muñoz-Blanco, Rick Mitchell, Guy Michael Anderson and his *Eh Toi!* archive, the Houston Community College System, the University of Chicago Folk Festival, Alligator Records, Tom Radai, Gary Hartman and the Center for Texas Music History, Steve Sucher and the Musicians Benevolent Society of Houston, Project Row Houses, KPFT-FM radio, the Houston Blues Society, the Reverend Carl E. Isaac and First Morning Star Missionary Baptist Church of Houston, the Reverend Francis X. Conroy and St. Pius Catholic Church of Beaumont, St. Anne de Beaupre Catholic Church of Houston, St. Francis of Assisi Catholic Church of Houston, St. Mark the Evangelist Catholic Church of Houston, the staff at the

San Jacinto Battleground State Historic Site, the administration and staff at the University of Texas Press (especially Theresa May), the many zydeco people we met and documented, and, as always, Marla and Connie.

All direct quotations in this book, unless otherwise indicated, come from interviews documented in the Appendix, which follows the main text.

Minor portions of this book incorporate revisions of passages from articles previously published by the author in the *Journal of Texas Music History* and the *Houston Press*. The writing of this book was supported in part by a Sabbatical Leave Award granted to the author by the Houston Community College System.

TEXAS ZYDECO

INTRODUCTION
Along the Zydeco Corridor

No matter where you may have lived or traveled or what your tastes in music might be, somewhere along the way you have likely encountered the uncanny sound of zydeco. For many people it is but a fleeting moment of exposure, leaving them slightly confused but somehow enthused by their sudden involuntary foot-tapping. For certain others it is an even more visceral awakening, the start of an ongoing relationship with a potent force. For some, there is no memory of their first encounter, for they have known it all their lives.

This music of black Creoles from the upper western coast of the Gulf of Mexico once percolated in obscurity. Even in the areas where it originated, the antecedents and early forms of zydeco epitomized the notion of a pure folk idiom: created, performed, taught, and appreciated only within a specific rural subculture. By the 1950s and '60s, however, that rustic sound was evolving, incorporating urban influences, and attracting some attention beyond its home region and primary ethnic group of origin, mainly among certain aficionados of American roots music.

By the mid-1980s zydeco had emerged here and there in the mainstream of popular culture, energizing the sound-tracks of various Hollywood films, television programs, and advertising spots as well as becoming widely available to an expanding fan base through a proliferation of audio recordings. Some of those recordings presented this vibrant music on its own terms; others used it to enliven genre-hopping productions by experimental rock 'n' rollers or pop singers. Whatever the case, it has been out there—in pure form or diluted—for many to hear, and not just as a commodity of the electronic media.

A late-twentieth-century renaissance of the intertwining of Creole and Cajun cuisines continues to sizzle nationwide, and this marketing phenomenon has spawned new venues (especially along the Gulf Coast) in the form of theme restaurants that regularly host the live performance of zydeco. As a consequence, countless people first hear this music simply because they crave some spicy seafood. And at the many multicultural festivals now produced throughout the nation, the appeal of zydeco strikes fresh ears every year, introducing them to the basic elements of an irresistible sound.

Foremost in that sound is the presence of the accordion, a unique musical machine not widely featured, and sometimes derided, in mainstream American pop music. But in zydeco, as in certain other ethnomusical subcultures, this hand-operated bellows-flexing wind instrument is absolutely essential. Moreover, its master players, who usually double as lead singers, are highly venerated. Whether they are pumping out a rapid two-step boogie or euphoniously easing through a slow-drag waltz, the men and women who wield the squeezebox are the kings and queens of this music.

But in contrast to other accordion-based forms, zydeco requires that its dominant instrument be paired with the highly percussive rubboard vest (also referred to as the scrub board and, in French, as *le frottoir,* from the verb *frotter,* "to rub"). Unlike the handheld washboard once common in jug bands and such, this device is not a household utensil but a customized modern musical instrument. Designed to hang from the shoulders of the percussionist, it allows for a much larger metallic surface to cover the torso—and liberates both hands to clutch the various implements used to conjure the genre's complex polyrhythms. Though now sometimes adopted by others, the rubboard vest was invented by and first popularized among zydeco players. With this tool they have defined the gritty chank-a-chank rhythms that are as fundamental to this music as the reedy chords and funky riffs coming from the accordion.

These days a typical zydeco band comprises five pieces. The seminal instruments, accordion and rubboard, are prominently featured. Electric guitar, bass, and drums most commonly provide the supporting accompaniment, coalescing with the primary duo to forge a distinctive mix. The songs draw from a traditional repertoire informed by blues, ballads, shuffles, and waltzes, now also often infused with a gumbo of other, postmodern influences. The vocalizing may be in English or French, though the latter grows less common with each generation of players. But this music has one priority far more compelling than linguistics or lyrics: it makes you want to dance.

Texas swamp, Chambers County, 2004.

Whether you have publicly succumbed to that impulse or not, you know the feeling, for you have heard that seductive sound.

So here is a question: what large metropolis of the upper Gulf Coast is arguably the most crucial, historically speaking, in the mid-twentieth-century development of modern zydeco? To put it another way: in which big city did the folk music of black Creoles from southwest Louisiana first undergo a major synthesis with urban influences to create, document, and codify that sound you have come to know?

If you answered New Orleans (the music capital of Louisiana and the largest city in that state), you are incorrect, though the Crescent City has done a splendid job of cashing in on zydeco's fairly recent popularity.

Actually, it was in Houston, now the nation's fourth-largest city, that black Creole immigrants and their descendants first prominently fused the old French Louisiana folk music known as la-la with urban blues to create the new sound that came to be known, spelled, and recorded as "zydeco." In fact, as this book will show, several key innovations in the evolution of this music—concerning not only its name but also its instruments, recording history, leading figures, and stylistic twists and turns—occurred initially in Texas, where numerous important zydeco artists reside and perform today.

The lower southeastern corner of the Lone Star State stretches westward from the Louisiana boundary at the Sabine River, following the coastal bend in a swath over one hundred miles wide and long, past Galveston. Among certain folks this region is jokingly referred to as "Louisiana Lapland"—that is, the place where a large piece of south Louisiana seems to have "lapped over" into Texas. And indeed in many respects this area often mirrors southwestern Louisiana more than it does the rest of the state of Texas.

Since the early twentieth century it has also maintained a sizable population of black Creoles, with fresh infusions immigrating regularly. Apart from the sense that the general environment of the upper Texas coast is a lot like home, black Creole families over the years have typically made the relatively short relocation to Houston and the surrounding area for a single reason: employment.

In search of improved living conditions, many of these Creoles (not to be confused with white Cajuns, a different ethnic group with whom they do have much in common) first settled in Texas enclaves such as the Frenchtown district in Houston's Fifth Ward or the village of Barrett Station, north of Baytown. Often having abandoned meager sharecropping arrangements back in rural Louisiana, they found higher-paying job opportunities in the multitude of large refineries, petrochemical plants, railroad yards, international shipping docks, and other industries concentrated in the greater Houston area, as well as in nearby Beaumont and Port Arthur. They brought with them the acoustic folk-music idiom called la-la, which soon was exposed to and absorbed new urban influences. In so doing it profoundly changed, morphing into early zydeco, the progenitor of that syncopated accordion-based sound that the rest of the nation discovered in the 1980s.

By leaving the insular culture of their people in south Louisiana and transplanting their families to industrial Texas cities, many black Creoles chose to reconcile themselves to change and adapt to a new kind of life, at least to some degree. The impact on the traditional folk music they imported from back home was immense. In its evolved form, this exciting offspring was soon exported back to Louisiana, profoundly influencing the subsequent definition of zydeco at large.

In reviewing and analyzing the history of this back-and-forth social-musical syncretism and its present ramifications, this book by no means intends to deny that Louisiana is the primal territory for black Creole culture of the Gulf Coast. Simply put, without Louisiana there would be no zydeco—yesterday, today, or tomorrow. It is the zydeco motherland. However, an accurate and complete appreciation of the heritage (and the future) of this music must include an understanding of certain people and developments in Texas.

By analogy, without the Mississippi Delta or similar regions in the Deep South, there theoretically would be no blues music. Yet consider how significantly blues was changed when Southern blacks, with their folk music traditions, migrated to northern industrial cities, most notably Chicago, birthplace of the modern form of the genre. And consider how it is precisely that newer, urban style that has since dominated popular culture, even back in the South. And finally consider where the larger concentrations of blues musicians live and work today. Thus, to understand fully what blues music is, what it has been, and where it is going, one obviously must recognize the role of Chicago.

In short, as Michael Tisserand acknowledges in *The Kingdom of Zydeco,* Houston's role in the maturation and popularization of modern zydeco is in many ways similar to Chicago's in relation to blues. Yet the Bayou City, like southeast Texas in general, rarely registers in popular consciousness as the zydeco mecca it has been for many years. Both its historical role and its ongoing vitality are typically overlooked in the common representation of this music as a purely rural Louisiana phenomenon.

One of the main reasons for that discrepancy is probably a lack of distance, both physical and sociocultural. Moving from southwest Louisiana to nearby Houston, Beaumont, or Port Arthur is not a particularly demanding journey, in terms of either miles or cost. Moreover, the proximity of Louisiana to southeast Texas allows for frequent trips back and forth, facilitating personal and cultural interchanges that have constantly reinforced the black Creole Texans' connection to their families' native parishes. For them the state line was and is merely a political boundary.

Today that portion of I-10 that connects the southeast Texas cities of Houston and Beaumont to the southwest Louisiana cities of Lake Charles and Lafayette might well be

Peter and Rita Manuel at home, Port Arthur, Texas, 2003.

proclaimed the zydeco corridor of the world. Extending an almost equal distance on either side of the Sabine River, this is a heavily traveled section of road familiar to practically every zydeco musician. While many of them play festivals nationwide and tour beyond the Gulf Coast whenever they can, this stretch of east-west thoroughfare demarcates their primary circuit. It is the main route to their regular gigs, families, and friends—and getting from one to another often necessitates crossing that Texas-Louisiana state line.

What is particularly exciting is that so many, though certainly not all, of the zydeco musicians who regularly traverse that corridor today are relatively young, not even yet middle-aged, a key point of contrast with the distinguished but now mostly elderly African American blues community of the same region. At the start of the twenty-first century, southeast Texas alone is home to hundreds of regularly performing zydeco players younger than forty, many in their twenties and some still in their teens or younger. It obviously bodes well for the future of this amazing music, but it did not happen by chance. The cross-cultural foundation was laid long ago, back when the black Creole music called la-la first came to the Lone Star State and transformed itself forever.

This book is the result of a close collaboration between two men who appreciate that music, the people who make it, and those who dance to it. Together we offer verbal and visual evidence to support the contention that the phrase "Texas zydeco" is not an oxymoron but a cultural fact.

Zydeco on the covered patio (with Billy Poullard and the Zydeco Combo),
Pine Tree Lodge, LaBelle, Texas, 2004.

One { SOUTHEAST TEXAS HOTBED

A flat-bottomed airboat roars around the bend, heaving its wake into mats of blossoming lily pads and thick stands of cattail reeds. Chocolate-milky water splashes over marshy banks, soaking the knotted roots of tall cypress. A snowy egret wings up and onto a moss-laden branch. Then, like the floating alligator that vanished only moments before, the fan-powered watercraft is suddenly gone, the noise of its engine fading as it speeds around the tree-shrouded curve. Here and there along the surface, turtle snouts poke through the murky liquid for air. The choral buzz of countless unseen insects resumes.

But there is another sound that never ceases during this transient disturbance of the scene. It comes from a large wooden building overlooking this oxbow branch of Taylor Bayou. There, where the dirt road dead-ends, parked automobiles, trucks, and motorcycles rim the clearing—their drivers and riders now disembarked and congregating on the spacious covered patio, close to the point of origin for this live music, a waltz.

While drums, bass, and rubboard maintain the classic pattern of three-quarter time, the guitarist extends his solo, making the strings articulate a mournful melody. Then, with a nod, he resumes the rhythmic chording and yields to a nearby accordionist, whose instrument promptly tells the sad story once again—not in words, but with a sound as old as the surrounding forest. Later, as he squeezes and pulls his way to the start of another chorus, the man with the old-style button accordion closes his eyes and earnestly sings in French, the language of his ancestors. And though many in his audience cannot literally translate the lyrics, everyone seems to understand and appreciate the dominant passions they convey. In return, he will perform many selections from his personal repertoire of *la musique française* over the course of this summer afternoon, a Saturday, at the Pine Tree Lodge.

This down-home restaurant is located in Jefferson County, Texas, in the relatively sparsely populated community of LaBelle, about ten miles south of Beaumont and twenty-five miles west of Louisiana. As Robert Wooster documents in *The New Handbook of Texas*, settlers have resided in this "fertile but flood-prone" area since the 1830s, but it did not acquire its proper name until 1888, when postmaster J. E. Broussard christened his isolated office "LaBelle" as a tribute to Mary Bell Bordages, his fiancée.

According to current coproprietor Norma Miller, LaBelle's original Pine Tree Lodge dates back to the 1920s, when it was first constructed on this same site. She proudly points to a framed copy of an old black-and-white photograph depicting a smaller, more rustic building, its façade covered with signs advertising Falstaff Beer, Royal Crown Cola, and other treats. Destroyed by fire twice in its history, the establishment was reborn in 1984 when Norma and her husband, Ken, purchased the property. They repaired, remodeled, and eventually expanded it to include the attached covered space where the music is now performed.

It is an open-air, rectangular-shaped patio room with a roof-support structure built of raw cedar and pine. Short fencing made of black metal bars forms partial walls on the three sides of the slab closest to the bayou. The one solid wall, where a door leads from this outdoor dining area into the primary restaurant, displays a large bulletin board covered with a green background material. Mounted on it are various snapshots of smiling people, and a sign: "1st Annual SE TEX BBQ COOK OFF WINNER / Pine Tree Lodge." Prominently affixed to the same bulletin board are the skull of a cow and, turned sideways, a large jawbone. Framed documents nearby include two *Beaumont Enterprise* Reader's Choice Awards for "Best Catfish." There are also similar prizes bestowed by other groups, including readers of the *Port Arthur News*. Such memorabilia attests not only to the quality of the country cooking served here, but also to the fact that many people from neighboring cities have made the trip down the rural road that ends at the Pine Tree Lodge.

Meanwhile, six ceiling fans churn the humid air, and strings of Christmas lights faintly glow along the edge of the ceiling. The band starts another number, introduced as "The Eunice Two-Step," immediately enticing couples back onto the cement floor in front of the stage. Wearing a heavy-duty bib-apron to protect his instrument from the sweat he generates, the accordionist works to bring forth the familiar tune, a classic shared by Cajuns and Creoles alike. At the end of the first verse he joyfully shouts, "I'm Billy Poullard, and I always like to dance!" And though he stays center stage to continue the song, he and the rubboard-player, his son, begin to sway sprightly from side to side in synchronized step. Soon the large

Billy Poullard, Pine Tree Lodge, LaBelle, Texas, 2004.

man on bass guitar joins in, and the threesome moves like a choreographed unit, locked in a happy groove with the music.

More patrons arrive, rushing straight for the dance floor or settling into the few remaining metal chairs around the tables. Among them are senior citizens, middle-agers (including a large contingent of motorbikers), and a few youngsters. Some of the black folks are Creoles, and some of the white folks are Cajuns; however, many of the patrons are not of French descent. Despite their differences in age, race, and ethnicity, it is evident that all of the people gathered here—that is, outside, beyond the air-conditioned sanctuary of the restaurant's interior—must really enjoy this music. And they seem to respect and appreciate each other too because of that common bond. For them, hearing these songs, dancing these steps, and seeing these friends make up an experience that matters more than the mugginess and occasional mosquitoes that come with it.

Later, while the band breaks briefly, some audience members focus on consuming and replenishing their drinks. Others return to plates of food now gone cold, edibles that had been promptly abandoned when the dance tunes commenced. Waitresses are summoned, and new orders placed. Folks throughout the room greet each other, old acquaintances and strangers alike. Almost everyone seems to be talking or laughing, contributing to this din of good-natured banter. But one gray-haired gentleman stands alone directly below one of the fans, facing upward toward the rotating blades, both of his arms slightly raised, grateful. He holds that breeze-induced posture for a full minute, as if in a trance. Finally he moves, swabbing his forehead with a white handkerchief. As he turns to shuffle back to his seat, he loudly proclaims, "Yeah, baby! It is *hot* out here today!" Then, after another pass of the cloth across his face, he adds, "But so is the zydeco!"

"LAST YEAR AT THIS TIME, THE PLACE WAS ALREADY PACKED," says Red, to nobody in particular. He gazes out at the preshow audience, over a thousand strong and still arriving, then glances momentarily toward the overcast sky and puddles of rain beyond the covered rodeo arena. He is standing on the dirt floor in the almost deserted side-stage area, directly beneath a banner that features a cartoon crawfish wearing a purple and gold vest and holding a sign that proclaims "Original Zydeco Jamm Festival 2004." It is a little more than half past noon, nearly a full hour before the first of eight groups is scheduled to perform in a marathon program that will conclude sometime after midnight. Clutching a sporadically blaring walkie-talkie in one hand and a bottle of water in the other, Red orchestrates the final preparations for this massive gathering of zydeco people, a phenomenon that occurs here every March.

"This time last year, you couldn't even see the bleachers. You couldn't even see the dirt," he proclaims to anyone within earshot. Given his professional and financial investment in this

Food vendors, Original Zydeco Jamm Festival, Crosby, Texas, 2004.

large-scale production, his fretting over the wet weather and its possible impact on attendance is certainly justified. But to most of the many patrons eagerly settling into this sprawling venue, the forecast for a rainy Saturday now provokes scant concern.

After all, they are fairly dry, protected overhead by a galvanized metal roof that runs the full length of the rectangular stadium. Now and then through the smudgy skylight panels there is a faint flash of lightning, but it is distant and nonthreatening. Spaced at regular intervals along the sides, cylindrical posts uphold the rust-colored crossbeams that span the underside of the huge roof. Otherwise, inside this structure there are no floor-to-ceiling walls, just chain-link fencing around the perimeter. So the breezes blow freely and, though chilled a bit by the moisture, are comfortable, approximately sixty to sixty-five degrees Fahrenheit.

On the south side of the arena is a large meadow, gradually dissolving to mud, where teams of attendants direct drivers to park their cars and trucks. To the north is a little impromptu village of RVs and tents where some patrons and many of the numerous independent vendors have camped out since Friday night—and where a few clusters of people still congregate under awnings and canopies, consuming food and drink. But most of the campers are already somewhere within the large pavilion, where Red supervises the constantly evolving last-minute preparations and surveys the gathering crowd.

Tall rows of aluminum bleachers line the north and south sidelines, yet for now only scattered people sit there. The most coveted space for the general audience is obviously the expansive field of dirt between the bleachers; that is where folks are congregating. The solid ground there makes it more conducive to stretching out, mingling, and dancing. Moreover, from that vantage point spectators directly face the front edge of the stage, which spans most of the east side of the facility.

On the opposite end of the arena field is another prime location—an elevated viewing platform packed with tables and chairs, enough to hold perhaps eighty to one hundred people. It is a second-story VIP room of sorts, reserved for event sponsors, their associates, and special guests. From an elaborate system of scaffolding, flooring, railings, and prefabricated stairways, it has been constructed especially for the occasion, to be dismantled in the aftermath. Positioned directly inside the main entrance gates, its skeletal columns straddle the dirt floor. They support a rarefied haven, which appears almost to hover over what will soon become a throng of bodies swaying to the zydeco beat.

On the ground directly in front of that privileged space is another temporary installation: a wooden dance floor, approximately forty by sixty feet. Now empty, it will later be filled with dancers competing in a formal two-step contest, complete with rules and judges. Closer to the stage is a layout of approximately eighty to ninety tables, each covered by a red or green tablecloth, and each accompanied by eight metal-framed hard-plastic chairs. The earliest arrivers, eschewing the bleachers for the most part, have already claimed much of this available ground-level seating and established their personal headquarters for the upcoming eleven-hour event.

"Hey-ey-ey-ey, zy-de-CO!" shouts a tall man, raising a plastic cup, prolonging the "hey" in an extended call to party, then emphasizing the final syllable of that magical word "zydeco," according to the traditional Creole pronunciation. His spontaneous exhortation provokes a series of whoops, whistles, and hollers that fade back into the buzz of hundreds of conversations taking place at once.

Along the margins and near the aisles, other folks are setting up their own portable lawn chairs, getting positioned for the show that will soon commence on the stage. Directly in front of it, lines of white tape affixed to the bare ground demarcate a spacious rectangle. That dusty territory has been designated as the primary public dancing area for the night, open to all comers. Whatever it may lack in refinements, it compensates by its proximity to the four-foot-high platform where a succession of bands will perform.

In vendors' booths back near the main entrance, smoke pours from big barrel pits; deep fryers hiss and sizzle. The smells of particular foods waft and merge, pervading the whole scene: boiled crawfish and shrimp, simmering gumbo, barbecued beef, smoked turkey, fried catfish, cotton candy, corn dogs, and more—all accented by a pungent undercurrent of red pepper sauce and beer.

The crowd is overwhelmingly African American, in all the diverse possibilities of skin tone that label can imply. They range in age from toddlers to adolescents to young adults to the middle-aged and even elderly. At some tables what appears to be several generations of a family are seated together, sharing food and—in a rare phenomenon in postmodern America—the same taste in music, at least for the day. Males and females are dressed in a variety of casual styles. Some evoke the look of rural cowboys duded up for a Saturday-night party, while others reflect more recent urban trends. In fact, on the floor near the stage there is an almost equal balance between those sporting crisply trimmed straw hats, tight jeans, rodeo-style belt buckles, and pointed-toe boots and those wearing do-rags, athletic jerseys, baggy pants, and Nikes.

What power draws all these black folks together in this relatively remote location, despite their differences in age and attire, and on a rain-soaked Saturday at that? As one festival attendee, a recent convert to the music, exclaims, "This zydeco, if you get hooked, it's worse than pot! . . . It'll take you over!" But there's clearly something much deeper than that.

"It's more than just music," asserts Gerald Wayne Joseph (b. 1956). "It reflects a culture of a people." A Houston-born Creole and devoted zydeco aficionado who has absorbed this

Boy with sign, Original Zydeco Jamm Festival, Crosby, Texas, 2004.

Dancers, Original Zydeco Jamm Festival, Crosby, Texas, 2004.

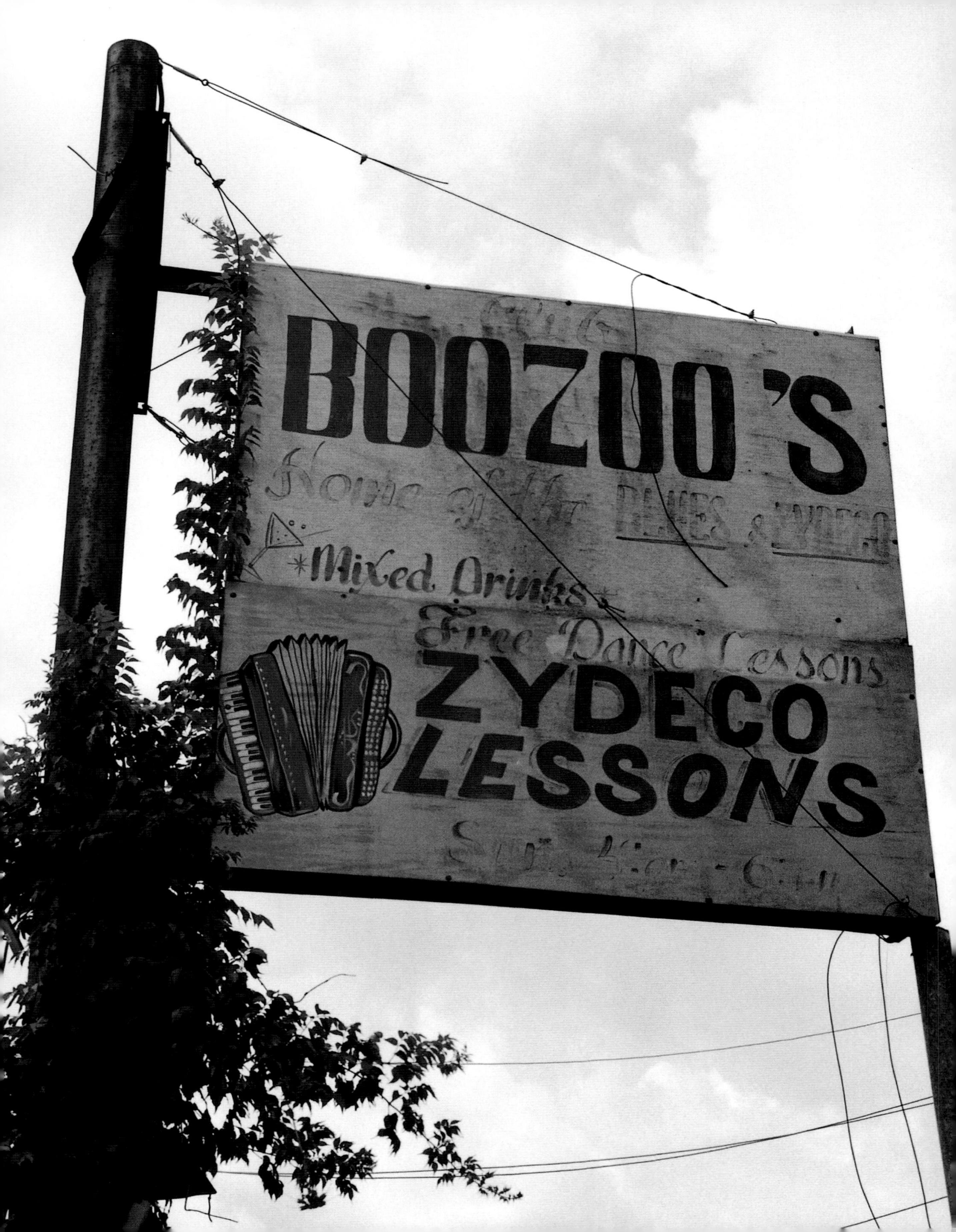
BOOZOO'S
Mixed Drinks
Free Dance Lessons
ZYDECO
LESSONS

unique experience since his infancy, he explains, "I guess the cliche would be that, 'I was zydeco when zydeco wasn't cool'—when it was not widely accepted or played on the radio." He adds that it is "more of a regional type of music" that has been "harnessed and kept within a group of people." To Joseph, it is a tangible, living embodiment of black Creole culture, a major conduit to his personal heritage. "That's what zydeco represents—more than just the music. It's indicative of a people."

What some outsiders, and even some zydeco fans nationwide, might not fully appreciate is the extended locus of that culture. Many of the black Creoles who have played key roles in the history of zydeco have done so here—not exclusively back in the neighboring ancestral motherland of south Louisiana, but here, where we are now, approximately one hundred miles due west of the state line in southeast Texas.

To be more precise, we are currently in Crosby, Texas, a working-class town of nearly 2,000 people, approximately twenty-five miles northeast of Houston, just beyond the San Jacinto River. It is located in far eastern Harris County, close to both Liberty County and Chambers County—an area long familiar to generations of black Creoles. As Roxanne J. Evans points out in *The New Handbook of Texas*, the disastrous 1927 flood of the Mississippi River once "sent blacks fleeing to Crosby" from south Louisiana, and "many of them were Catholic," a fact implying an increased likelihood of their Creole descent.

Today, however, many of the people actually residing within the Crosby city limits are not African American. Yet less than three miles to the south, down the main road, is the predominantly black town of Barrett, known historically as Barrett's Settlement after the emancipated slave who founded the community, and often referred to colloquially as Barrett Station. The current population there numbers almost 3,000, many of whom have been involved with the Crosby festival—as producers, performers, and fans—since its inception.

Among the several zydeco musicians who were born or raised in Barrett, the most prominent is probably Brian Terry (b. 1973), the leader of Lil' Brian and the Zydeco Travelers. As he explains, "Whenever my mom and dad moved from Louisiana, that was the one spot they stopped at and made home. . . . Basically you can almost call it a little Louisiana."

For him, as for many people who support the annual Original Zydeco Jamm Festival, places such as Crosby and Barrett are distinctive small towns yet also, in some ways, an extension of metropolitan Houston. In 1997, Terry paid tribute to that collective scene in the song "H-Town Zydeco," the opening track on his groundbreaking CD, *Z-Funk*, on Rounder Records. While the lyrics celebrate the vibrancy of Houston's (i.e., "H-Town's") burgeoning zydeco culture, they also include a reference to "the Crosby Fairgrounds," a line that some listeners probably still don't fully comprehend. But zydeco insiders can readily decode the allusion. For over a decade now, Crosby has established itself as home to one of the nation's premiere zydeco festivals, providing a major showcase for talent from the cradle land of

OPPOSITE PAGE: *Club Boozoo's sign, Barrett, Texas, 2004.*

southeast Texas and southwest Louisiana. For instance, as San Francisco–based Andrea D. Rubinstein has written of her experience at the 2001 version of the gathering in Crosby:

I witnessed an event unlike any other zydeco festival I have been to in the 7 years I have been a fan of this music. If you can imagine zydeco presented in a stadium, rock & roll style, with overhead video screens, over 10 TV monitors presenting the on-stage action to the fans in the stands, laser light shows, explosions of flashing lights and smoke machines on stage, fabulous stage costumes on the performers, second line marching bands & karate acts sharing the stage while zydeco acts played, and a squad of dancers looking like cheerleaders choreographed to zydeco music, you only have a small sense of what it was like to be at the Zydeco Jamm, with a crowd of nearly 10,000 other zydeco fans.

"Man, I tell you, we started small in Crosby, but it's just gotten huge," says event cofounder and promoter Steve "Red" Delasbour. "We take a rodeo arena and convert it to a concert theater. The normal arena capacity is approximately 10,000, but we reconfigure the place, enlarge it so the grounds can hold even more."

Delasbour proudly claims to offer one of the largest single-day gatherings of "some of the hottest zydeco bands in the world," usually ranging in number from eight to eleven groups. And while you might expect such hype from a festival promoter, a quick scan of the lineup for any given year generally supports that claim. It also reveals what, to some, may be a surprising fact: the face of zydeco is getting younger. With a few exceptions, the old-timers who first introduced zydeco to popular consciousness are passing on and being supplanted by a new generation of players, many still in their twenties or thirties, and many of those possessing an image-savvy sensibility that speaks to mainstream urban audiences.

As Delasbour is quick to point out, his festival draws fans of all ages. But its rapid growth through the late 1990s and into the twenty-first century follows directly from the emergence of numerous youth-culture-friendly Texas zydeco acts with band names such as the NuBreedz, the Outlaws, the Floaters, or the Badboyz. Part of Delasbour's success undoubtedly lies in his willingness to cater to this younger crowd, and doing so, especially at such a large-scale event, requires the right technology. "Traditionally in zydeco, a lot of promoters don't have good sound production," he says. "But we're spending a lot of dollars on sound, lighting, stages, and curtains. It's going to be quite a show." Indeed, the quantity and quality of equipment and technicians are consistently first-rate, and the overall production values, though perhaps not the setting, rival those of any major-league pop concert.

Such a state-of-the-art high-tech installation in the midst of a no-frills decades-old rodeo arena is in some respects emblematic of today's zydeco culture itself—simultaneously

Brian Jack and the Zydeco Gamblers, Original Zydeco Jamm Festival, Crosby, Texas, 2004.

progressive and traditional, sophisticated and rustic, urban and folksy. And that, along with the numerous performers, is part of the appeal of the annual festival in Crosby, an event that draws fans from all over the upper Gulf Coast and beyond.

In some instances those fans have had little previous direct connection to Creole culture beyond their initial fascination with its music. But the power of that music can be profound, as the case of Thomas Wills, a native of Baltimore, Maryland, illustrates. A middle-aged African American jazz and R&B musician, Wills enthusiastically relates his recent life-changing encounter with zydeco:

I never heard it till I went to Fairfax [Virginia] and I heard Buckwheat [i.e., Stanley Dural, b. 1947, the prominent touring artist known as Buckwheat Zydeco]. I said, damn, this is what I need to know how to play!

Then I heard Buckwheat again, over in Alexandria, Virginia. Then he played in Baltimore, Maryland. . . . I heard him there. I fell in love with it. This was just two years ago!

So I said, "Buckwheat"—when I got a chance to meet him—I said, "Look, man, I want to learn how to play this. . . . I'm a sax player." And he said, "Well I'm going to tell you something. This is how you do this: You go down to Houston to the ghetto . . . then you can learn all the zydeco you want. . . ."

[I had] never been to Houston before. Never been down South! But I come here two years ago, and I've been here ever since! And I went straight to Crosby, to the big festival. . . . I met a bunch of zydeco guys there. I met a whole bunch of them. . . . I ran up into zydeco, and now I can't play nothing else but that!

Wills's intensely delivered personal testimony is probably unique among patrons of "the big festival," but not his understanding that the Crosby Fairgrounds is, for one weekend each March, perhaps the ultimate contemporary zydeco extravaganza. Heeding Buckwheat's advice to go to Houston to find a large concentration of zydeco culture, Wills quickly discovered this gathering. And from now on, he claims, "I'll be there every year."

Among his many new friends who have performed on that stage is Leroy Thomas (b. 1965), the Houston-based leader of the nationally touring Zydeco Roadrunners. For his 2004 set there, Thomas wears a black cowboy hat and neatly pressed black cowboy shirt with the Wrangler logo stitched in red and gold trim over the left-hand chest pocket, as well as in larger letters across the upper back. His black pleated slacks are held in place by a western-style belt crowned by a large rectangular metal-plate buckle decorated with a full-color replica of the Texas state flag. While this partial description may bring to mind the consummate cowboy, note those fine dress pants he wears in lieu of jeans, as well as his formal footwear—not

Jazz musician Kyle Turner and Leroy Thomas,
Original Zydeco Jamm Festival, Crosby, Texas, 2004.

Ballou Family musicians, Original Zydeco Jamm Festival, Crosby, Texas 2004.

boots at all, but impeccably shined black Oxford-style shoes. Generally speaking, the pop-cultural norm dictates that a musician's choice of clothing is somehow a visual signifier of his or her style of music. So what to make of Leroy Thomas, whose look fuses rodeo chic with downtown business attire?

Yet that apparent contradiction is in a sense reflected in his performance, which deftly mixes down-home elements with urban cool, blending the folksy and the hip. On one number, for instance, Thomas pumps a simple riff on a single-row accordion with bellows that have been painted in the motif of the flag of the United States. But joining him onstage is one of the top jazz saxophonists in Houston, Kyle Turner. Over the musical foundation that Thomas is cranking out on this, the least sophisticated of the old-style squeezeboxes, Turner improvises a series of scorching horn solos that push the range of chromatic possibilities. It is truly an odd coupling of sounds, but somehow it befits Leroy Thomas and the Zydeco Roadrunners, a band that has played venues such as the Manhattan nightclub called La Belle Époque, as well as the dirt-floored rodeo grounds in a small East Texas town.

Historically, zydeco music has thrived because of its capacity to reconcile disparate influences and synthesize them into something unique. And perhaps the fundamental theme of the Original Zydeco Jamm Festival in Crosby is that whatever zydeco is, it is still evolving. In ways both obvious and subtle, you see it and hear it in almost every band that crosses that stage.

There is Cedryl Ballou, frontman for the Waco-based Zydeco Trendsetters, a band composed entirely of members of his Creole family (including his father, Cedric Ballou, on five-string bass and his grandfather Classie Ballou, b. 1937, a well-known veteran blues musician, on guitar). Wearing diamond studs in each ear lobe and a jersey from the National Football League's Washington Redskins, the young accordionist stands center stage and vocalizes on original pop-flavored numbers such as "Eye of the Tiger."

Meanwhile, the elder patriarch sits on a stool and deftly strums his red Gibson guitar, content to play a supporting role in this band. Not far away on the stage, thirteen-year-old Cranston Ballou commands the drum set like a seasoned pro, nodding his head in time as he works the sticks. Four-year-old Cam'Ron Ballou, Classie's great-grandson, grips a spoon in each hand and scrapes the handles against a rubboard custom-designed to fit his small frame. He is precocious, but still a kid, lapsing between intently strumming rhythmic flourishes on the board and giving way to momentary distractions, during which he simply gazes and grins, losing the beat then regaining the groove and refocusing on the musical performance. Where else in secular culture would you see so many generations of a single family performing for such an audience? That, too, is part of the reason for zydeco's ongoing evolution—its capacity to bridge the proverbial gap between age groups, uniting the past, present, and future in the creation of music that is simultaneously new and old.

ABOVE: *Cam'Ron Ballou, Original Zydeco Jamm Festival, Crosby, Texas, 2004.*
OPPOSITE PAGE: *Jerome Batiste, Original Zydeco Jamm Festival, Crosby, Texas, 2004.*

Over the course of the festival, the interplay between a traditional repertoire and fresh musical influences is perhaps the ultimate indicator of how and why zydeco not only survives but flourishes in the twenty-first century. Jerome Batiste, who lives in Crosby, leads his group, the ZydeKo Players, in a set that includes a tribute to Wilson "Boozoo" Chavis (1930–2001), whose death from a heart attack (following a performance in Austin, Texas) signaled the end of an era. Playing the triple-row button accordion, Batiste sings "Paper in My Shoe," his cover of the 1955 regional hit record by Chavis on the Goldband label. In the style of "the Creole Cowboy," as the venerable Chavis was often called in his later years, Batiste sports a white hat, plaid long-sleeved shirt, and blue jeans—a traditional rodeo look, for sure. But he and the ZydeKo Players inject a funky backbeat to the old song, almost suggesting reggae. Of the five musicians on stage, only the bassist does not vocalize as they sing together, often engaging in a call-and-response mode in which Batiste articulates a lyric and the others voice it again.

In contrast to Batiste, Houston's J. Paul Jr. and the Zydeco NuBreedz embody the look—and in many respects the sound—of a contemporary R&B ensemble. Dressed in FUBU or NFL jerseys, head scarves, and other accoutrements of hip-hop fashion, the cast of supporting musicians (including, for this gig, a guest keyboardist and a female backing vocalist) works through a sustained musical buildup, a kind of grand chorus without words. The wiry, hyperanimated rubboard player, his red stocking cap pulled down to the eyebrows, dashes and leaps around the stage, enkindling the crowd's enthusiasm. Then he suddenly stops, broadly grins, and unleashes an explosion of percussive effects, his blurred hands frantically scraping short drumsticks across his rubboarded chest. While the guitarist improvises a sequence of jazz-rock licks and the keyboardist escalates a heavily pulsing organ riff, the female singer's soft wailing gradually evolves into an emphatically repeated rhetorical question: "Are you rea-ea-dee? Are you rea-ea-dee?"

The rubboard man rushes to the microphone stand and shouts, "J. Paul! J. Paul! J. Paul!" Red lights immediately saturate the stage, and there he is. His braided hair pulled back and held in place by a black headband, the dynamic young bandleader emerges, each hand gripping the triple-row button accordion strapped across the front of his torso. As he reaches to plug in his instrument, the band initiates a driving shuffle beat, keyboards accenting each line like a horn section.

What follows is a nonstop medley of J. Paul Jr. and the Zydeco NuBreedz songs, one of which interweaves a short passage quoted from the R&B classic "Can't Get Next to You." This is by no means a rote cover of the '60s hit by the Temptations (a Norman Whitfield–Barrett Strong composition), but a new J. Paul original that more or less alludes to it in passing. The first phase of this sustained performance culminates in a lover's plea repeated like a mantra. Then, with zydeco rhythms still churning underneath, J. Paul (the stage name of

Rubboard player, Original Zydeco Jamm Festival, Crosby, Texas, 2004.

J. Paul Jr., Original Zydeco Jamm Festival, Crosby, Texas, 2004.

Paul Lawrence Grant III, b. 1973) calls out for "a special man in the house," the guest rapper known as Nuwine, who promptly takes the cordless mic and spews forth words in cascading rhymes, working back to the previous "Can't Get Next to You" theme on each chorus.

Minutes later when Nuwine, rhymes spent, eventually departs the stage, the accordion-led instrumental accompaniment still does not cease, but segues straight into a starkly reinvented version of the climactic passage from "Use Me," the Bill Withers hit pop song from the early '70s. J. Paul's gospel-tinged delivery enthralls the crowd as he closes his eyes, picks out a vocal line, then repeats it over and over, seemingly probing some psychic state more than singing some scripted song, obliviously connected to raw emotion. At last the protracted opening sequence of material comes to an end, however, and the band members temporarily swig drinks and wipe towels across their faces while the audience bellows its appreciation.

Stepping back to the main microphone, J. Paul shouts three times the query, "Do we have any *soldiers* in the house?" Six young black women then march onto the stage, lining up directly behind the accordion-wielding bandleader and the rubboard player, who remain front and center. The women are dressed in matching uniforms: military-style camouflage-print fatigue pants, form-fitting black tank tops, and black baseball-style caps. The music to J. Paul's original composition "Where My Soldiers At" pulses to life, and they begin to dance in choreographed frenzy. They all have yellow bandanas protruding from their right hip pockets, flowing behind like tail feathers.

The "soldiers" referenced in the lyrics are, in fact, the now deceased "zydeco architects," as J. Paul says—that is, key figures in the early history of the genre. While the backup singers articulate the chorus, the six dancing girls reach into their side pockets on cue, pull out and activate flashlights encased in yellow and black plastic, and they dance with wild yet synchronized energy while waving to the crowd. As soon as the song stops, they vanish off stage.

Over the course of the rest of his set, J. Paul indulges in slow ballads rendered with heart-stirring vibrato as well as up-tempo shuffles on which he shouts in call-and-response with both band and audience. There is also another rap interlude provided by a guest artist called Flip, who concludes his segment by handing the microphone back to the previously featured Nuwine. The general crowd response, even among many of those dressed like cowboys, is loud and protracted. Yet except for the scraping of the rubboard and the tastefully interjected notes on accordion, the dominant sound of this music—like the look of its players—is profoundly urban, more obviously influenced by contemporary R&B, hip-hop, and popular culture at large than by Creole folk tradition.

An even more pronounced example of MTV-style influence on this genre occurs with Nooney and the Zydeco Floaters, another Houston band. The band members first take the stage dressed in the type of hooded protective coverall suits associated with work involving hazardous exposure. However, each of these white outfits has been artfully tagged with colorful spray-painted graffiti, including the wearer's personal nickname scripted across the back. So they look kind of like some squadron of hip-hop spacemen as they mill about and wave to the crowd. Then one hollers, "It's getting kind of hot," and they all quickly slip out of the incongruous costumes, exposing their actual performance apparel, a less outrageous ensemble of NBA jerseys over T-shirts and baggy blue jeans.

The bass begins a deep, rumbling introduction that is soon joined by the other instruments amid lots of shouting from the rubboard player. He gets the crowd to respond on cue: "Noo-ney! Noo-ney!" Offstage the bandleader begins playing the opening lines of a tune on his accordion before finally strolling to the front microphone, waving his arms and yelling to the crowd: "They say zydeco is over in Louisiana, but we got it right here!" He squeezes the buttons on his single-row accordion, and the song begins, prompting a flurry of dancing and prancing on stage. At one point Nooney (the stage name of Frank Young Jr., b. 1970) cuts the music to address the audience again. He then disconnects the microphone from its stand, holds it in his left hand, and waves his right hand to introduce a call-and-response chant.

"When I say 'Boo,' y'all say 'Zoo'," he shouts. Then, after a pause, "Boo!"

"Zoo!" the people resound.

"When I say 'Beau,' y'all say 'Jocque.' . . . Beau!"

"Jocque!" they shout.

"Boo!"

"Zoo!"

"Beau!"

"Jocque!"

This ritual of vocalizing collective appreciation for two deceased icons of Louisiana zydeco works through several cycles of vigorous reiteration.

Then Nooney launches into a song that instantly sounds more traditional than anything he has performed thus far. His playing now emulates the styles of the late Boozoo Chavis and Andrus "Beau Jocque" Espre (1954–1999), the two figures cited in his previous cheerleading. Nooney's impulse to pay homage to these two men seems widely shared. After all, during the 1990s both Chavis and Beau Jocque were commonly acknowledged to be zydeco royalty, and their rivalry for the ultimate crown (following the death of its previous claimant, "Rockin' Dopsie," the stage name of Alton Rubin, 1932–1993) is the subject of Robert Mugge's 1994 documentary film, *The Kingdom of Zydeco*. Moreover, both Chavis and Beau Jocque were particularly active and influential during the era when many of today's younger players, such as Nooney, were first learning to play this music. These two zydeco icons were also players of the button (as opposed to the keyboard) accordion—just like practically every one of the bandleaders featured at this year's festival.

J. Paul Jr. and some members of the Zydeco NuBreedz,
Original Zydeco Jamm Festival, Crosby, Texas, 2004.

Nooney (Frank Young Jr.), Original Zydeco Jamm Festival, Crosby, Texas, 2004.

It is significant to note, however, that over the course of the evening, with the exception of J. Paul's roll call of zydeco forefathers in "Where My Soldiers At," nobody else on stage ever mentions the original and the only undisputed "king of zydeco," Louisiana native and former longtime Texas resident Clifton Chenier (1925–1987). And except for one song performed by Leroy Thomas at this event, nobody chooses to play the larger piano-key accordion, the instrument with which Chenier defined the classic zydeco sound.

Instead, throughout the afternoon and into the night, it is a steady procession of button accordion players, alternating among single-row, double-row, and triple-row models. Backstage, one of the young bandleaders explains that he prefers the button accordion simply because he can move his fingers more rapidly over the small buttons than over the piano-style keyboard. And the capacity to play at a fast tempo seems to be a high priority for these twenty-first-century zydeco stars. Their repertoire, generally speaking, is a mix of traditional and contemporary two-steps, R&B ballads, and hip-hop beats. And although some of these bands certainly do so elsewhere, at this festival none of them chooses to perform a twelve-bar blues or a waltz, two mainstay components of Chenier's classic style.

Nevertheless, for his next-to-last song and without any fanfare or commentary, Nooney begins to play his own version of "Hot Tamale Baby," a fast-paced zydeco shuffle that was first recorded by Chenier—and remains widely recognized as one of his signature compositions. Thus, though nobody calls attention to the fact, Chenier is indirectly acknowledged here in Crosby, no more than thirty miles from where he once lived on the east side of Houston.

Yet Nooney's treatment of Chenier's dance-hall favorite soon abruptly shifts gears, diverging into a nonmelodic chorus of group shouting and bluntly macho posturing in the style of gangsta rap. This jarring sequence culminates with Nooney screaming profanely a six-syllable line (in the same meter as the title phrase of Chenier's song) meant to disrespect "the competition." He bellows it repeatedly, as if other zydeco bands were rival gangs that he feels compelled to intimidate with R-rated verbiage. Then in a surrealistic moment, the instrumental melody suddenly emerges from the cacophony, the rhythm locks in, and the band segues back into Chenier's "Hot Tamale Baby" for a closing flourish.

Perhaps no other performance at the 2004 festival in Crosby better illustrates the occasionally uneasy symbiosis between the different generations and diverse styles that all claim connection to zydeco culture in the twenty-first century. Yet despite such elements of hip-hop extremism in the music of some contemporary Texas Creoles, there are still strong ties to the customs and sounds of the past.

For instance, although none of the young performers ever fully engages with the blues at the 2004 festival, there is a hint of that Chenier-like quality in the performance of Brian Jack and the Zydeco Gamblers. This high-energy band generally performs in a more traditional,

though heavily percussive, style. In fact, though not necessarily represented by his performance at this particular event, the clean-cut and bespectacled bandleader, Jack, is actually one of several young Texas-based zydeco players actively exploring the roots of his musical and linguistic heritage. Yet it still comes as a surprise when Jack (b. 1980), a native of the nearby town of Dayton, releases his hands from the single-row accordion in midsong, pulls a harmonica out of his pocket, puts it to his mouth, and proceeds to blow a solo. This humble instrument, long associated with blues and country music, has rarely been featured in the popular sound track of Jack's generation, including the youth-oriented zydeco subculture. His willingness to master the harmonica and incorporate it into his music underscores both his respect for what some of his peers might consider an old-timey African American musical tradition as well as his impulse to redefine zydeco in his own image, to make it new.

Later in the evening Step Rideau and the Zydeco Outlaws play the festival's closing set, illustrating once again the confluence of an ancestral tradition and a progressive urban vibe. A native of tiny Lebeau, Louisiana, Rideau (b. 1967) has now lived for most of his adult life in Houston. As such, his musical influences range from old folk songs to classic rhythm and blues to rap and beyond. Though he was born in St. Landry Parish and surrounded by black Creole culture from his infancy, it wasn't until he relocated to Houston in the mid-1980s that Rideau began to play the accordion. Today he is widely acknowledged—on both sides of the Sabine River—as one of the living masters of the instrument. He has also established himself, over the course of multiple CDs and countless festival appearances nationwide, as one of the most prolific and passionate zydeco recording artists, songwriters, and live performers in the region.

Part of Rideau's appeal is that he brings a true singer's sensibility to zydeco—not just shouting out the lyrics but also soulfully engaging with them to articulate the songs, both in English and in Creole French. In that respect, he is served well by his bandmates, who provide not only skillful instrumental accompaniment but also unusually rich and melodious vocal harmonies, especially in the case of his drummer, Houston native Jean-Paul Jolivette (b. 1974). Collectively these players make music that respects the art of the human voice in song as much as it respects the driving rhythms, funky beats, and accordion riffs of contemporary zydeco.

On the stage at Crosby that three-way harmonizing is especially impressive, as is a precisely executed jazz-style drum solo by Jolivette. But what really sets Rideau and his band apart from those that preceded them at this festival is the simple fact that they sing at least some lyrics in French. Though a few of the other performers are also known to do so from time to time, on this night Rideau alone chooses to communicate in the root language of his ethnic heritage. And this ratio of French to English at a major zydeco event is not unusual in the twenty-first century—in Texas or Louisiana.

OPPOSITE PAGE: *Brian Jack, Original Zydeco Jamm Festival, Crosby, Texas, 2004.*

Step Rideau, Houston, Texas, 2003.

Jean-Paul Jolivette, Original Zydeco Jamm Festival, Crosby, Texas, 2004.

For example, Chris Ardoin (b. 1980), the only Louisiana-based artist to perform at the 2004 festival, is a descendant of perhaps the most storied French-speaking family in the history of Creole music. He summarizes his lineage in a backstage interview: "A great-great-cousin of mine was Amédé Ardoin, and they say he's the father of Creole-Cajun music. Then my grandfather was Bois Sec Ardoin. And you know, my uncles and my father [Lawrence 'Black' Ardoin] played. I'm the next generation." Yet this lifelong resident of Lake Charles also points out, "I sing only in English. I don't speak French." Though he descends from famous Francophone singers such as Amédé (1898–1941, who first recorded in 1929) and "Bois Sec" (the nickname of his grandfather Alphonse, b. 1916), Chris Ardoin is in other respects like most of his professional peers today in that, with the exception of perhaps a few well-known catchphrases, he is completely monolingual in his articulation of zydeco lyrics. It is the over-whelming norm, especially among the younger players.

It is that reality that makes Rideau's French-inclusive festival set of special note. After a period (perhaps best illustrated by his 1999 CD, *I'm So Glad*) of experimenting effectively with R&B and rap fusions with zydeco, Rideau has focused anew on developing a repertoire that incorporates elements of a more traditional sound, including more vocalizing *en fran-çais*. His 2003 CD, *From: Step 2 U*, for instance, consists of ten originals plus four numbers that reach back to Chenier, Chavis, and another famous patriarch, John Delafose (1939–1994). Rideau sings in both English and French, sometimes within the same song. Decades ago, when Chenier was the reigning king of the genre, such bilingual vocalizing was the norm. But among today's younger zydeco artists—most of whom grew up watching music videos and listening to rap—the unique patois of their ancestors has generally disappeared.

But there are exceptions, both in southwest Louisiana and southeast Texas, where some zydeco musicians in their twenties and thirties are making a conscious effort to learn, speak, and sing—at least a little—in Creole French. In Texas these neotraditionalists include the aforementioned Rideau and Brian Jack, as well as the Houston-born Corey "Lil' Pop" Ledet (b. 1981) and the Sealy, Texas, native Cedric Watson (b. 1983), as well as their common mentor, James B. Adams (b. 1956) and others. And there are, of course, some older musicians—such as Wilfred Chevis (b. 1945) in Houston and, especially, Billy Poullard (b. 1937) and Ed Poullard (b. 1952) in Beaumont—who still regularly perform songs in French.

The Original Zydeco Jamm Festival 2004 concludes with the performance by Step Rideau and the Zydeco Outlaws—one that is unique not only because of the French singing but also because of an extended and sophisticated drum solo delivered by Jolivette midway through one of the final numbers. Taken out of context, it might sound like a rollicking snippet of classic jazz. But here it soon builds to a climax that merges seamlessly into the zydeco flow as the other instruments join in to resume the song. It seems the perfect way to punctuate the end of this festival, an annual event that embodies the ongoing syncretism of Creole folk traditions and popular culture in southeast Texas.

IT IS NOW SUNDAY EVENING, less than twenty-four hours since the conclusion of the 2004 festival. On the prominent southwest Houston thoroughfare called Kirby Drive, near the edge of a fashionable retail district, is an establishment called The Big Easy Social and Pleasure Club. The midsized room is packed with adults of various ages, races, and affiliations—all listening, and many of them dancing, to live zydeco. Some of them were approximately thirty miles east of here at the Crosby festival the night before. Like those, most of the patrons are regulars at this weekly event, a casual gathering of fans and musicians. Though any one of several local bands may be hired to host the gig, following the opening set it usually evolves into a jam session with lots of participants.

Sunday night zydeco at The Big Easy draws a diverse group of musicians from all over the metropolitan area. There are usually performances by some of the older accordionists, such as (until ill health recently slowed him down) Wilbert Thibodeaux (b. 1927) or Chester Papillion (b. 1941), as well as rubboard players such as Joseph Lavergne (b. 1937). And there are always plenty of younger players too, accordionists such as Robert "Ra-Ra" Carter (b. 1983) or rubboard players such as Melissa Mays (b. 1980).

These long-established Sunday night events bring together Texas zydeco players from three different strata: accomplished professionals who tour and perform full-time, veteran musicians who opt to maintain day jobs and play mainly on weekends, and confident amateurs who are eager to share the stage and show what they can do. For instance, C. J. Chenier (b. 1957), the son of Clifton Chenier, is an internationally known star and recording artist, one of the biggest names in contemporary zydeco. Though he has lived in Houston for most of his adult life, he rarely plays actual gigs in local clubs, such as The Big Easy, instead booking most of his concerts out of state or overseas. But when he is home between tours, he has occasionally shown up unannounced to sit in and jam—especially when his friends in the Zydeco Dots, a popular local band, host the event. Similarly, Leroy Thomas, Step Rideau, and others of their status sometimes appear when they have an open date—their unexpected presence on stage stoking the usually already energized crowd.

On this particular Sunday evening the customers are enjoying a lively session hosted by Wilfred Chevis and the Texas Zydeco Band. A native of Church Point, Louisiana, Chevis has lived in Houston since 1969 and is now one of the more experienced zydeco bandleaders working regularly in the Lone Star State. The music he and his cohorts create on the Big Easy stage sounds older, more traditional, and remarkably different from those frenzied shuffles and hip-hop-inspired beats that seemed to dominate the festival in Crosby yesterday. Apart

LEFT TO RIGHT: *Arthur "T-Put" Carter and Chester Papillion,*
The Big Easy Social and Pleasure Club, Houston, Texas, 2004.

LEFT TO RIGHT: *Martin Chevis and Wilfred Chevis,*
The Big Easy Social and Pleasure Club, Houston, Texas, 2004.

from any subjective interpretations regarding Chevis's personal performance style, there are several crucial distinctions.

For one, the Excelsior accordion that he pumps and stretches is not only larger and heavier than the smaller instruments favored by the younger set. It is a full-sized piano accordion, the same general type that Clifton Chenier, the original king of zydeco, used to play.

That is, it is not a button-operated squeezebox, which plays only in a limited range of certain musical keys, but a more versatile instrument with a larger bellows and a right-hand keyboard that can produce any note in the chromatic scale.

The late king's son, C. J. Chenier, provides additional insight on this important distinction:

You know, the button accordions are diatonic [i.e., capable of playing only a fixed pattern of intervals], and the piano-note [accordion] is chromatic. . . . For the most part, almost everybody else around here, except for just a few, these days plays just the button. Now if you take the piano accordion and play just the black notes, just the black keys, that's similar to the way a button accordion sounds. I mean, it don't have no sharps and no flats. You've got to kind of cross it to make it be able to play the blues.

And to me, Clifton Chenier being the only person I'd ever paid attention to—and my daddy played the blues—the piano-note is the only accordion I ever thought about playing.

As the younger Chenier's commentary suggests, the majority of (but not all) zydeco accordionists are either piano-note players or button players—that is, one or the other, not both. Moreover, there are far more people in the latter group. For instance, in addition to Chenier himself, there are only a few other nationally prominent stars—most notably, Buckwheat Zydeco and Lil' Brian Terry—who typically play the piano accordion.

However, at the start of the twenty-first century the Houston scene alone still retains a small cadre of men who follow the example of Clifton Chenier and choose to play this style of instrument. Some of them are retired or semiretired from active work as professional musicians—including Wilbert Thibodeaux, Willie Davis (b. 1930), and Dan Rubit (b. 1942). Among the local piano-accordion players who remain professionally active are Raymond Chavis (b. 1944), Charles "Lil' Reb" Wilson (b. 1949), the artist known mainly as Jabo (i.e., Donald Glenn, b. 1954), and Otha Sanchez (b. 1955), as well as the aforementioned Chester Papillion, Wilfred Chevis, C. J. Chenier, and Brian Terry. And then there are younger players, such as Leroy Thomas or Corey Ledet, who have primarily utilized the button accordion to date but also increasingly play the piano-key instrument, onstage and in the recording studio.

But back at The Big Easy there is more than the choice of the now less-common type of accordion that makes Chevis's performance there such a counterpoint to the prevailing sound track of the previous day's festival in Crosby. For along with the expected two-steps and boogies, Chevis plays some almost defiantly old-style waltzes. Moreover, he engages, again and again, with twelve-bar blues. And to top it all off, on many of those numbers, he sings in French. The composite effect is a powerful syncretism of musical forms that calls to mind the classic bilingual Creole repertoire of Clifton Chenier, a sound largely abandoned by many of the youthful bands that now tend to dominate Gulf Coast zydeco festivals.

Like Chester Papillion, who follows him on the Big Easy stage and also performs blues and waltzes with French lyrics, Chevis has made this kind of music for most of his life. It is no wonder, for he was influenced directly by its greatest innovator. As Chevis relates,

I've been playing zydeco since I was nine years old. I got started with my father. My father taught me, in southwest Louisiana. I was playing a little squeezebox then, and the music was called la-la. It wasn't called zydeco then; it was called la-la.

Then at the age of twenty-four, I met Clifton Chenier. He introduced me to the big accordion. He sold me one, and he taught me how to play the keyboard accordion. He said that was going to be something different, and when he recorded, he called his music zydeco. That's how zydeco got started.

I came to Houston in '69. I was introduced to Houston, Texas, by Clifton Chenier. I came with him. He used to take me with him over here, and he played festivals and at Catholic halls. He played at Miller Outdoor Theatre for Juneteenth festivals. He introduced me to the people and always let me play about a half hour or forty-five minutes with him. And then people started booking me, so I moved down here.

Now based in the Bayou City for more than three decades, Chevis has regularly performed and recorded in both Texas and Louisiana, remaining an active traveler along the zydeco corridor. In fact, you could say that he has extended it, to some degree, by making several well-received appearances (to primarily Hispanic audiences) on down the Texas coast in Victoria and Corpus Christi and, on at least one occasion, as far south as McAllen, near the Mexican border. However, for Chevis as for many other Gulf Coast zydeco musicians living west of the Sabine River, most of the gigs are in the many nightclubs, restaurants, church dances, festivals, and private parties to be found in Houston. For instance, at The Big Easy the veteran accordionist is part of the long-established rotation, performing with his full band once a month (on average) at the Sunday night zydeco party.

However, even when he is not the featured artist, Chevis—like a large number of other Houston zydeco players—usually shows up at The Big Easy for this end-of-the-weekend gathering. The club provides a comfortable, fairly centralized place for musicians to socialize, network, and, if so inclined, sit in on the jam session that inevitably occurs. For rather than being perceived, as some venues are, as the more or less private turf of certain players, The Big Easy offers a consistently friendly (and affordable) environment where everyone, musician or not, seems to feel at home.

The credit for that ambience goes to this popular establishment's cofounder and sole proprietor, Tom McLendon. Though the venue name and decorative theme (including a purple and gold façade on Kirby Drive) reveal McLendon's love of New Orleans, the booking policy almost exclusively focuses on the southeast Texas blues and zydeco scene. As such, it is a place where local musicians find it easy to intermingle with one another and with fans. McLendon explains that the club's slogan—"The House of Mixology"—refers not to the well-stocked bar so much as to the mix of musical styles and the diverse customers who enjoy them. But the key to the success of his Sunday-night zydeco shows is a policy with implications both economic and social: "The only cover [charge] I require," he says, "is respect, respect for your brothers and sisters."

Every Sunday night The Big Easy provides even the most casual observer with the opportunity to observe harmonious cultural diversity evolving organically on the dance floor. While the sounds of zydeco fill the room, the open space in front of the raised stage is likely to be overcrowded with couples, some of which might elsewhere be considered oddly matched. At any given moment there might be senior citizens paired with younger adults, blacks with whites (as well as people of other races), college-educated professionals with working-class folks, heavy drinkers with teetotalers, off-duty musicians with fans, and accomplished dancers with uncertain beginners.

Of course, the real spectacle occurs when any two of those who have truly mastered the fine art of zydeco dancing pair off and reveal some of its multiform wonders. Utilizing a repertoire of traditional steps and moves, often embellished with personal idiosyncrasies and improvised flourishes, they communicate a key part of the legacy of this music—which in its essence is dance music above all else—and the culture that originated it. In certain ways, their spirited presence is almost as crucial to the event as the music itself, and they typically are the focus of much respect and delight from other dancers and observers.

In some cases these amazing dancing couples consist of a man and a woman who know and see each other primarily only through these Sunday-night gatherings at The Big Easy. There they meet in an informal weekly ritual, one that demands much physical energy yet seems also to revitalize them and the many onlookers who follow their movements across the floor. Among the most consistently present and impressive of such dancers is the quietly effervescent Gay Ann Gustafson, an elementary-school librarian who also enjoys ballet and opera. But her passion for zydeco is obvious when she arrives at The Big Easy and greets her many friends.

OPPOSITE PAGE: *Jabo (Donald Glenn),*
The Big Easy Social and Pleasure Club, Houston, Texas, 2004.

Tom McLendon, proprietor, The Big Easy Social and Pleasure Club, Houston, Texas, 2004.

Sunday night zydeco at The Big Easy Social and Pleasure Club, Houston, Texas, 2004.

Some of her favorite dance partners are serious practitioners and promoters of the art form, such as the young Louisiana native named Willie Bushnell, who originally learned to dance from his Creole grandmother. Since moving to Texas many years ago, Bushnell has taught the history and techniques of zydeco dancing at workshops and demonstrations across the nation, including an appearance with Gustafson in 2000 for the Texas International Folk Dancers. Another of Gustason's regular dance partners is the venerable Emmit Goodwin, a longtime resident of the old section of Houston known as Frenchtown. Once a personal acquaintance of Clifton Chenier, the now elderly Goodwin insists that he has "really slowed down" since suffering a stroke some years ago. Yet through 2005 this elderly gentleman, always decked out in a white cowboy hat and shiny black boots, remains a vital force on the Big Easy dance floor whenever it is zydeco time.

On this particular night, as another Sunday evening crosses that midnight line into the earliest moments of a Monday, there is a temporary break in the music making. Then the local bandleader known as Bon Ton Mickey (the stage name of Louisiana-born Mickey Guillory) leaves his bar stool, fetches his accordion case from the assembled equipment stacked in one corner of the room, and saunters onto the stage. While strapping on his instrument and plugging into the amplifier, he nods, smiles, and exchanges words with the randomly assembled supporting musicians who join him for this closing set.

His three-song performance commences with a zydeco blues shuffle sung in English, then yields to a waltz sung in French. An instrumental two-step marks the grand finale, climaxing with an extended sequence of improvised soloing. Following a flurry of churned accordion riffs, bent guitar licks, and funk-strutting bass lines, Guillory shifts the band into "break-down" mode (that is, playing nothing but the rhythmic core of the song) and then leans toward the microphone to shout, "You know where the old-time zydeco come from? It's when the drums and the scrub board got together and had a party!"

With those words the room suddenly explodes with percussive energy. As longtime Zydeco Dots member Joseph Rossyion (b. 1965) unleashes a frenzied pattern behind the drum kit, an unannounced female rubboard player maniacally assaults the metal plate—her hands and arms pumping up and down in an accelerated blur, almost like hummingbird wings. Intensely they pound, strike, scrape, and stroke this number, as well as this night, to its proper climax. One final chorus with all the other instruments serves as the denouement, and then it is over.

Dancers and patrons shake hands, trade hugs, and bid their peers farewell—in most cases fully expecting to see one another again, right here, next week. The remaining musicians stow their instruments and gather gear. Some of them depart immediately; others stand and converse, and a few settle down at a table for a round of drinks with friends. Although they all ultimately must depart for their respective domiciles, it is clear that almost

Emmit Goodwin, The Big Easy Social and Pleasure Club, Houston, Texas, 2004.

Bon Ton Mickey (Mickey Guillory), Houston, Texas, 2003.

everyone who has been part of this evening—musicians, fans, dancers, and barflies alike—feels "at home" here at The Big Easy.

Along with a few other clubs in twenty-first-century Houston (such as the predominantly African American establishment called C. C.'s Hideout in the Sunnyside neighborhood and the Silver Slipper in Fifth Ward), The Big Easy offers the weekly possibility of a homecoming of sorts, every Sunday night, for the many zydeco people of southeast Texas. For this coastal region, stretching from Houston eastward to Port Arthur, is truly the second home of zydeco music.

Texas zydeco is a complex phenomenon that has both drawn from and contributed to the black Creole culture of Louisiana for many generations. It is not so much a particular stylistic designation as a simple geographic reality. And it has been so, whether widely recognized or not, since the modern form of this lively music first emerged over half a century ago.

Leroy Thomas, Juneteenth Music Festival, Beaumont, Texas, 2003.

There's a saying: "The bee fertilizes the flower that it steals from." See, that's the essence of acculturation. . . . This truly is the march of history.

—MACK McCORMICK, TO THE AUTHOR

CHANK-A-CHANK AND SOCIAL CHANGE

Two

The Early Years

A little more than two centuries ago, the North American territory known as Texas was ruled by Spain, and that called Louisiana was governed by France, two longtime adversarial nations. In fact, there had previously been a Spanish presence in Louisiana and a French presence (as far back as 1682) in parts of Texas, so each government controlled land once possessed by the other. Back in Europe as well as on the New World soil that they claimed, these empires were rivals—not only political or military or economic competitors but also linguistic and cultural rivals as well. Along and beyond the coastline of the Gulf of Mexico, each spawned distinctive social structures informed by various indigenous influences and landscapes.

Then in 1803, the year of the Louisiana Purchase, the shape of the upstart nation called the United States of America radically changed, suddenly expanding to abut the eastern and northeastern borders of the *Provincia de Texas*, as it was labeled on a map ("A Map of New Spain") from 1804. In 1812 the current boundaries of Louisiana were drawn, and it joined the nation as its eighteenth state. By 1821 New Spain had become the independent nation of Mexico, which maintained control of the Texas territory. Then in 1836 a confederacy of Euro-American colonists and Tejanos broke from Mexico to form the independent Republic of Texas. One decade later Texas joined the expanding United States as Louisiana's larger neighbor to the west.

Since then, Texas and Louisiana, two places steeped in their own mythos, have in fact shared much history and culture as members of the same nation. Yet despite myriad common ties, they sometimes seem as contrary as Spain and France at the height of their rivalry.

In popular understanding today, Texas and Louisiana are often perceived to be strikingly different. It is no wonder, for over the years various media have directly or indirectly propagated certain romanticized caricatures as personifications of these places: the leather-fringed cowboy urging his horse across the open plain, or the mysterious Creole poling his bateau across some murky swamp, for instance. Nostalgic stereotypes linger in the collective consciousness, and such overly simplified images surely affect perceptions of the people and the landscapes of both states (especially among outsiders who have never spent much time in either place). In reality, however, Louisiana has its share of cowboys and prairies, and southeast Texas is home to many Creoles and swamps. The natural environment and the human population, at least in that approximately one-hundred-mile-wide swath on either side of the state line, do have their differences, but they also have much in common with each other.

As the writer John Graves observes in *Texas Rivers*, for himself and many other Texans this fact causes that eastern edge of the Lone Star State to seem especially strange, like some exotic land:

For those of us who live in the more open country of the central and western parts of the state, the wooded zone along our Louisiana border can be a little daunting. Blessed with copious rainfall, laced with perennially flowing creeks that feed strong rivers, shaded by forests except where they have been cleared, peopled with folk whose traditional attitudes, ways of living, and even manner of speaking hark back directly to the Deep South, the region at times seems foreign to persons accustomed to the drier prairies, plains, rocky hills, and the dialects of the rest of the state.

This particular sense of the "foreign" is especially evident in that part of Texas bounded by the lower Sabine, which runs from the bottom of the Toledo Bend Reservoir down past Port Arthur to the Gulf of Mexico. In the area between that segment of the river and Houston, the "Louisiana Lapland" phenomenon is most pronounced, adding distinctive Creole and Cajun elements to the more generalized Deep South ambience that Graves perceives.

Those Creole and Cajun influences, like the people they come from, often share similar distinctions, most obviously a French linguistic heritage but also certain traditions in religion, food, music, and more. However, it is important to recognize that Creoles are not Cajuns and, as the title of an essay by Louisiana-based writer Herman Fuselier bluntly proclaims, "Zydeco Is Not Cajun Music."

Despite their multiform diversity, the Creoles who came to Texas from southern Louisiana all connect, directly or indirectly, to a lineage from the Franco-African (or Franco-Afro-

Caribbean) slave class. This sociobiological legacy marks the key point of contrast between them and their close neighbors the Cajuns, who descended from late-eighteenth-century French emigrants from eastern Canada. In short, the inherent contrast between Africa and Canada suggests a fundamental difference between Creoles and Cajuns, as the terms are mainly used today in reference to both music and people along the upper Gulf Coast. As Fuselier states,

Simply put, Cajun music is the waltzes and two-steps played by the white descendants of the Acadians, who were exiled from Nova Scotia in the 1700s. Zydeco is the R&B-based accordion grooves of black Creoles.

Creole has 100 different definitions. But when it comes to Zydeco, it refers to the descendants of slaves, free people of color and mixed-race people of this region.

Indeed, much popular confusion exists about the term "Creole" because that word has been used historically to designate so many different types of people in North America. In the preface to their book *Creoles of Color in the Bayou Country*, Carl Brasseaux, Keith P. Fontenot, and Claude F. Oubre assert that "few words in American English are as misunderstood or as frequently misused," explaining also that the term can mean one thing to a linguist and another to a social historian.

The folklorist Barry Jean Ancelet, in his essay "Cajuns and Creoles," explains that the Creole label in colonial Louisiana and the Caribbean originally referred to descendants of white French settlers: "Those born in the colony called themselves Creoles, a word meaning 'home-grown, not imported,' to distinguish themselves from immigrants." In his prefatory essay for *Creoles of Color of the Gulf South*, James H. Dormon adds the etymological insight that the word "Creole" derives "from the Latin *creare*—'to beget' or 'create.' New World Creoles were indeed 'created' as the byproducts of the European colonial process." Joan E. Supplee notes in *The New Handbook of Texas* that in New Spain a cognate of the word, *criollo*, was used to describe those born there of European parentage. And Dormon, in fact, suggests that the word may have first emerged in Portuguese as *crioulo*.

Back in Louisiana during the era of French colonization (1699–1803), the term "Creole" was first applied mainly to Caucasian New World natives descended from European-born parents, a socially elite class (at least on American soil) based in the famous *Quartier Français* in New Orleans or on plantations that capitalized on the regional trade in cotton, sugar, and slaves. The ethnic class of black Creoles, whose progeny would ultimately invent the music known as zydeco, resulted from the union of some of those aristocratic white Creole men and their African and Caribbean slave women, producing offspring referred to in French as *noir*.

Known in English as black Creoles, or Creoles of color, these people possessed a unique mixed-race identity among the other French-speaking people of South Louisiana. Before emancipation, however, most of them remained slaves—despite the fact that their fathers (or grandfathers, great-grandfathers, etc.) usually were free white men. Such realities were the norm throughout the antebellum South. The great abolitionist and autobiographer Frederick Douglass (1818–1895), who himself was born into slavery as the result of such a sexual union, defines the general situation at the time:

Slavery had no recognition of fathers, as none of families. That the mother was a slave was enough for its deadly purpose. By its law the child followed the condition of its mother. . . . The father might be a white man, glorifying in the purity of his [Caucasian] blood, and the child ranked with the blackest slaves.

However, while enslavement was inevitable for most of them, not all black Creoles suffered that fate. Some were known instead as *les gens de couleur libres*, or "free people of color" (a phrase that Ancelet notes, in *Cajun Music and Zydeco*, "implied mixed blood; *negres libres* were free persons of pure African ancestry"). These free persons of color generally enjoyed the same legal rights and economic opportunities as most nonblack citizens of the region: they could own businesses, plantations, and, in some cases, even slaves. As Gary Hartman points out in *The Handbook of Texas Music*, "These French-speaking free blacks soon spread across the region from New Orleans throughout southwestern Louisiana and into East Texas."

From the postemancipation era to the present, many people who have continued to identify themselves as black Creoles have procreated with people of other ethnic groups and races, producing offspring of various skin tones, physical traits, and linguistic orientations. As a consequence, the term "Creole" today can evoke a wide range of syncretic possibilities regarding human genetics and culture. Thus, Dormon cautions that "the continuing evolution of the term's usage renders a perfect consistency of usage impossible. Such terminologies, like ethnic groups themselves, are never static, unchanging, immutable realities."

Yet in the more narrowed context of a review of the mid-twentieth-century development of zydeco music, the phrase "black Creoles" is a bit less problematic. For our purposes, it refers historically to the predominantly farming-class people of some French ancestry, however vague, who socially and legally have been classified as Negroes along the upper Gulf Coast. Most of them descended from former slaves in southwest Louisiana, but they did not always stay there.

Since the days of the earliest settlements, interchange has regularly occurred across the lower Sabine River. As a result, generations of southeast Texans have been profoundly

Gene Rideau, zydeco promoter, Crosby, Texas, 2004.

influenced by Louisiana culture; conversely, the proud culture of southwest Louisiana has also been deeply affected by the place referred to in a famous Cajun song as "Grand Texas." As the folklorist Carl Lindahl notes in *The Accordion as King*, the lyrics to this and other songs from southwest Louisiana "describe Texas both as a land of opportunity and as a place of painful separation; this mixed message reflects the long history of the Cajun settlement of East Texas." In this case, the Cajuns' experience in many respects mirrors that of their African American counterparts, the black Creoles of the region. Both groups have been part of that ongoing interchange. But the role of Texas in one of its most significant musical consequences has rarely been recognized for what it is.

ALONG THE UPPER GULF COAST, the home of the purest forms of the folk tradition of *la musique française* unquestionably is, and always will be, the Acadiana region of southern Louisiana. It is the place where Cajun music and the early form of black Creole music known as la-la, the predecessor of zydeco, originated. Zydeco as we know it today, however, is not exactly a "pure" form, and neither is it solely a cultural production of Acadiana.

Rather, zydeco is a product of the black Creole diaspora of the twentieth century, a music conceived by Louisiana people who were often living out of state in urban centers, and were thus subject to new influences and opportunities. As John Minton asserts in a 1996 article for the journal *American Music*, an accurate historical definition of zydeco describes "a postwar popular music that first made its mark in Texas cities such as Port Arthur, Beaumont, Galveston, and Houston" before gaining widespread popularity and acceptance among the many Creoles back in Louisiana. Zydeco is a doubly syncretized musical phenomenon, a hybrid that required transplantation and cross-pollination to come into existence. As such, it is both an import to and an export from the Lone Star State.

It is easy to comprehend why ingrained assumptions and general observations might cause some people to cast quick skepticism on such assertions. After all, zydeco is a thriving musical genre in South Louisiana, highlighted at many annual festivals and other venues across the state. Most of its biggest stars were born (and in many cases died) there. Moreover, Louisiana-specific references and motifs have always been common in zydeco song lyrics and social gatherings, wherever they occur. The music and the people who regularly enjoy it—in Louisiana as well as in Texas, California, and elsewhere—often celebrate an idealized vision of the ancestral past in the Creole homeland. As Minton points out in *American Music*,

Both as a musical and linguistic idiom, zydeco is distantly tied to a culture approximating the ideal "folk society." In reality, though, as both a musical genre and a generic term, zydeco was coined by urban wage-earners, more specifically by professional musicians not in rural Louisiana—the "back home" of the zydeco ethos—but in urban Texas.

To be clear: zydeco was, and in most cases still is, created by black Creole natives of Louisiana or their descendents. However, many of those people live, or lived, in the Lone Star State for much of their lives. Some of the key figures in the music today (including established artists such as C. J. Chenier or Brian Terry and rising stars such as Corey Ledet or Cedric Watson) are Texas-born Creoles. More to the point, some of the crucial innovations that ultimately defined zydeco as a modern popular form first occurred on Texas soil.

An overview of the most significant of those innovations begins with a 1934 recording session at the Texas Hotel in San Antonio by the Louisiana man who first performed the early black Creole folk music of his people on a record. Then in the 1940s Houston was the site of the very first recordings (one by a Texas native and the other by an immigrant from Louisiana) ever to feature lyrics using variants of the seminal word "zydeco" in reference to a particular style of music. Also, the Bayou City, not Louisiana, is the place where the now universally recognized spelling of that odd word (z-y-d-e-c-o) was coined and first established. Moreover, the original king of zydeco, Clifton Chenier, lived for many years and made a large number of his most famous recordings in Houston, his primary residence during what was arguably the major phase of his career. Before that, however, Chenier had also lived for a while in nearby Port Arthur, the city where he and his brother first conceived, invented, and played the modern form of the essential zydeco percussion instrument, the rubboard vest. More generally, it was in such southeast Texas urban centers as these that Chenier and other Creole immigrants began the process of blending their ancestral French music called la-la with Texas blues and early R&B to engender the fundamental prototype for modern zydeco. And it was there that they found a large share of the audience, venues, and cash on which much of the early popular success of this new music would ultimately depend.

Just as the post-war northern industrial city of Chicago served as the crucial setting where the African American southern folk music known as country blues would evolve into its urbanized, electric, and dominant form, the booming port city of Houston served as the primary incubator in which the black Creole acoustic music called la-la would assimilate new musical possibilities and evolve into zydeco. As I previously wrote in *The Roots of Texas Music*,

As modern musical phenomena, both blues and zydeco first occurred following African-American migrations from specific rural regions to specific industrial cities. Thus, any understanding of the notion of the true "home" for either of these two types of music (and certainly for others as well) is complicated by the reality of ethno-cultural mobility. Where does the blues come into being? In Chicago? In the Delta? In Africa? Where does zydeco come into being? In Houston? In the part of Louisiana known as Acadia? . . . The answer to all of these questions might be yes, depending upon how one defines "being." The facts of movement and syncretism often belie the myth of some ideal-

ized cultural purity with timeless roots planted firmly in one particular place. And especially for any people correctly defined as Creoles, understanding the culture—as a means of understanding its music—necessitates an appreciation of mobility, confrontation, assimilation, and change.

Concerning the difficulty of precisely locating the advent of zydeco, additional research and experience have ultimately convinced me that the wisest insight may well be this: for black Creoles of the upper Gulf Coast, the Sabine River historically has been mainly a landmark, a geopolitical boundary, but no obstacle to the natural interstate flow of their lives. After all, the physical distance between downtown Houston and Acadia Parish (the heartland of Creole and Cajun heritage) is less than two hundred miles. The phenomenon of modern zydeco happened in significant part because the ancestors of black Creoles moved from old postemancipation homesteads in rural areas, abandoning the agrarian lifestyles they had inherited, to live and work in the largest cities in the region. There they met, socialized with, and made music for (and with) other African Americans who were not Creole. This experience, along with their increased income and access to modern musical instruments and technologies, profoundly changed their music. That the biggest city these people mainly gravitated toward happened to be in Texas was (and today is) far less important to them than the fact that it offered good wages and amenities. That it was so close to their families' parishes of origin was a bonus, making it easy for each generation to maintain cultural ties with Louisiana even when residing in Texas (as many have done throughout their lives).

Although the majority of black Creole immigrants came to Texas after 1920, some had lived west of the Sabine River many decades earlier. In *The New Handbook of Texas*, Diana J. Kleiner documents one such case, observing that "wealthy aristocratic Creole planters from Louisiana arrived in Liberty County with their slaves in 1845." This point may well account to some degree for the relatively large number of black Creoles located there (even today), especially in the town of Raywood. However, the earliest presence of black Creole communities in southeast Texas is perhaps most effectively traced through its correlation with the rise of black Catholicism (the dominant religious affiliation of these people) in the state.

In an article on the Catholic diocese of Beaumont, Steven P. Ryan provides the fundamental insight that "traditionally the Catholic Church in Texas had been under the direction of bishops in Mexico" until the war for the independence of Texas in 1836 alienated that relationship and "the Texas church came increasingly under the influence of French Catholics in Louisiana." Roxanne J. Evans, in *The New Handbook of Texas*, also establishes that most of the black Catholics who have resided in Texas throughout its history have come from Louisiana or descended from those who did, and that their ancestors were generally slaves who originally had been proselytized and baptized by their French owners. She notes particularly that many of these black Creoles were transported from Louisiana to Texas during the Civil War (1861–1865), but also that much voluntary migration across the state line soon followed.

Mary H. Ogilvie points out in *The New Handbook of Texas* in an article on Bishop Nicholas Aloysius Gallagher (1846–1918) that by 1882, various Catholic dioceses in southeast Texas under his general administration were working specifically to expand their ministry to the numerous black Catholics coming into the region from Louisiana:

One of Gallagher's first concerns was to increase the role of the church in the development of the black community. In 1886 he opened a school for black children, in cooperation with the Dominican Sisters, in Galveston, the first school of its kind in Texas. The project was so successful that Gallagher had to erect a new building two years later to accommodate the number of applicants. As an outgrowth of this school Holy Rosary Parish, one of the first black parishes in Texas, was established in 1888. . . . Bishop Gallagher [also] initiated parish churches for blacks in Houston, Beaumont, and Port Arthur.

Evans says that "the first known black parish" was established in Houston in 1887 by this same Bishop Gallagher, who likewise "dedicated a small elementary school in the city's Third Ward for the education of black children."

Evans also observes that by 1887, "nearly 10,500 of Houston's estimated 28,000 residents were black," a statistic that suggests one of the essential reasons the Bayou City would be a popular destination for African Americans, Creole or not, who were abandoning the fields where they had once served as slaves. This trend would accelerate in the ensuing decades of the post–Civil War era. In *Black Dixie*, Howard Beeth and Cary D. Wintz show, for instance, that the black population of Houston "increased from 3,691 in 1870, to 23,929 in 1910," mainly from immigrants who "arrived from rural areas in Texas and Louisiana." Surely many Creoles were among these numbers too.

However, the first truly large-scale wave of voluntary Louisiana-to-Texas immigration occurred just after the turn of the century, ignited by the history-changing discovery of oil near Beaumont. As Paul E. Isaac explains in *The New Handbook of Texas*:

The Spindletop oil gusher of 1901 produced a boom that left Beaumont with a doubled population (20,640 in 1910), great wealth, and a petroleum-based economy that expanded as refineries and pipelines were built and new fields discovered nearby. . . . Three major oil companies—the Texas Company (later Texaco), Gulf Oil Corporation, and Humble (later Exxon)—were formed in Beaumont during the first year of the boom. The Magnolia Refinery [which would later become part of the Mobil Oil Company] became the city's largest employer. . . . Discovery of a new oilfield at Spindletop in 1925 brought another burst of growth.

Juneteenth Music Festival (with Step Rideau),
Cardinal Stadium at Lamar University, Beaumont, Texas, 2003.

Not only did Spindletop create thousands of new jobs in the oilfields; it also produced a colossal ripple effect on related industries, such as seaport construction, channel dredging, shipbuilding, and such—not only in Beaumont but also in Port Arthur and especially in Houston. It provided an unprecedented positive economic impact that would permanently alter the fortunes of southeast Texas and, arguably, the nation.

John W. Storey documents the effect on Port Arthur, a city located approximately seventeen miles southeast of Beaumont on the west bank of Sabine Lake. It, too, quickly became home to large refineries and their various satellite industries, all of which required an infusion of workers—drawn mostly from the surrounding countryside in southeast Texas and southwest Louisiana. As he writes in *The New Handbook of Texas*,

Pipelines tied the city to Spindletop, and petroleum products soon were shipped through the canal. By 1909 Port Arthur had become the twelfth largest port in the United States in value of exports, and by 1914 it was the second largest oil-refining point in the nation. Development as a major petrochemical center was reflected in population growth. From 900 residents in 1900, Port Arthur expanded to a population of 7,663 in 1910 and 50,902 in 1930.

As Michael Tisserand acknowledges in *The Kingdom of Zydeco*, Spindletop's impact would alter the course of American music: "Starting almost immediately, and peaking through the years of World War II, black Creoles migrated to Texas in search of jobs, bringing along their accordions and French songs." Situated near the Gulf of Mexico and close to the state line, the so-called "Golden Triangle" area of Beaumont, Port Arthur, and Orange first drew many of these immigrants to the relatively high-paying employment in the new oilfields, chemical plants, and shipbuilding yards of the region—as well as to more traditional means of earning a living in the suddenly expanding field of municipal services or on rice farms or shrimp boats. However, the city whose fortunes would be most profoundly affected by the discovery of massive oil deposits in southeast Texas is the place where the largest number of black Creoles would ultimately settle.

Located 112 miles west of the Sabine River, the metropolis of Houston, already established as a major railroad and commercial center, soon became the petrochemical capital of Texas and the nation.

In the latter half of the nineteenth century, the city had initiated work to improve access to and from the sea via its main natural waterway, Buffalo Bayou. Following the devastation of nearby Galveston by a hurricane in 1900, that project took on even more importance, for it would eventually provide the area with a grand shipping port located almost fifty miles inland and thus far better protected from hurricanes than Galveston had been, as well as

being closer to rail lines and an eventual network of highways. As David G. McComb asserts in *The Portable Handbook of Texas*, the opening of the Houston Ship Channel in 1914 "made Houston a deepwater port variously ranked second or third largest in the United States, with access to the shipping of the world."

Although the discovery of oil at Spindletop in 1901 had its first socioeconomic impact on the cities in the immediate vicinity of the Golden Triangle, its long-term effect soon caused Houston to surpass them all. The oil companies and related industries eagerly constructed refineries and plants along the new Houston Ship Channel, which provided more accessibility to land-based shipping and safer harbor from Gulf storms than Port Arthur. McComb adds, "By 1929, 40 oil companies had located offices in the city." Roger M. Olien points out in *The New Handbook of Texas* that by that same year, "27 percent of all manufacturing employees in Harris County were employed by refineries. Between that date and 1940, the capacity of all of the installations in the county increased four-fold." He further notes that the biggest of these Harris County refineries was the Baytown-based Humble Oil complex, which "expanded steadily until 1940, when it was the largest installation in the United States."

World War II, and the American prosperity that followed, also hastened the development of heavy industry and shipbuilding (and consequent employment opportunities) in Houston, attracting even more immigrants to the area. McComb explains the basis for this phenomenon:

Nearby coastal deposits of salt, sulfur, and natural gas supplied the ingredients for petrochemicals, and the United States government provided the war materials. On this foundation after the war Houston developed one of the two largest petrochemical concentrations in the United States with such companies as Dow, DuPont, Shell, Sinclair, Monsanto, and Goodyear.

Yet, though Houston was the business and population center of it all, the economic windfall reached cities and towns all the way to, and in fact (especially after the discovery of oil in Louisiana in 1934) across, the Louisiana border through a network of interrelated industrial complexes that stretched along the upper Texas coast. Olien summarizes the result:

All of the activity in the Gulf Coast region expanded the economies of cities and villages, especially after service, supply, and related manufacturing companies located plants and distribution facilities in the Houston-Beaumont-Port Arthur area, thereby diversifying the economy of the region.

That newfound economic diversity was the magnet that pulled French-speaking people, both Creole and Cajun, from their Louisiana homeland to a new way of life, often in Texas. Rural

OPPOSITE PAGE: *Houston Ship Channel, 2005.*

black Creoles especially had experienced a growing dissatisfaction with their traditional roles as members of the sharecropping underclass. That angst, coupled with the opportunity to earn significantly higher wages and benefits, made the relatively short relocation to Port Arthur, Beaumont, or Houston an attractive option for many.

Guitarist and singer Sherman Robertson (who played with zydeco patriarch Clifton Chenier in the Red Hot Louisiana Band for over three years in the 1980s) recalls the postwar situation that prompted his own Creole father (who had been Chenier's childhood friend) to come to Texas:

My father was a sharecropper who went off to fight World War II, a man who was driven to be some-body. I was born in 1948, after he had returned from the War in '46. When he came to Houston [in 1949] from Breaux Bridge [Louisiana], he left the mules and the plow hitched. He abandoned his field. Because he had been to World War II, and then to come back and say 'I've got to get back in the sharecropping groove,' well, he just didn't fit that groove anymore. . . .

To my family, Houston offered a way out, a new way to live.

Like the elder Robertson, and both before and after him throughout the twentieth century, thousands of black Creoles embraced that "new way to live" by moving to Texas.

As acclaimed Creole accordionist and zydeco bandleader Lonnie Mitchell (ca. 1925–1995, a native of Liberty, Texas) put it, "Wasn't nothing going on in Louisiana but farm work hardly. . . . But you know people could come from Louisiana and go to work in a refinery or any of them big old jobs over here. That's why so many people moved here."

Another source of steady jobs was the civil service. For instance, Alcide "L.C." Donatto Jr. (b. 1953), the son of the deceased Houston zydeco accordionist known mainly as L. C. Donatto (1932–2002), recalls that after his parents moved from Opelousas, Louisiana, to Houston's Fifth Ward in the 1950s, his father found immediate employment at the Todd Shipyards before taking what he considered to be a better position, "working with the city." Likewise, former bandleader Dalton Broussard (b. 1911)—the patriarch of a clan than has produced several generations of zydeco musicians—left Louisiana around 1960 and eventually secured a good career for himself with the City of Houston, where he served for over twenty years. "I was working on a farm, and I left the farm and come here to Texas just to make money, yeah," he says.

However, Creole migration to the Lone Star State did not occur exclusively in urban centers. For example, Dan Rubit (b. 1942), another zydeco accordionist born of Creole parents who had migrated from Louisiana, points out, "I was born here in Texas, in Liberty . . . around Raywood. . . . My daddy bought some property up there . . . and we made a good homestead out there, farming. So I grew up on a farm."

Dalton Broussard (with family portrait) at home, Houston, Texas, 2005.

Nevertheless, by as early as the second decade of the 1900s the majority of the Creoles arriving in southeast Texas tended to gravitate toward the largest cities of the region—and especially to Houston and its near-northeast-side neighborhood known as Fifth Ward. First established in 1866 on land that had been settled by emancipated slaves, Fifth Ward by the 1920s had become home to the city's highest concentration of black Creole residents. The enclave where they primarily clustered, near DesChaumes Street, soon became known as Frenchtown.

In his *American Music* article, Minton notes that by 1922 Frenchtown covered about "a dozen or so city blocks" containing approximately five hundred residents; however, "as Creole migration increased, especially after the great Mississippi River flood of 1927, the district expanded accordingly, eventually including three times its original area."

Carol Rust, in a 1992 *Houston Chronicle* feature story on the history of Frenchtown, includes a profile of three sisters (Lena Mouton, Mabel Guillory, and Sarah Patt) who were part of that influx:

Like most of the elderly Creoles who live in Frenchtown, the sisters came here after the Mississippi River flooded southern Louisiana in 1927, destroying crops and homes and drowning livestock.

After the flood, fields and barns north [and west] of the Mississippi's waters were thick with refugees who camped there until they figured out where they would go. Like many other Creoles, the sisters' parents, sharecroppers south of Lafayette, gathered up their nine children, boarded a train and headed for Houston, where cousins and friends had told them there were jobs, shorter workdays and better salaries.

Their father landed a job at a meatpacking house, and the children enrolled in school. No one in Houston had ever heard their language, a melodic French peppered with Spanish and slang. And they'd never seen the light-skinned and sometimes blue-eyed and blond Creoles. . . .

"They told us we were too white to be black and too black to be white," Mabel Guillory says. . . . "Up until then, we didn't know we were different from anybody else. In Louisiana, all the people we knew were Creole."

But the Creoles in Houston banded together in Frenchtown, where their food, music and culture—and even their own French newspaper—thrived in spite of the distance from south Louisiana. A community of modest wooden houses sprang up, with neighbors helping one another build their homes in return for gumbo, home brew and music.

Despite having relocated to the big city, the first generations of Frenchtown people often retained some of their country ways. Because the neighborhood was located on what was then the edge of town, it still offered them access to a natural, quasi-rural environment in which some elements of their ancestral lifestyle could survive. A 1989 *Houston Post* article by David Kaplan illustrates the point, beginning with a comment from former Frenchtown resident Bob Lee:

"On the other side of the street (in Fifth Ward), the guy's gonna wanna talk to you about basketball and how well he shoots pool. In Frenchtown, he's gonna talk about his horses or hunting or dominoes. . . . They've still got a ruralness in them."

Frenchtown was a tightly knit community. "They all built each other's houses," says retired blacksmith Charles Broussard, a 73-year-old Creole who grew up a half mile from Frenchtown, but spent a lot of time there.

In its first decades, Frenchtown had a country atmosphere. "There was good hunting, mostly quail and rabbit," says Broussard. . . .

"If someone killed a hog, they'd spread the meat, spread it around to the neighbors," says Leroy Ellis, a 46-year-old Frenchtown carpenter.

George "Pap" Alex, a 69-year-old Frenchtown resident, remembers seeing lots of chickens, pigs and gardens in the neighborhood too.

Though Frenchtown was a residential and small-business district, many of its black Creole inhabitants found good jobs nearby, especially at the various plants and docks along the upper portion of the Houston Ship Channel, as well as at Southern Pacific Railroad's huge Englewood Yard. "We used to joke that you couldn't get a job at the rail yard unless you were a Frenchman," longtime Frenchtown resident Catherine Trahan told Rust.

An accordion player named Anderson Moss (who died in Houston in his eighties in 1996) was one those immigrants, having arrived in Frenchtown from Maurice, Louisiana, in 1928. As he told Michael Tisserand in *The Kingdom of Zydeco*, "Louisiana people took over this town. . . . All you had to do was say you was from Louisiana, and they would hire you right there." Tisserand also cites Ernest Henry, a friend of Moss's, who adds his agreement: "They know you sweat in the field with the cotton, sweet potato, cane. . . . Myself, that's how I got hired. The man wouldn't hire nobody if he wasn't from Louisiana."

Although they did on occasion labor side by side with non-Creole blacks (and although not all of Houston's black Creoles lived in or near Frenchtown), during the first half of the twentieth century Frenchtown people tended to work and socialize primarily among themselves, maintaining their unique cultural identity within the larger African American community of Houston. As Kaplan writes, "Frenchtown was once like a miniature foreign country."

One reason that many Texas blacks evidently considered Frenchtown people to be somewhat exotic was their almost universal devotion to Catholicism and its rites and lore. As the Texas-based cultural historian Mack McCormick (b. 1930) recalls from his own firsthand observations of Frenchtown in the late 1940s and the 1950s:

Frenchtown was heavily family people. Steady jobs were predominant, and they were regular church members. They were Catholic, as opposed to Protestant or nothing, which is always a big factor in communities. . . .

A community is often defined by other people more than by itself. And hearing about French-town from other blacks, they would talk about them as Catholics. Sort of amazed, like, what is all this? At the time, you know, the Latin mass was still there and so on. . . . I guess a lot of blacks sort of thought of Catholics as a foreign religion, or some peculiar kind, you know, that people from Louisiana dealt with. . . . They knew it was just alien, or thought of it that way.

Houstonians also found Frenchtown residents unique because some of their physical characteristics set them apart from other blacks in Texas at the time. Given the racially mixed lineages that defined them collectively as Creoles, they were uncommonly diverse in appearance. "Some were as black as a black shoe with curly hair. Some looked like Indians. Some looked Spanish. Some looked white. I saw kids with blond hair and blue eyes," restaurateur and Frenchtown denizen Phyllis Jarmon told Kaplan.

However, despite the wide range of skin tones and physical traits among them, a sense of rich ethnic heritage surely united the people of Frenchtown, as it did most Creoles in the region. Strong cultural ties distinguished them from practically every other group in southeast Texas. No one talked the way they did, blending the French idiom of their ancestors with uniquely accented English. Few if any others at the time practiced or fully appreciated their distinctive culinary traditions. Their fervent Catholicism often estranged them from other blacks. And when they made music, intoning lyrics in a strange patois while accompanied by an uncommon instrument, they simply sounded like nobody else.

THEY MAINLY CALLED IT LA-LA MUSIC—that strange, nonamplified, accordion-based folk tradition that the black Creoles brought from rural southwest Louisiana to Texas destinations such as Port Arthur, Beaumont, and the Frenchtown neighborhood. In the 1920s, '30s, and '40s, it was mostly performed solo or with fiddle accompaniment, usually backed by some improvised percussion on household utensils such as the washboard. It was an informal music, a sound one would not have heard in the fine nightclubs of black Houston during the first half of the twentieth century. It had never featured a drum kit, an electric guitar, or a bass—and certainly not a horn section or a keyboard. It was music performed on back porches and under shade trees at Creole house parties and picnics, music wrought by nonprofessional players, almost exclusively males, working-class men who had learned the old tunes (and how to play the basic instruments) from their fathers and uncles back in southwest Louisiana. At the time, nobody called it "zydeco." When Creoles and others in the region did not refer to it as "la-la," they called it simply "French music." But the social

changes that these westwardly mobile Creoles were starting to experience would profoundly alter that music, leading it eventually to assimilate new influences and evolve into a lively modern form.

The terms "la-la" and "zydeco" are sometimes still used interchangeably today, mainly by elderly Creoles, to refer to the older, more traditional styles of the dominant music of their culture. In common usage those terms also have designated not only the black Creole music itself but also the exuberant dancing that typically accompanies it, as well as the social events at which that kind of music is performed. (People might speak of "doing the la-la," or "going to a la-la," or being "at the zydeco," for instance.) Both words, "la-la" and "zydeco," also function readily as either nouns or verbs, in the latter case signifying the action of performing or dancing to that music. (For example, the city of Beaumont has recently promoted itself, along nearby portions of I-10 as well as in print ads in magazines such as *Texas Monthly*, with the slogan "Beaumont Rocks—and Zydecos, Too!")

Clarence Gallien (d. 1989), a native of the Louisiana town of Opelousas who moved to Frenchtown in 1953, illustrates one such application of the flexibility of the term "la-la" in his comment to Alan Govenar in *Meeting the Blues*:

They didn't call it zydeco at that time, it was la-la. They used to give different la-la at the house or at a little cafe. La-la was a house dance when thirty, forty, fifty people get together and have a good time. . . . Any time anybody plays the accordion, we call it a la-la, a country la-la.

Longtime Houston-based professional musician Robert "Skin Man" Murphy (b. 1927), a Dallas-born drummer who accompanied Clifton Chenier (among others) on recording sessions and regional tours, provides a vivid description of his first encounter with such a "country la-la," an experience made possible after he married a Creole bride. Note how his anecdote utilizes the multivalent term to refer both to the event as well as the style of music he heard there:

When I first met [Chenier] he played nothing but what they call now zydeco, but when I first heard of it, it was called la-la.

I was introduced to it by my brother-in-law. When my wife and I first got married [in 1949], we went to visit her people in Parks, Louisiana. It's right out of Breaux Bridge. And my wife's grandmother lived on a little peninsula. Well, actually it was an island, in Bayou Teche, that old bayou there. We had to cross over a bridge to get to her house. . . . She was as dark as the ace of spades and couldn't speak a word of English but "Ah-lo" [i.e., "hello"]. . . . She started speaking that patois then, and I got lost. . . .

We left there and they said, "They are having a la-la up in Parks."

And I said, "What's a la-la?"

They say, "Come on; you'll see." . . . When we got to this place, I saw all these cars and all these people. And it was a long shotgun-type place. It was a club, but it was made in the style of a shotgun house—just long and rectangular-like. And I heard this stuff going on, and the place looked like it was just moving from side to side, you know.

I walked up and peeked in the door. There were old people on this side sitting down, and there were old people on that side sitting down, and all the youngsters and the dancers are out in the middle of the floor.

I could see over their heads. There was a violin, a rubboard, and an accordion. And I had never seen or heard anything like that in my life. That was an experience! I stayed there and listened to it. . . . Man, those people, oh, they were having a good time! And that was my introduction to la-la, which they started calling it zydeco later on.

Houston accordionist and bandleader Wilfred Chevis further explains the relationship between the two terms by recounting his earliest experiences learning about the music of his Creole heritage:

Traditional la-la music started way back, man. . . . Like my dad explained it to me, they started with harmonicas. Back then they couldn't even afford an accordion or nothing. The French-Cajun people played the little [i.e., button-style diatonic] accordion. And when they would break, they didn't know how to fix them. So they would throw 'em in the trash, and the black people pick 'em up out of the trash and patch 'em up. That's how they learned the accordion. They'd patch 'em up and fool with 'em, and that's how they learned how to play. Back then it was called la-la.

La-la wasn't like the zydeco. The zydeco is more exciting. La-la was a traditional type of music, was laid-back, you know. . . . It was a slower type of beat. Zydeco has an up-tempo, with a little touch of blues to spice it up.

As Chevis also relates in a 1990 *Houston Chronicle* article by Marty Racine, la-la was music made by friends and family, and it mainly served as the informal sound track to various social gatherings:

Mostly backyard parties . . . We did a lot of weddings and birthdays. People have a lot of parties. Most of those were outdoors, because they didn't have too many clubs and halls. We were of the generation that they wouldn't allow into clubs. Every now and then we'd play a church fair . . . and they'd have family get-togethers. That'd be once a year, and everybody'd look forward to that. . . . Back then I played it because of my dad—he really wanted me to play it. . . . But I didn't really like la-la too much at that time. I didn't see any future in it at all.

Button accordions on stage, Original Zydeco Jamm Festival, Crosby, Texas, 2004.

The youthful experience of Chevis, a professional musician and recording artist for most of his adult life, likely parallels that of many other Creole players who started out performing in the la-la style they inherited from the older generations. This early manifestation of—kind of a prequel to—zydeco "fits the classic definition of folk music very precisely," as Lorenzo Thomas points out in *Juneteenth Texas*. He adds the key criteria: "It is casual, related to a specific social function, has a traditional repertoire that is also traditionally transmitted in a master/apprentice mode that, more often than not, exists within the family."

During the era in which large numbers of Louisiana la-la players embarked on urban migrations, some of them also began to move beyond the sonic limitations of the single-row diatonic accordion, the kind that Chevis calls the "little squeezebox," which was first mastered in south Louisiana by Cajuns. This form of the instrument (invented in the 1820s by Germans) does not have a piano-style keyboard or even multiple rows of buttons. Instead, it offers only one row of ten buttons for primary notes in a major scale and three for bass; as a result, it plays a full tonal range in only one key.

In an article on his Web site for Savoy Music, Cajun musician and accordion builder Mark Savoy of Eunice, Louisiana, traces the history of this potent squeezebox in the rice-farming regions of the upper Gulf Coast:

It arrived in Louisiana with the immigration of German farmers, and its popularity in the mid 1850s soon created such a demand on the local business establishments that music companies such as C. Bruno and Sons (est. 1834) in San Antonio, Texas, began supplying a variety of retail outlets. Louisiana stores that sold clothing carried "German style" accordions. Stores that sold farm implements sold them also. Almost every business place had accordions for sale. The accordion was found not in the fishing and trapping communities of the bayou country but rather in the flat, fertile rice farms around Crowley.

As Richard Stewart documented in a 1994 *Houston Chronicle* article, native Texan accordion builder Jude Moreau—like Savoy, a Cajun by birth—has proudly dedicated himself to crafting these old-style instruments at his home-based shop near Beaumont. "I do it out of love to preserve my heritage," Moreau says, before going on to explain the narrow musical range of these small hand-made accordions: "There's no half steps [i.e., no way to play sharps or flats]. . . . There are some notes they just won't make. There's a lot of music you can't play on them because the notes aren't there."

Because of such fundamental limitations, the single-row accordion was unable to perform a diverse repertoire with other instruments that could produce any note in the chromatic range. Consequently, as time passed and accessibility to new styles of music (especially blues, R&B, swing, jazz, country and western, and pop) increased, the more progressive black Creole accordionists—especially those who had moved to large cities—often began utilizing the more versatile double-row and triple-row accordions. Such models allowed the instrument, up to a point, to play in multiple keys, making it easier to collaborate with other types of accompaniment. This development, which would later be accelerated by Chenier's use of the fully chromatic piano-note accordion, was one of the necessary steps toward the eventual synthesis of a new, urbanized form of black Creole music. But despite the importance of advances in accordion technology and harmonic versatility, the essence of that music, its most distinguished quality, was its rhythmic foundation. And those rhythms were, for the most part, nothing new, but almost as old as the people themselves.

THE FIRST DISTINCT FORM OF BLACK CREOLE MUSIC IN LOUISIANA, predating la-la and the popularization of the accordion, was a type of intense, ritualized chanting accented by heavy syncopation provided by clapping and makeshift percussion. As the Creole fiddler Canray Fontenot (1922–1995) told Tisserand in *The Kingdom of Zydeco*, "They used to have that where didn't have no musicians. . . . but them old people would sit down, clap their hands, and make up a song. And they would dance on that, them people." This pre-instrumental, improvisational music was an early style of Creole gospel singing known as *juré* (from the French verb *jurer*, "to testify") that, as Fontenot recalls, often included special dance steps. Minton in *American Music* describes it as "a localized form of the African American 'ring shout,' consisting of a counterclockwise procession accompanied by antiphonal singing and the shuffling, stamping, and clapping of the dancers."

Although some researchers describe the music as completely a cappella and, as Grace Lichtenstein and Laura Dankner assert in *Musical Gumbo*, "most common during Lent, when instruments and dancing were taboo," Minton says (again, in *American Music*) it was "occasionally supplemented by simple percussion such as the ubiquitous metal-on-jawbone scraper or its descendant, the washboard." In *Cajun Music*, Ann Savoy, among others, concurs in an analysis that links the rhythms that define the form to impulses both secular and religious:

The early Creole music was often made without instruments since money was scarce. People would make "marches," rhythmic stomping of the feet, for entertainment. Late at night the stomping could be heard across the flat fields as the feelings got intense. A party could center around a man clicking two spoons together with one hand and banging his cane with the other. Religiously speaking, "juré" singers were powerfully inspirational. They praised the Lord with hand clapping, foot timing, and calling and singing of testimonies to the Lord interspersed with cries of "Jurez, my Lord." Mule jaws, washboards, and sticks rubbed on wood were other popular early instruments.

While Minton, Savoy, and others state that juré singers commonly, perhaps spontaneously, utilized whatever primitive tools may have been at hand for percussive effects, most sources seem to agree that other, more sophisticated musical instruments were absent. Canray Fontenot (in response to Savoy's interview question, "What is a juré?") offers further insight concerning the dearth of instrumental accompaniment in the performance of juré:

It's something they used to do in Lent time. They'd get together and sing and clap their hands. I believe they'd do some kind of march. . . . I remember after Mardi Gras people had this idea that it was bad luck to play music during Lent. I couldn't touch my fiddle during Lent as long as my mama was living.

Given such a seasonal prohibition against handling real musical instruments (which still were relatively rare among impoverished black Creoles of the pre- and early la-la eras), it is not difficult to imagine how juré performers might have naturally supplemented their plaintive vocalizing and hand-clapped or foot-stomped rhythms by tapping, scraping, and pounding on a variety of suitable objects at hand. Spoons, bottle openers, washboards, and other kitchen tools provided ready means to call forth the complex rhythms and polyrhythms of the Creoles' African or Afro-Caribbean ancestry. And while such percussive effects would eventually inform the secular music known as la-la and its successor, zydeco, it is important to note that they originated primarily as a form of intense religious expression.

However, Lent and other Catholic observances were not the only contexts in which juré occurred in rural southwest Louisiana. In fact, a variation on the juré tradition also flourished among Protestant black Creole sharecroppers, who were mainly affiliated with the Baptist Church. For this group, a distinct minority, a juré was a type of ritualized thanksgiving celebration that followed a successful harvest. Joseph "Little Joe" Doucet (b. 1942), a Creole native of the countryside outside of Ville Platte, Louisiana (and a longtime Houston-based guitarist who worked with Clifton Chenier in the 1960s), relates his understanding of juré as it survived in his community:

I was raised up on a farm, sharecropping. . . . Every time we'd get through with our crop, well, they would have a party at somebody's house. And they'd play all night long, all with a harmonica. And they was doing jurés; it was known as a juré. . . .

They'd say, "We're going to have a juré tonight at so-and-so's place," and everybody would hear about it. . . . A juré would happen and people would cook a lot of food, after their crop. You come out good on your crop, and they would have a cooking, and everybody would eat. And after they would eat, they'd get drunk. Get drunk and eat. Uh-huh, after the crop, kind of like thanksgiving, you know, but it was a juré. . . .

And people would stamp their foot and roll that house. And they would keep that time up with their foot . . . inside the house. And you could hear that [he stomps his feet in time on the wooden floor]. And everybody would do that, and they was blowing on that thing. They had the harp [i.e., harmonica]. They was doing the rhythm and everything together with just one person [playing the harmonica]. . . . And everybody kept on doing the singing just all night long, all night! Yeah, they would sing and play that harp, yeah. Uh-huh. No accordion, just a double harmonica, a double harp.

Doucet, who grew up in a French-speaking family and "had to go to school to learn how to speak English," goes on to explain that the accordion was particularly banned at every juré he ever witnessed—and not because of Lent. As he points out, the folklore of his tightly knit black Creole community prompted some people to view the squeezebox as a powerful tool of evil.

The jurés, the thing that they would do, they was scared to have an accordion inside the house, because they thought it was the devil. They was religious people. And they would be saying thanks to God, you know, for being successful with the crop. . . . They was mostly Baptists. . . .

Zydeco was a disgrace to them kind of juré people. They called it the devil. Because the accordion and stuff, they wasn't hip to that type of music. So therefore they was scared of it. If they can't understand it, they get scared of it. And so therefore, the accordion wasn't too much welcomed because they would play them in clubs. The juré people didn't go for that because they didn't like no clubs. They kept mostly to themselves.

Despite such prejudice against the essential Creole musical instrument and the social context in which it often was played, these Protestant "juré people"—like their Catholic counterparts—could nonetheless surely generate some intense rhythms at their ritualistic gatherings. As Doucet quips with a smile, "That's where I got my timing from." And his former bandleader concurs, for as Clifton Chenier once told Alan Govenar in *Meeting the Blues*, "The beat came from the religion people."

Barry Jean Ancelet, in *Cajun Music and Zydeco*, argues that the syncopated beat Chenier refers to is the essentially defining characteristic of the genre:

The clues to the origins of zydeco are the field recordings made by folklorists John and Alan Lomax for the Library of Congress between 1934 and 1937. In these recordings, groups of black Creole singers can be heard performing what were called jurés . . . essentially Louisiana French shouts accompanied only by improvised percussion (clapping hands, stamping feet, spoons rubbed on corrugated washboards) and vocal counterpoints. . . . Later, black Creole musicians, most notably Clifton Chenier, transformed the juré tradition into full-blown dance music, stepping up to a chromatic piano accordion and

OPPOSITE PAGE: *Joe Doucet, Houston, Texas, 2005.*

adding elements from the blues, rock, and swing. Nevertheless, the essence of real zydeco remained firmly rooted in the highly percussive juré style, which was never commercially recorded.

That juré-inspired polyrhythmic foundation is, in fact, the signature trait differentiating the music of black Creoles from that of white Cajuns. Ben Sandmel reports in *Zydeco!* that Alan Lomax "called juré 'the most African sound I found in America.'" Starting with something as simple as the skillful clapping of hands, those beats were soon replicated and amplified by the manipulation of wood, metal, and bone objects commonly found on Louisiana farms of the nineteenth and early twentieth centuries.

Today, of course, Creole musicians use fabricated metal instruments, as well as full drum kits, to generate and creatively explore those intricate rhythms. In contrast, traditional Cajun music follows standardized European time signatures with a regular beat. Though most Cajun bands now include a drummer (reflecting the influence of country music and western swing on the genre) and a few have even adopted the rubboard vest pioneered by their Creole counterparts, it is telling to note that the primary percussion instrument in old-style Cajun music was the iron triangle. It was simply a metal bar (usually no more than one-quarter inch in diameter) bent in a tricornered equilateral shape, suspended by a string held aloft in one hand. Tapped at regular intervals with a small metal stick gripped by the opposite hand, the triangle marked the measured rhythms for ballads, waltzes, and two-steps with an even pattern of "ding-ding-ding." Hence, compared to the much louder and more complex rhythms conjured by Creole performers on the kind of devices that originated in and evolved from juré, traditional Cajun percussion often seems subdued and unremarkable. In his essay in *Juneteenth Texas*, Lorenzo Thomas elaborates on this cultural difference:

Even if some listeners are unsure about the difference between Cajun and zydeco music, it is not hard to hear the element that makes zydeco unique. . . . African percussion in the guise of the frottoir, or "rubboard." The traditional Cajun percussion instrument is the triangle. . . .

While the triangle can be a fierce instrument in the right hands, the zydeco band's corrugated washboard played by tapping and rubbing is capable of a wider range of polyrhythmic effects and seems to be utilized in a fundamentally African approach. . . . With such performers the frottoir has a function similar to the grooved quiro or bead-shrouded gourd (chequeré) used in Cuban and Puerto Rican salsa orchestras.

Thus, African and Afro-Caribbean rhythms and the legacy of juré imbue the music of Gulf Coast Creoles with its own distinctive textures. Like the a cappella Negro spirituals and field hollers that predated and strongly influenced the emergence of blues in the Deep South, juré is the root of the black Creole sound.

Vanessa Davis, Original Zydeco Jamm Festival, Crosby, Texas, 2004.

WHILE THE SYNCOPATED SUBSTRUCTURE OF JURÉ WAS PRIMAL, it originated as a form of group expression, usually religious in nature. La-la, on the other hand, established not only the central importance of accordion-based melodies but also the notion of the lead soloist, the lone individual whose secularized singing and playing (borrowing heavily from the Cajun French repertoire) dominated the music. Typically performed alone or supplemented by only one or two supporting instruments at most, acoustic la-la resulted from a confluence of Creole and Cajun music traditions. As such, it formed the second major phase in the three-part evolution of black Creole music into zydeco.

Singer and accordionist Amédé (also sometimes spelled Amédée) Ardoin (1898–1941) is universally acknowledged as the key figure in the early development of the intertwining of Creole and Cajun music traditions. He is particularly important for the documentation of those Louisiana folk traditions in sound recordings, a phenomenon that first became technologically and economically feasible in the Deep South in the two decades immediately following World War I (and that would come to a temporary halt nationwide during World War II).

Ardoin is likewise significant in matters of race. As Ann Savoy writes of this black Creole's central importance, "Respected by white and black alike and applauded by all as a virtuoso musician, his music laid the groundwork for Cajun music as we know it today. His tunes and words are still sung nightly by dancehall bands." Tisserand adds further explanation for Ardoin's exalted reputation, pointing out that this pioneering figure "brought the blues into Cajun like nobody else before him. His impassioned vocals and syncopated accordion work defined the Creole style and pointed the way toward zydeco."

A native of Eunice, Louisiana, whose father had been born into slavery, this groundbreaking musician is generally credited as the first Creole—and certainly the first Creole accordionist—to make a record (though Ann Savoy notes that a black fiddler named Douglas Bellard may have recorded before Ardoin's 1929 debut on wax). Whatever the case, Ardoin obviously heard, absorbed, and skillfully imitated the early strains of French Cajun music in the countryside and small towns of southwest Louisiana—so much so that many listeners, past and present, have heard his seminal recordings (produced between 1929 and 1934) without realizing that he actually was a black man. His high-pitched vocal style with nasal intonation (as opposed to the open-throated technique common in much African American singing) especially prompted such confusion.

Arhoolie Records founder Chris Strachwitz (b. 1931), who would reissue many of those recordings on compact disc in 1995, provides one such example. In his liner notes to *Zydeco: Volume One, the Early Years*, he reports, "It wasn't until Clifton Chenier told me that 'Amédé Ardoin was the first colored to make French records' that I realized Amédé was of African-American background. To my ears, the recordings of Amédé Ardoin did not sound all that different from . . . Cajun accordionists I had heard on records."

Various accounts, including Tisserand's published testimony by relatives such as Milton Ardoin (Amédé's nephew) or Bois Sec Ardoin (Amédé's cousin), establish that this great Creole musician began playing the accordion in his childhood, and from that point on throughout his short life, utilized his musical prowess on the instrument to make a living—an evidently unprecedented career decision in the agrarian economy of the time. Canray Fontenot told Tisserand that Ardoin, "didn't want to work" and thus would hitchhike on a daily basis from the countryside to any neighboring town, adding that "he didn't give a damn which direction it was—he'd go somewhere he could pick up a few nickels." Though the personal details of his life are sometimes vague, it is widely reported that Ardoin never married, perhaps a consequence of the roving lifestyle he maintained as a musician.

To survive primarily by making music, Ardoin would perform for anybody who might pay him; it did not matter whether those nickels came from black folks or white folks. He also would readily collaborate with other musicians who played French music, especially the white Cajuns from whose culture the old songs largely emanated. His partner on many of the records he made, for instance, was the legendary Cajun fiddle player Dennis McGee (1893–1989), making them a biracial duo at a time when such pairings were exceedingly unusual—in fact, practically unheard of (and not only in the South). As Ann Savoy declares in *Cajun Music*, "In early Louisiana history, a black man rarely received the social acceptance and respect that Amédée is cited as having had. He was *the* musician to hire for country house parties, and he would bring huge crowds to the dancehalls in which he played."

According to popular consensus, however, it was on the stage of one such Cajun dance hall that Ardoin allegedly infuriated some racist observers by taking a handkerchief offered to him by a white female and using it to wipe the perspiration from his face. Lore has it that this public action was interpreted, by a few people at least, as defiance of the segregationist customs of the era—in which a black man might be tolerated as a performing musician at an otherwise all-white social function, but crossed the line of acceptability when any suggestion of personal intimacy with a white woman, however slight, was implied (or misconstrued). Though the subsequent explanatory details are imprecise and inconsistent, most people who knew Ardoin (or who have since researched his tragic life) seem to accept the premise that such an action resulted, later that night, in a bushwhacking by unknown assailants, a brutal beating that left Ardoin brain-damaged and broken. Some years later, in 1941, he reportedly died in an asylum in Pineville, Louisiana.

Yet his recordings and his reputation as the consummate performer of traditional Louisiana French music remain, and therein lies an early connection between black Creole musicianship and the Lone Star State.

On August 8, 1934, sound engineers (employed by the Victor Corporation to produce material for phonograph records on the Bluebird imprint) had summoned a variety of regional folk musicians to the Texas Hotel in downtown San Antonio. Among them was Amédé Ardoin, accompanied by his partner on fiddle, Dennis McGee. Despite the duo's experience performing the waltzes and two-steps of the white French music of rural southwest Louisiana, the six tracks they would record there included some special characteristics that hint at Ardoin's posthumously realized role as the true patriarch of black Creole music.

Of special significance, the titles of two of those songs include the magic word "blues," suggesting the early synthesis of traditional Cajun material with African American forms: "Les Blues de Voyage" ("Travel Blues") and "Les Blues de Crowley" ("Crowley Blues," named after a southwest Louisiana town). Both songs, but especially the latter, are reminiscent of the crudely emotive style common in early country blues recorded during the same era in the Mississippi Delta. Yet because Ardoin's take on the blues featured French lyrics sung by an accordionist, they seem simultaneously exotic and familiar, foreshadowing the subsequent synthesis at the core of early zydeco. It is especially noteworthy that an overview of Ardoin's recording career reveals that his song titles specifically invoke "blues" only four times among the thirty-four tracks he is known to have documented. This one session at the Texas Hotel therefore accounts for half of his total output of such overtly blues-inspired numbers.

Moreover, on all six of the tracks produced that day in San Antonio, there is a form of discrete yet primal percussion. It is a simple sound that was surely common in the performance of such music at social functions, but it had never before, or after, been captured on any of Ardoin's recordings. No, this sound effect did not emanate from an actual instrument. It simply came from the rhythms of the accordionist deliberately tapping his foot, the most organic form of percussion known to man. As such, the Texas session serves as a kind of symbolic harbinger of the role that percussive effects would take in the subsequent history of recorded black Creole music.

Jared Snyder's essay "Amédé's Recordings" provides the explanation that "Eli Oberstein, who was in charge of the recordings, chose not to damp the sound of Ardoin's foot tapping in time to the music. Foot tapping was a critical part of the performance and was something normally eliminated by recording on carpeted floor." Whatever his motivation, Oberstein did posterity a favor. His unusual engineering decision produced a sonic document that replicates more accurately the way Creole music would have been performed and heard at social events.

For example, Louisiana-born accordionist Willie Davis (b. 1930) compares the sophisticated foot tapping that he heard in early la-la performances to drumming: "It was just accordion and washboard, but they was playing drum with their foot on that wooden floor, you see, on that old porch. That would keep the beat, you see, yeah." At some such gatherings the vigorous tapping of feet would also, as Snyder points out, often be amplified, inadvertently or not, by the house-party tradition of having the musician stand and play on a sturdy wooden table in one corner of the room. The primary function of such an improvised platform might have been simply to provide a makeshift bandstand that would elevate the featured artist. That way it would improve both the viewing of the "stage" from the audience as well as the projection of the instrumentation and singing across the room. However, it also obviously established a resonating surface that highlighted any secondary foot tapping or stomping by the performer. Some folk musicians might well have valued such a means for deliberate enhancement of the beat, whether it came from a tabletop or floorboards underfoot.

For instance, in an interview published in part in my book *Down in Houston*, the guitarist and singer known as Texas Johnny Brown (b. 1928) reveals that the classic blues figure Sam "Lightnin'" Hopkins (1912–1982)—who, as will be shown, has his own place in the Texas history of zydeco—schemed to achieve a similar effect in the ACA recording studio in Houston:

And I remember Lightnin' used to take a board, put a board down underneath his feet. And if he didn't have a drum, he'd just pat his feet real hard—on that board—and play right along with it. It always amazed me how he did it, because his timing was his own timing as far as rhythm is concerned.

As this anecdote suggests, at least some country-style folk singers in the Texas-Louisiana region in the early twentieth century (and particularly those who mainly performed solo or with minimal accompaniment) might have desired some type of foot-tapped soundboard for producing their own rhythmic accompaniment. We do not know whether any suggestion from Ardoin might have influenced Oberstein's technical priorities for recording the session; however, it is tempting to imagine that the Creole accordionist could appreciate the outcome (i.e., the fact that we hear his tapping foot) and its implications.

Granted, Ardoin's foot tapping on the San Antonio recordings, though discernible and significant, is nonetheless subtle in comparison to the types of percussion inherent in modern music in general, and black Creole forms in particular. Yet the result of Oberstein's quirky decision, intentional or not, implies the prominent role of rhythmic accents in Ardoin's cultural legacy (harking back to juré), as well as their increasing importance in the subsequent evolution of la-la into zydeco.

In the decades following Ardoin's brief tenure as a recording artist, black Creoles in Louisiana and Texas would utilize various percussion devices made of metal to create even more pronounced syncopation, eventually adopting the wood-framed corrugated washboard (scraped by a spoon or fork) as the main tool for doing so. La-la, in turn, would increasingly come to emphasize its Afro-Caribbean rhythmic framework, in which accents shift fluidly to different beats. The rubboard too would begin to evolve as a serious instrument with its own performance theory of sorts, the better to fashion the chank-a-chank sound. And the songs performed by musicians wielding rubboards and accordions (increasingly, the more versatile double-row and triple-row models) would begin to expand beyond the traditional French music of southwest Louisiana to incorporate elements of the popular African American form known as blues.

BY THE DECADE WHEN AMÉDÉ ARDOIN PREMATURELY DIED, Americans of all races and regions were participating in the generalized rural-to-urban and east-to-west migration trends of the nation. While rural black Creoles continued to relocate mainly to southeast Texas cities such as Houston, Beaumont, and Port Arthur, some also moved (especially after World War II) to the Pacific Coast. In his chapter "Gulf Coast West," Tisserand relates how thousands of black Creoles trekked westward in search of jobs, not only in Texas but also in California. There they tended to settle in big cities such as Oakland (or other communities in the San Francisco Bay Area) or Los Angeles. Over subsequent decades they would develop a California Creole subculture personified by resident zydeco musicians such as Ida Guillory (b. 1929, known by the stage name of "Queen Ida") and Danny Poullard (1938–2001)—both of whom had been born in Louisiana but, like so many other Creoles, raised to adulthood in Texas.

The family of Ida Guillory had moved from Lake Charles to Beaumont when she was nine years old. After her older sister's husband got transferred to the West Coast, her father first visited there in 1945. Tisserand quotes Guillory's summation of what next transpired: "He left this hot weather in Texas, and when he came back, he told my mother she might like it in California. . . . and we moved in 1947."

Poullard's family had departed Louisiana for Beaumont when he was thirteen years old, and today branches of that family still maintain a significant musical presence there through his younger brother, the distinguished Creole fiddler and accordionist Ed Poullard, and his cousin, accordionist Billy Poullard. However, unlike most of his relatives and fellow Texas-based Creoles, he decided independently to leave the Gulf Coast forever. Following a period of military service that took him beyond the region, he briefly returned—only to be disillusioned with the Deep South attitude about race. Soon he settled permanently in California.

Whatever their motivations, large numbers of black Creoles headed west in the postwar era and the decades that followed. Although some of those, as illustrated above, ended up settling as far away as the mythic Golden State, far more chose the relatively easier relocation to what would soon become the fastest growing major city in America, Houston. Many of these immigrants found sufficient reasons to stay there—most obviously, the financial advantages of a higher wage and the lifestyle it could support, but also the already established sense of community in Creole enclaves such as Frenchtown and a network of black

Catholic churches. However, the big-city environment, whether in California or in Texas, and the rewards it could offer also increased the opportunities for them to work with, socialize with, and be influenced by people beyond their primary ethnic group of origin. It thus became more and more common for black Creoles, especially those with good jobs and money to spend on entertainment, to mix with the general African American population.

In Houston, a city that remained largely racially segregated until 1963, that mixing occurred most prominently at first-class black-owned venues such as the Bronze Peacock nightclub in Fifth Ward or the venerable Eldorado Ballroom or Club Ebony in Third Ward. At establishments such as these, immigrant Creoles witnessed firsthand the excitement of professional floor shows, swinging big bands, and nationally touring stars. Accustomed as they were to acoustic la-la music and the informal house-party culture that nurtured it, they now experienced something vibrant and new: dressing in the latest fashions for a night of sophisticated dancing and grooving to live jazz and electric blues. Concurrently, it became more common for these particular black Creoles, not far removed from the sharecropping lifestyle of their ancestors, to own and listen to radios and phonographs—those great conduits of popular culture. And most of the records they heard and purchased featured artists such as Louis Jordan, T-Bone Walker, Count Basie, or others who epitomized this newfound notion of urban cool.

In contrast to many family and friends who may have resisted the migratory temptation and remained in relative isolation back in rural south Louisiana, most of these recently citified Creoles were rapidly expanding their musical tastes beyond the la-la music of their upbringing. And among those who played the traditional instruments and sang on the porches of Frenchtown, some began adapting this old-style music, blending in elements of the latest sounds to concoct something simultaneously familiar and brand-new. This musical metamorphosis, like their transformed selves, would ultimately become a product of both the Louisiana countryside and the big-city streets.

However, these people—bounded not only by music but also by religion, language, food, and more—were by no means abandoning their Creole heritage. French songs performed la-la style composed a major element of their sense of ethnic identity and pride. Through most of the 1940s, la-la, although it was already in an early stage of change, remained the dominant sound track of the house parties and backyard gatherings of Frenchtown. It was theirs and theirs alone, unique folk music performed by Creoles for Creoles—not the kind of stuff the general public, black or white, heard elsewhere in the city. It provided an instantaneous aural link to a homeland in southwest Louisiana, a connection to specific people and places now (at least for the moment) left behind. But over time, as these Creole immigrants grew more accustomed to the ubiquitous language and music of popular culture, the backwards-focused repertoire of old-style French la-la would start to seem, to some of them at least, somewhat quaint. Among the more adventurous black Creole musicians, there were record shops and bandstands full of cool new sounds to explore.

This phenomenon is perhaps best illustrated by one of the patriarchs of Frenchtown accordion playing for much of the twentieth century, Anderson Moss. Tisserand calls him "one of the early Creole arrivals to Houston." Born in southwest Louisiana, Moss had grown up with the old-style la-la of Amédé Ardoin, whom he reportedly once saw perform. Yet by the time he moved to Houston, in 1928, and, years later, started learning to play the accordion, he was more interested in urbane, jazz-inflected Texas blues than in any old tunes from the Creole or Cajun tradition.

One of the first two songs he mastered well enough to perform in public was the 1945 hit "Driftin' Blues," written and performed by Texas City native Charles Brown (1922–1999), a pianist and singer. The other was "Stormy Monday," which had been immortalized on a 78 rpm disc in 1947 by the Dallas-born guitarist, singer, and songwriter T-Bone Walker (1910–1975). Both of these records had been produced in California and were hugely popular with black audiences nationwide. There was nothing rural or French about their distinctively hip, modern sound. Yet Tisserand reports that Moss specifically credited his early success in finding gigs at Frenchtown parties with his novel ability to render those two songs on the accordion.

In the late 1940s and the '50s the independent folklorist Mack McCormick observed Moss firsthand in some of his Frenchtown performances. He provides additional insight on the Creole accordionist's progressive repertoire:

Anderson Moss was particularly interesting because he introduced swing-band instrumentals. He was very fond of them. He played "Jumpin' at the Woodside" or "In the Mood" and stuff like that. Now, you know, a lot of musicians broaden their repertoire to please every faction that may be in the place. That may be an element of what he did, but he also just enjoyed playing those instrumentals—and could do an amazingly good job on accordion. He was a superior musician and capable. I mean a fully capable musician. You could have asked him for "The Star-Spangled Banner," I imagine. I don't know what his background or training was, but he just had a command of music, and he could drop into these different things.

While the self-taught Moss may have possessed a rare musical sensibility, the venues where he performed in his prime catered almost exclusively to black Creole patrons. As Tisserand writes, "Moss played everywhere there were French people to hire him." That his sophisticated, urbanized approach to accordion music was so popular with this audience underscores just how much Frenchtown tastes were evolving. Though it featured the familiar figure of a black Creole on accordion, this newer sound was not la-la anymore. Thus, in

Ashton Savoy, Houston, Texas, 1995.

those years immediately following Word War II, as Creole accordionists like Moss learned more jazz and blues numbers—and especially as they began on occasion to socialize and even perform with local blues musicians—a new label gradually emerged among Frenchtown people to signify this uniquely syncretized music.

For a while nobody really knew exactly what to call it. Then when a common word from an old Creole folk expression finally stuck, few could agree on how to spell it—or in some cases, even how to pronounce it correctly. As Ancelet (especially in his essay in *Creoles of Color of the Gulf South*), Spitzer, Tisserand, and others have previously documented and theorized about, some of the early variations in orthography (and hence, by implication, in pronunciation) include "zarico," "zordico," "zologo," and "zodico." Moreover, the earliest known writing on the Frenchtown neighborhood, Marie Lee Phelps's 1955 item in the *Houston Post*, refers to a Creole house party as a "zottico." But eventually—and, significantly, in Houston rather than in Louisiana—the spelling and pronunciation now recognized universally as "zydeco" would come to the fore.

Ashton Savoy (b. 1928), a black Creole guitarist from Louisiana who began working the southeast Texas music circuit in the late 1940s before eventually settling permanently in Houston, remembers the transition. As he explains in Minton's 1996 article, "Houston Creoles and Zydeco": "They used to call that 'French la la.' . . . 'Well, we going around to listen at the French la la tonight,' you know. . . . well then they started playing the blues, they started mixing that stuff up then, you know. Well, that's when they started calling it 'zydeco' then."

RESEARCHERS GENERALLY CONCUR that the strange Creole word *zydeco*, however it may have been spelled or spoken in the past, originates from the standard French term for beans (in south Louisiana, especially what are called snap beans): *haricots*. In particular, they point to an old expression, "*Les haricots sont pas salés.*" It is a statement that occurs in various Creole folk songs, first documented in the 1934 juré field recordings made by John and Alan Lomax. The line translates as "The beans are not salted," a declaration that once functioned as a folksy metaphor for poverty (in a material sense, for sure, but also perhaps connoting emotional, even sexual, deprivation). On the literal level, it signified the absence of cash with which to purchase salt (or salted meat) for seasoning the homegrown vegetables that provided Creole farming families with their fundamental sustenance.

As such, that coded expression, like the powerful *z*-word that would ultimately be derived from it, is analogous in some respects to the original African American sense of "the blues." Like a man who's "got the blues and can't be satisfied," a man who can't salt his beans is understood to be in a certain emotional state, one tinged with some measure of anxiety, but he is licensed by his sad situation to pursue the desire to escape it (through music, dancing, imbibing, or other diversions). Ancelet cogently observes (in *Creoles of Color of the Gulf*

South) that the line about unsalted beans "seems also to appear in [lyric] situations that feature frustrated courtship or unhappy relationships." But like blues music, the form now known as zydeco offered an outlet for articulating personal suffering and, thereby, through the creative act, for deriving some release from it.

Understanding the evolution of the term now spelled z-y-d-e-c-o begins by noting the way the first two words in the statement "*les haricots sont pas salés*" are commonly pronounced in Creole patois. In French, the plural definite article, *les*, produces an elision that makes a *z* sound when it fuses with the subsequent vowel sound in *haricots* (a word in which both the initial *h* and the *t* are silent). The result is that the French phrase *les haricots*, when translated phonetically into English, sounds somewhat akin to "lez arico" or "le zarico." Ancelet, in fact, has compiled additional etymological research to suggest that "zarico," or a close cognate, could be a term (like "gumbo") of African origin.

Whatever the case, the orally transmitted expression (given here in standard French spelling as "*les haricots sont pas salés*") is known to have surfaced spontaneously in colloquial interchanges and the early folk-music forms of juré and la-la. Significantly, in those occurrences it seems to have referenced an actual vegetable, hard times in general, or more figuratively perhaps, an unfulfilled love affair. However, along the Gulf Coast through the World War II era, neither that line nor its two key words were commonly known to refer to any particular type of music (or music event or dancing). But by the late 1940s, that changed, and the transformed sense of a new word, metamorphosed from *les haricots*, was documented on a record first in Houston, the same place where in the 1950s the now standard orthography initially materialized in print to designate the fused music of Frenchtown.

THE FIRST TWO RECORDINGS TO OFFER EARLY VARIATIONS of the nascent term "zydeco" in reference to something other than unsalted beans were not produced in Louisiana. Moreover, they did not feature any accordions or rubboards played in the la-la style. They were both sung in English, not French. One came from a native Texan and the other from a Louisiana-born Creole who had moved west to the big city. As such, these postwar Houston recordings mark a crucial moment in the early fusion of black Creole tradition and popular culture.

To most fans of American music, the name "Lightnin' Hopkins" calls to mind the quintessential Texas blues troubadour, yet he is in fact one of the first two artists ever recorded using an approximation of the word "zydeco" to refer explicitly to a style of Creole music. How did that come to be?

Born in cotton-farming country near the East Texas town of Centerville in 1911 or 1912, Sam Hopkins first visited Houston in the 1920s before settling permanently in its historically African American neighborhood called Third Ward, located southeast of downtown. It was

Curley Cormier, proprietor, The Silver Slipper, Houston, Texas, 2003.

there that this singer and guitarist would become known by the nickname "Lightnin'" and would launch a career of recordings and performances that qualify him as one of the true blues giants of the twentieth century. As John Wheat notes in his essay in *Juneteenth Texas*, Hopkins is of special importance as a "transitional figure in the migration of Texas down-home blues to urban settings," adding that he became a spokesperson of sorts "for rural blacks, as well as those who had migrated to the city yet still retained their country ways."

Hence, even though he did not come from southwest Louisiana, Hopkins had life experiences that in some respects paralleled those of the many black Creoles who were migrating from remote farms to the city. In fact, in Houston this former cotton picker would meet and marry one such Creole transplant, his Louisiana-born wife of many years, Antoinette. As Curley Cormier, Robert Murphy, and other eyewitnesses attest, Hopkins also spent much time in the Frenchtown community, located just a few miles north of Third Ward. Cormier, for instance, remembers the guitarist performing and hanging out at Alfred's Place, the old club (founded and still operated by the Cormier family) that survives today as The Silver Slipper. There and elsewhere, including during some regional tours in the 1960s, Hopkins would sometimes perform with his wife's cousin, a fellow Houston resident, Clifton Chenier. As Murphy, a former drummer for Chenier, recalls:

There was a place in Third Ward, right around the corner from where Lightnin' used to live. Clif and I played there on Sunday afternoons. And Lightnin' would come around from his house. He'd walk around there with his guitar. It was a house that had been converted into a beer joint. It was close to McGowen [Street], a two-story house. . . . And we'd sit there, and Lightnin' would come around to join in with us, and man, we would have us a jam session! . . .

In the summer of '61, I got on the road with Clifton Chenier, Lightnin' Hopkins, and Sonny Boy Williamson. We had a thing going all through Texas and right on the outskirts of Oklahoma. When we got off of that, that's when we started all these Louisiana trips.

Yet years before any such professional collaboration on road tours, and possibly before Hopkins even met Chenier (who first moved from Louisiana to Port Arthur in 1947), Houston producer Bill Quinn (1903–1976) recorded the blues singer improvising an extended allusion to zydeco. It happened in one of several sessions that occurred sometime between 1947 and 1950 at Quinn's Gold Star Studio (incidentally, the same place where Quinn taped the 1946 hit record of Louisiana expatriate Harry Choates singing the popular Cajun anthem "Jole Blon"). Among the many Hopkins tracks that Quinn documented there is one with the bizarre title "Zolo Go."

The "Zolo Go" title was surely assigned by Quinn after the session, most likely based on his misunderstanding (he was a Caucasian native of Massachusetts, after all) of the exotic word he had heard Hopkins articulate in the studio. As Chris Strachwitz says in his liner notes to the CD *Lightning Hopkins: The Gold Star Sessions, Vol. 1*, "The curiously titled 'ZOLO GO' needs a bit of explanation but as soon as you hear the song you realize that Lightning is singing about his impressions of going out to a zydeco dance. When Bill Quinn heard this, he probably had no idea what zydeco was or how to spell it."

On this track Hopkins also does something exceedingly rare, abandoning his trademark guitar and instead performing solo on the organ. Why? The better to sonically impersonate an accordion, of course—a sound that he had implicitly been exposed to at Creole gatherings around Houston. In its musical structure, "Zolo Go" is a standard eight-bar blues, a form that Hopkins had been hearing and playing all his life, dating back to his early experience as a protégé of the seminal Texas blues figure Blind Lemon Jefferson (1897–1929). But he performs this unusual track with an atypically syncopated beat, and his improvised lyrics make several explicit references to zydeco as a type of music, dance, or music-related social gathering.

The extant version of this recording (on an Arhoolie CD) includes a spoken introduction that was reportedly omitted from the original release on a Gold Star 78 (as the B side for the single "Automobile"). Yet in that opening passage, Hopkins tells his audience exactly what he is going to do. As his left hand plays the basic chords and the right fills in with a simple riff, Hopkins states, "I'm going to zydeco for a little while for you folks. You know, young and old likes that." Note that he first utilizes the Creole word as a verb—and that he observes, presciently, that this particular style of music possesses cross-generational appeal (a fact that holds true in zydeco today). The subsequent lyrics that he sings include specific mention of a "zydeco dance" as well as a description of a woman character who is consumed by the urge "to zydeco." The vignette concludes with one female character advising another that they should "go zydeco."

Strachwitz offers an important sociohistorical context for considering the full significance of "Zolo Go." In particular he tells us that none of the late-1940s Gold Star recordings by Hopkins were ever widely distributed, but they were popular staples on jukeboxes in black-owned establishments throughout southeast Texas, and especially in its largest city. This fact suggests that many of the African American customers at such places, whether they possessed Creole blood or not, evidently understood the cultural phenomenon of going to a zydeco event. Likewise, they recognized the distinct instrumental sound that Hopkins evokes on this unique track. Perhaps nobody knew for sure how to spell that funny word, but as this important recording reveals, Houston was already becoming a zydeco town.

Though, like Hopkins, not a zydeco musician per se, southwest Louisiana native Clarence Garlow (1911–1986) was a Creole by birth, and in 1949 in Houston he too waxed a widely popular single that speaks of going out to the zydeco to have some fun.

Garlow grew up surrounded by old-style string-band music and la-la. His father, Compton

OPPOSITE PAGE: *Lightnin' Hopkins, Chicago, 1970.*

*"Bon Ton Roula" by Clarence Garlow, original 78 rpm disc
(from the collection of Andrew Brown).*

Garlow, played the fiddle, and his mother was a Broussard (one of the most common French surnames in southern Louisiana). Yet when Clarence was only five months old, his family, like so many others before and after, left Jefferson Davis Parish and moved to Texas, settling in the boomtown environment of early-twentieth-century Beaumont. Sheldon Harris in *Blues Who's Who* notes that Garlow was "interested in music early, learning fiddle at eight years of age," and, later, acoustic rhythm guitar and accordion as well, talents that enabled him to work as a youngster in his father's string band. However, as Alan Govenar explains in *Meeting the Blues*, "when he heard the 'amplified sound' of T-Bone Walker, his attitude changed. He wanted to play electric guitar."

Garlow's choice to follow the dynamic lead of the suave Texas-born blues showman T-Bone Walker was shared by thousands of other guitarists, including many Creoles such as Ashton Savoy and Curley Cormier. Harris quotes Max Jones's assessment of the profound influence Walker had on postwar popular tastes: "He was a figure of major importance . . . playing the kind of lean, biting guitar licks and solos which turned a generation of blues and R&B exponents around in new directions." Following his own epiphany, Garlow acquired an electric guitar and learned to play it in this newfangled style, forsaking the music of his father's generation. Thereafter he soon quit his job at the Beaumont post office, formed an R&B combo, and went to Houston to gig regularly on the area nightclub circuit. There in 1949 Macy Lela Henry (1912–1991), who was in the process of creating her own independent record company, discovered Garlow in one such venue and signed him to a deal. The Macy's Recordings label would survive for less than three years, but it did produce two nationwide hits: "Wintertime Blues" by Houston guitarist-singer Lester Williams (1920–1997) and the oddly titled "Bon Ton Roula" by Garlow.

Though Garlow's career-defining record was an up-tempo number featuring a modern R&B band (comprising electric guitar, bass, drums, piano, and saxophone), it offered a national audience a glimpse into some of the mysteries of Creole culture. Its title, like the "Zolo Go" Gold Star recording by Hopkins, reflected a naïve attempt by a studio producer to spell a well-known phrase from the Creole idiom (a trend that continued in 1953 when Garlow recorded a song listed as "Jumping at the Zadacoe"). In proper French, the formal spelling for "Bon Ton Roula" would be "Bon Temps Rouler"—from the declaration "*Laissez les bon temps rouler*" (i.e., "Let the good times roll"). The track opens with six bars featuring rumba-style percussion and a funky bass groove, which is soon punctuated by the exclamatory phrase "*Eh toi*"—an expression (translation: "Hey you!") still so common in black Creole culture that five decades later it would became the name of a Houston-based zydeco magazine (originally *Hé! Toi*, later changed to *Eh Toi!*). In the lyrics, the singer introduces himself as "one smart Frenchman" and then volunteers information about how to have a good time in a "Creole town." Subsequent Creole-specific references include "crawfish," "Louisiana," "church bazaar," and "French la-la." But the climactic line advises his fun-seeking audience to head out of town to the countryside and "to the zydeco."

Although Clarence "Bon Ton" Garlow (as he came to be known) spent much of his professional life performing and recording in various towns (especially along the zydeco corridor that runs from Houston to just east of Lafayette), Beaumont remained his home for most of his life, the place where he died at age seventy-five. It was also where in the 1950s he had owned and operated The Bon Ton Drive-In, as well as where he had worked as a popular radio DJ. Starting around 1955 and continuing into the '60s, Garlow hosted a succession of programs—each of which typically featured "Bon Ton" as the name of the show—on Beaumont stations KJET, KLVI, and KZEY. Though he was arguably a one-hit wonder (and some people would later erroneously credit the song "Bon Ton Roula" to Clifton Chenier, who also recorded and often performed the number), Garlow's signature composition marks an important step in the early introduction of zydeco to a mass audience.

As this section illustrates, two 78 rpm records issued by small labels in Houston demonstrate that by the late 1940s the defining concept of zydeco, a word whose formal spelling had yet to be fixed, was well established among blacks along the western portion of the upper Gulf Coast—and not as a reference to beans. As Hopkins and Garlow utilized the term, some might have perceived it as a mere novelty; however, those groundbreaking allusions to zydeco also underscored a social reality. As artifacts, they indicate that creative interchange and syncretism was occurring between certain Creole folk traditions and black popular culture in urban southeast Texas.

Nevertheless, during the period when these records were first being featured on area jukeboxes, accordion-and-rubboard-based black Creole music was still mainly heard only in the informal context of house parties in places such as Frenchtown or other enclaves. Though Hopkins or Garlow might sing knowingly about such gatherings, they were not yet an entertainment option for the general black population that patronized local clubs. But on Christmas Day 1949, that situation changed, altering further the course of Texas music.

BY THE LATE 1940S, thousands of black Creoles were already well established in jobs and residences in Houston, a demographic fact that facilitated the assimilation of regular waves of new arrivals. And they continued to come, not only from Louisiana but also from rural southeast Texas communities such as Liberty, Raywood, Ames, Barrett, Orange, Mauriceville, and Double Bayou. These Creole newcomers brought with them their folk-music traditions; hence, anytime another button accordionist or rubboard specialist showed up in Frenchtown or in one of the African American wards, it could stimulate a minirenaissance, of sorts, of the la-la sound and the culture that nourished it.

During that era, Willie Green was to emerge as the city's first widely recognized master of the la-la or early-zydeco accordion. He had been living in the Bayou City since the 1920s, and by midcentury he reigned, as the folklorist Carl Lindahl described him at the First International Accordion Festival in 2001, as the "king of Houston zydeco." Though he reportedly died in the late 1960s, his name is still mentioned with reverence among some local zydeco people. Among the many distinctions attributed to Green, he is perhaps most significant for having been, as John Minton writes in *American Music*, "the first Houston Creole to perform French music in a public venue."

Green, who typically performed with only a second accordion and old-style washboard for accompaniment, had since the mid-1940s developed an informal master-apprentice relationship with another accordionist. This younger man had been christened Alcide Donatto back home in Opelousas, but after migrating west, he had become known publicly as "L. C." Donatto (based on his Texas employer's nickname for, or miscomprehension of, the French name his parents had originally chosen). Like other Creole musicians newly arrived from Louisiana, Donatto played old-fashioned la-la. In an interview from the 1980s with Alan Govenar for *Meeting the Blues*, Donatto avoids calling this music la-la, but defines it instead as "the real zydeco," by which he seems to mean the original style of Creole music before it fused with urban blues:

I moved to Houston in 1944, and brought the same zydeco I heard when I was coming up. When you talk about adding saxophones and horns like they do now, that really is not zydeco. The real zydeco was accordion, violin, rub board and an angle iron, a triangle. . . . I heard a lot of it coming up, and I still love it.

Donatto goes on to explain to Govenar how, shortly after his arrival in Houston, he came to work with his longtime mentor: "Willie Green was playing and I stood over at the bandstand. He said, 'You know anything about this?' And I said, 'Oh, a little bit.' He said, 'I'm going to let you try,' and I got on there. Everybody was surprised, I was a small boy."

Over the next few years Donatto played regularly with Green at house parties and Creole gatherings around town. Then a breakthrough moment occurred, and the two suddenly found themselves playing their presyncretized zydeco for the general public. Nothing like that had ever transpired in Houston before, and when it happened, it did so by sheer chance.

Govenar's interview with Donatto gives one account of the circumstances that culminated in Green and Donatto playing at Irene's Café, a venue that would (from 1949 until Green's death) provide them with a regular gig:

And then one time, we were driving around on Christmas morning in Sixth Ward, playing that accordion, and somebody on a front porch banging on a guitar stopped us and went in the house and

L. C. Donatto Jr. (with photo of his father) at home, Houston, Texas, 2004.

asked his wife if we could play some of that [i.e., as an ensemble on the porch], and she said, "I'd like to hear some of it myself." And before you knew it the yard was crowded. They stamped all the lady's flowers in the ground, but she didn't pay no attention to it. She said, "Forget about the flowers, you all." So Miss Irene heard us and came around and seen all the people in the yard.

Reportedly accompanied also by an unknown washboard player, this serendipitously organized band's ability to draw an appreciative audience obviously caught the attention of Miss Irene, the proprietress of a nearby café. As Donatto further explains, this time in an interview with Minton for *American Music*,

She heard that, and she come on 'round there, her and her husband, and seen all them people, said, "Well, why don't y'all come to the café?" And we started from that day. Started from that, and Count Basie or Benny Goodman couldn't draw no bigger crowd than that. . . . And we were the first ones played, that's right, zydeco in Houston.

With the young Donatto as one of his various partners, Green would play his stripped down, acoustic, la-la-style music at Irene's as well as other venues around the city.

While many of the details of Green's legendary local tenure exist only in aging memories, a sample of his playing (at Irene's in 1961, twelve years after his spontaneous premiere there on Christmas 1949) is preserved on one of Chris Strachwitz's field recordings (available on the Arhoolie CD *Zydeco: Volume One, the Early Years*). The four tracks on which Green appears, singing and playing the accordion, with Joe Savoy on second accordion and Edmund Savoy on washboard, are, in fact, the earliest of what Arhoolie describes (on the back cover of the CD box) as "the first historic live recordings of Zydeco music as it evolved in Texas and southwest Louisiana." Those tracks give a glimpse into Green's repertoire as it evolved in the early '60s, a song list that includes the popular Cajun-Creole ballad "Jole Blon" as well as the blues standard by Big Joe Williams, "Baby, Please Don't Go." Such a mixing of styles accounts in part, perhaps, for this music being considered zydeco.

But what's especially striking about these recordings is their primal, spare, old-fashioned sound. It is starkly different from the larger, more instrumentally diverse, amplified, and Creolized R&B that, following the lead of Clifton Chenier, was soon to emerge—and the sound that most people today associate with zydeco. Though Green's late la-la-style music and Chenier's full-force modern zydeco are obviously related, they are as far apart in tone and texture as the simple acoustic African American folk music of the Delta cotton fields of the 1920s is from the evolved, electric urban sound of a Chicago blues combo in a 1950s-era South Side lounge.

Yet within a few years of the 1949 public premiere at the down-home Irene's Café, even one of the most upscale entertainment establishments in Houston was featuring Willie Green's raw brand of early zydeco. Located on Dowling Street, the most prominent thoroughfare in Third Ward, Club Ebony billed itself, as a 1953 Yellow Pages advertisement documents, as "Houston's Beautiful, Exclusive Colored Night Club . . . One of the Nation's Finest." Offering "Dancing Nightly" as well as "Orchestra and Floor Show At Least 3 Nights Weekly," this club typically presented sophisticated big band music by nationally touring artists or local jazz greats such as Milt Larkin (1910–1996) or Arnett Cobb (1918–1989). However, a 1954 item in the local African American newspaper the *Informer* shows that Willie Green and his la-la cohort played there too.

It features a photograph (credited to Marvin Gardner) of three nicely dressed men holding instruments on a bandstand, a microphone stand placed front and center. The fellow on the left, wearing a coat and necktie, holds a double-row button accordion. The man in the middle sports a tuxedo with a bowtie, yet he has a common washboard utensil in one hand and a spoon handle posed in the scraping position in the other. The third figure is shorter, and his jacket is removed, exposing a white dress shirt and necktie. He is smiling broadly as he grips a large piano-key accordion, bellows partially opened to form a V-shaped pattern. Beneath this photograph, the caption reads as follows:

"JAMBALAYA AND CRAWFISH PIE?" Well perhaps not, but the Zodicos "put it in the wind" anyway. This group, composed of two Savoys, Edmund Sr. and Edmund Jr., and the "way-out" man Sam performed for the pre-Lenten Zodico dance at the Club Ebony last Tuesday night. Willie Green, whose name the band bears, was not around for the shot.

Common knowledge suggests that Green and his "Zodico" group (which may have added a supporting member for this special gig) likely rarely if ever played at the swank Club Ebony during the regular year. Yet for a Mardi Gras celebration, Green's rustic Creole music was apparently deemed worthy of gracing its high-profile stage. How so? Such an event would obviously appeal most directly to Catholics of French heritage among the larger black population that the nightclub served. And the annual tradition of gathering for a grand party on a Tuesday (that is, an early weeknight when the regular "Orchestra and Floor Show" would not have been featured) probably facilitated Green's ability to obtain this booking at such a first-class venue. On weekends and during the rest of the year, he would more likely be found in a less formal context, such as Irene's Café.

Mack McCormick, a key figure in documenting early zydeco (and much more) in Houston, recalls the context in which he personally first encountered the kind of music that Willie Green typically played at Irene's:

I guess it was some time in the late '40s here in Houston, I came across [la-la] and wasn't interested as such, at that time, because that was the period I was primarily interested in jazz. . . . I kind of vaguely remember a fiddler and an accordion player, somewhere. That's probably my first encounter.

I didn't hear the word "zydeco" until some time in the '50s. Because I remember when I started hearing it, it was hard to understand what people were saying. I found that the French-speaking people pronounced it better than the other black people. They tended, well, they just didn't pronounce it well enough that you could hear it. It was just such a strange word in the middle of a sentence. And they struck my attention, wondering what it was they were talking about. And then I realized, I've heard the music. . . .

In Sixth Ward . . . near the [former] rice mill on Waugh Drive, just to the west, there used to be a very old little community in there. It was kind of surrounded by just grassland. There was a place in there called Irene's, which people would come to from all over town, and it had zydeco once or twice a week. And it was close to where I lived . . . on the other side of the bayou, just a little short drive. I heard, well, a number of different groups in there. . . .

Irene's would have zydeco one or two nights a week, but the other time, she had practically everything—a jazz combo, a blues band, individual singers. And they would have dancing contests for whatever kind of music they had.

McCormick's description of where Irene's Café was located, as well as the diversity of musical genres that were featured there, is particularly important, for Sixth Ward was not a Creole enclave. As he says of the place, "This is nowhere near the center of Frenchtown, but I imagine the French-speaking people had spread out over most of Houston, away from one particular center by then." Thus, Green and Donatto's initial, ground-breaking performance at Irene's, like their subsequent long-running gig, occurred in a neighborhood that was not predominately black Creole. As McCormick surmises, by the mid-twentieth century, immigrants from Louisiana (and their Texas-born descendants) were so numerous and diverse that they were no longer confined by tradition to one particular district, but instead were becoming part of the fabric of black Houston at large.

Strachwitz's 1961 field recordings of Green at Irene's Café also document a casual house-party atmosphere that perhaps evokes some of the traditional social context of an old la-la. Even though Irene's was a commercial establishment that was surely angling to make a profit, Green and his band seemed to have encouraged patrons to feel completely at home there—to the point of staying overnight to sleep off a drinking binge, if necessary. In a spoken announcement between songs, Green or one of his band members addresses (what would seem to be, judging from background noise on the recording) a room full of happy customers. In a distinctive Creole accent, he encourages them to be comfortable, to order food, maybe to buy the musicians a beer, and so on. But he also embeds a history lesson, as this partial transcription from the Arhoolie disc shows:

We play old zydeco or Louisiana rhythm. You'd better hurry up and "ah-ha," oh yeah!

Ladies and gentlemen, we play right over here every Saturday night. Don't forget about us. If you get hungry, or you get tired, anything, you just order what you want; you will be served. They got barbecued chicken and ribs, gumbo, hamburgers. You know they've even got some chili, hot as it is. I know people that's drinking, you know, they like chili. . . . Just order what you want; you will be served!

You know, you're at home over here. This is where we got started with our zydeco, right over here. We've been playing over here off and on for twelve years. The zydeco got started when we did that jam with that push-and-pull and rub-and-scrub. Right over here at Miss Irene's. It was a Christmas morning—you'd better hurry up and knew it! So we're still over here—you'd better knew it.

We've got a whole lot of food. And if you get tired and can't go home, we've got a whole lot of room back there! Where you can go to rest till in the morning. You'd better hurry up and knew it. Ain't no nothing wrong with that! She's got something for everybody. . . . Cold beer, too. And we drink beer too, back here. Oh yeah, don't forget about that! [laughs]

In the years following Green and Donatto's Houston introduction of early zydeco music at Irene's Café, it became increasingly common for other Creole players to find gigs in clubs and cafes around town. By the 1950s, as the item from the *Informer* demonstrates, the local scene for Creole music was not limited only to Frenchtown or Irene's in Sixth Ward, but extended to Third Ward, the city's largest predominantly African American neighborhood. In fact, several of the additional tracks on *Zydeco: Volume One, the Early Years* were recorded in Third Ward at the beer joint known as the Dow-McGowen Lounge. These include performances by accordionists Albert Chevalier and Herbert "Good Rocking" Sam. Like Green, these accordion players also sing (sometimes in French, sometimes in English) and are accompanied by only one or two subordinate players.

However, the lone track by Sam (who would later be known to many as the patriarch who sired the members of the 1970s-era Houston-based group Sam Brothers Five) is a progressive up-tempo number in a blues-shouter style. Perhaps even more significantly, his lone accompanist is a real drummer (Harold Joseph), not someone scraping a washboard. As Sam's "Good Rocking" nickname suggests, the song has a raucous, early rock-and-roll feel to it. As such, it foreshadows a stylistic direction that many Texas zydeco players would soon start to explore, for the old-style zydeco introduced at Irene's was giving way to something new.

ALFONSE LONNIE MITCHELL (CA. 1925–1995), who is far better known by his middle name than his first, is a key transitional figure in Houston zydeco history. His active career there spanned the second half of the twentieth century, and his repertoire ultimately bridged from the retro style of Willie Green to the progressive dynamics of Clifton Chenier, both of whom had been his informal stage partners on occasion. From the time of his arrival in Houston (in a year he gave variously as 1946, 1947, and 1950) until his death, Mitchell was a true stalwart of the city's music scene, performing almost exclusively in his adopted hometown. As Lorenzo Thomas writes in *Juneteenth Texas*, "Though he became a major figure in zydeco music, Lonnie Mitchell remain[ed] a local musician. Unlike 'Lightnin'' Hopkins and many others, Mitchell . . . never toured Europe even though he has been invited. . . . Because he did not play outside of the community, Lonnie Mitchell served the music in several ways." In addition to the localized stature inherent in having performed in one city for almost fifty years (and through several phases of social changes affecting the contexts for his gigs), Mitchell is also well known for his longtime affiliation with Houston's most historically significant zydeco venue, as well as for serving as a respected mentor figure to at least two generations of players in southeast Texas.

Born in a Creole community near the town of Liberty, approximately fifty miles northeast of Houston, Mitchell grew up surrounded by the rural la-la culture his people had brought with them from Louisiana. Around the age of twelve, while observing the goings-on at one of the house parties regularly sponsored by his uncle, Mitchell developed an urge to play the accordion. It was triggered after he had witnessed a musician (believed to have been named Joe Jesse) expertly working the squeezebox. As Mitchell himself related in a 1993 interview:

I've been playing accordion, putting on dances, since I was seventeen, but I started playing on one when I was twelve. . . . I'm from Liberty, Texas. My uncle stayed in a little town they call Raywood, five miles on the other side of Liberty. Well, this guy would play for my uncle, my dad's brother, every other Saturday. Cornelius Mitchell, that's my uncle, and he was giving dances every other Saturday, about two miles due south of Raywood, right off of that country road. And when I was about twelve, my mother would take me. It was house dances then, you know. Very few people had a hall or, you know, a big club. They'd give dances in houses, take all the furniture out of the living room. Most of the people had big living rooms, you know. And they'd take all the furniture out of the living room and dance right there in the living room, when I was a kid.

One day at such a gathering, young Mitchell grew transfixed by the featured player's accordion skills and by the music echoing across a room full of dancers. During a break, he approached the elder and asked if he could try to play the accordion. The older musician's supportive response, offering to let the boy experiment with the instrument during the overnight aftermath of each party, changed Mitchell's destiny. As he continues the narrative:

And that guy . . . he said, "Go ahead and try it. Just don't go hard on it." So what I did, man, I would get up before day in the morning, me and that accordion. I would pull that accordion till damn near time for him to leave to go, to come back here to Houston where he stayed.

So after I started learning, my mother bought me one. I was about twelve . . . and child, from then my mother would have to make me go to bed! It would be about twelve, one or two o'clock in the morning, and me and that accordion was just whirling! And I learned. And when I was seventeen years old, I was playing good enough for the dances.

As he matured, Mitchell played at Creole house parties in Liberty, Raywood, Ames, and other small towns in the area. Following the la-la traditions he had inherited, he typically presented the music as a solo accordionist-singer with only washboard accompaniment:

Years ago French people called it la-la music. . . . You'd hear 'em telling one another: "Where you going now?" "I'm going to a la-la!" . . .

When zydeco started, that's all they ever used, scrubboard and accordion. . . . Way back when I was a kid, nobody had a guitar or a bass guitar or a drum, stuff like that. Just that washboard.

Though he developed a solid reputation as a performer, Mitchell would eventually give up playing, at least temporarily, while still in his prime. "And then I married," he explains. "And my wife, she belonged to the Baptist Church, and I had promised that when I married I would quit playing accordion." However, after deciding to follow the example of many other Creoles by leaving Liberty County farm life for a job in the city, he immediately resumed. "So I stayed [and did not play the accordion] for ten years, until I moved here to Houston, before I started back again."

Within a few years of his Houston debut, Mitchell had earned the status—along with Willie Green, L. C. Donatto, and a few others—as one of the best players in the city. It was a distinction he would maintain even as the defining progressive sound of zydeco began to evolve, in large part because of the influence of his friend, the future king of zydeco. As he related in a 1992 *Houston Chronicle* article by Rick Mitchell, "In those days, it was just me and Clifton and another guy named Willie Green. We used to play all during the week. Cliff would come sit in with me, and I'd sit in with him. He was the best I ever heard."

Mitchell's special relationship with Chenier, and his strong connection to the Houston zydeco community at large, would be grounded in not only his role as a skilled and steady performer but also his tenure, during a key five-year period, as the proprietor of what is arguably the single most important zydeco house in Texas history. In the heart of French-town, the place originally known as Johnson's Lounge had been established in the 1940s as a neighborhood entertainment venue. In its earliest stage of operations, however, it had featured small-scale versions of the swing-band floor shows that were popular in urban black culture of the era. But after the events at Irene's Café had demonstrated the viability of Creole folk tunes as commercial entertainment, the owner, Charley Johnson, decided to offer some of Frenchtown's indigenous music at the nightclub.

Mitchell started playing his country la-la-style music at Johnson's Lounge around 1951. Later, following the death of the founder, he leased and managed the business himself, renaming it Mitchell's Lounge. He raised the profile of Creole music by hosting live shows there as often as six nights a week, sometimes performed by his band but also featuring Chenier and other talents from all along the zydeco corridor. When Mitchell's five-year lease expired, the property reverted to Johnson's heir, his granddaughter Doris McClendon (1936–1997), a native (born Doris Marie Clifton) of Natchitoches, Louisiana.

McClendon's family had settled in Frenchtown in 1947, when she was still a child. Because her grandparents lived in the second-story space above it, she grew up spending much time at the club. As she related in a 1989 article by Marty Racine, "I would be there all the time. When the police would come, they would hide me in the kitchen. I was too young, but I was doing everything helping out, anyway. They showed me how to run the bar." Even though the instrumentation was limited ("just a rub-board and an accordion," she says), her grandfather's lounge attracted large numbers of patrons. "The crowd would be so big, you'd have to get there by 5 o'clock on Saturday to get a seat," she recalls.

Because of her close association with the establishment, McClendon gladly assumed control of the nightclub at the expiration of Mitchell's lease. She promptly changed its name to the Continental Zydeco Ballroom. Naturally, however, she continued to hire her friend Mitchell as one of the main bandleaders for years to come. As Minton states in "Houston Creoles and Zydeco," the Continental, "often featuring Mitchell six nights per week," main-tained and enhanced its reputation as "Houston's premiere Creole nightspot."

In a 1993 interview, McClendon summarizes some of the history of this Frenchtown insti-tution (and its ever-expanding physical structure) from the time it first switched formats to highlight the Creole music indigenous to the community:

My grandfather, Charley Johnson. . . . He started the Continental Zydeco Ballroom with just accordion and a scrub board. . . . Way back there, zydeco was real popular all around the French-town area, and people was playing it all in the backyards. So he had a small place called Johnson's Café, back in that day. . . . He had a small building there, so he had a scrub board and accordion at twenty-five cents at the door. So that brought the people out the backyards in the Frenchtown

area. They would come around and zydeco on Friday, Saturday, and Sunday, and Monday, during that time.

It got crowded, it was so popular. So he expanded to the building and opened a bigger ballroom. At one time, it was a grocery store and an icehouse and a small place there, hold about seventy-five people, or sixty people, I would say. Then he extended it, icehouse on one side and a small ballroom on the other side, where they could come in, and they had the accordion and the scrub board on the inside. As the Frenchtown community growed, he added a little bit more to the ballroom.

Eventually the price went to fifty cents at the door. And during this time, the Catholic halls was not having zydeco. So that was the only place to zydeco, right there in the Frenchtown area.

From those early days of operation until McClendon's death in 1997, the Continental Zydeco Ballroom reigned as perhaps the largest and most well-known place in Texas to hear the music on a regular basis. Practically every major artist in the genre, whether a resident of Texas or Louisiana, performed there. As Stephen Harris, who worked at the club for twenty-one years, conveyed (in an impromptu roll call during a 1998 interview outside the building):

All of them started in Houston right here: "Buckwheat" [Stanley Dural], "Boozoo" [Wilson Chavis], "Rockin' Dopsie" [Alton Rubin], "Rockin' Sidney" [Simien], John Delafose, Clifton Chenier—he played his last [Texas] gig right here. . . . "Beau Jocque" [Andrus Espre], Paul Richard, Wilfred Chevis, L. C. Donatto, Wilbert Thibodeaux. Lonnie Mitchell, he played his last gig here too.

In its final decade of operation, the Continental Zydeco Ballroom also cultivated a younger generation of musicians. As Brian Terry put it in a 1997 article by Carol Rust: "I didn't get my start there, but I got my jump start. Playing there was like being in the hall of fame."

Mitchell provides his own account, from 1993, of his experiences at this Texas zydeco landmark:

All the while I was doing paint and body work [i.e., his day job for thirty-two years], I was playing at the Continental Lounge. It used to be Johnson's place, way back years ago. That lady, Doris, what's running it now, that was her grandfather, Mr. Johnson.

So I was first playing there three nights a week—Friday, Saturday, and Sunday. . . . After I played there about five years, something like that, that place you couldn't hardly walk in the place, there was so many people. People coming out, from all over from Louisiana. And that was the zydeco place here in Houston. . . .

I played there, and then after the old man [Johnson] died, I took it over. I ran it about five years. Five years, and played at my own dances. . . . After my lease ran out, [Doris McClendon] wanted it,

OPPOSITE PAGE: *Doris McClendon, proprietor, Continental Zydeco Ballroom, Houston, Texas, 1996.*

so I let her have it. And I have played for, I don't know how many years, for her. . . . For old man Johnson, myself, and Doris, all together I have played there a long long time.

Unlike the elder Willie Green, however, Mitchell did not forever limit his accompaniment to mainly a rubboard, in the tradition of la-la. Under the influence of his increasingly popular colleague Clifton Chenier, Mitchell eventually modernized his sound by adding the standard blues-combo support (electric guitar, bass, and drums) and dubbing his group the Zydeco Rockers. As he told Minton for a 1995 article in the *Journal of Folklore Research*, "It makes it sound better, you know, a guitar and drums, to me. . . . I don't know if I could play now with just a washboard. . . . But you know, when you got a guitar and drums and all that, it just, I don't know, give more pep to the music." Of special importance to Mitchell was the musical support provided by a good drummer. As he emphatically proclaimed in the 1993 interview,

You can't play zydeco without drums, you can't. Got to have somebody that knows that timing!
. . . The drum and the accordion is the leader on zydeco. If that drummer ain't right, and he ain't in there with that accordion, he sound like hell. But if he right in there, got the right beat, there you go!

When the rest of the world began to discover Gulf Coast zydeco in the 1980s, Mitchell gained notoriety beyond the Bayou City among some researchers and field-tripping enthusiasts. However, as he witnessed how his friend Chenier graduated from the club circuit along the zydeco corridor to tour widely and enjoy unprecedented commercial success, Mitchell declined to go along for the ride. In that same 1993 interview he explains some of his reasons, drawing both similarities and contrasts between Chenier and himself:

We [Clifton Chenier and I] started playing here in Houston the same time. He had a washboard— it's that scrub board, you know—and an accordion with no amplifier. And that's what I had. And we just got to be big friends, big friends. See, during the week time, when he was playing somewhere, and I wasn't playing, I'd go meet him. And he did the same thing for me. We were just like two brothers. And we'd play together, played together.
See now, he got big, and went to playing out. But see, I had three kids. . . . See now, I didn't want to leave my family. And that's the reason I just stayed right here in Houston to play. If I had wanted to go, I could play just as good as he could. He was playing the piano accordion then. I mean, he always did play it. And I was playing that button accordion. . . . And I could put just as many people on the [dance] floor as he could with that piano accordion.
Only thing that was different, he could really sing, but I ain't got no good voice anymore. I have to have somebody sing for me. I can't bring my voice up and down. That's why he got so big. . . .

He started going around, different places, and they started hiring him overseas. . . . Many of times they tried to get me to go, but I wouldn't go. I didn't want to leave my family. See, I had promised my wife that I wouldn't go off.

Mitchell claims that he never regretted trusting his nesting instinct. His experience with Creole music had always, dating back to the Liberty County house parties of his childhood, been communal as much as commercial. He was accustomed to playing in familiar places for audiences composed largely of people he knew (some quite well), and he preferred it that way. And while the pay and benefits of the automotive body-shop job he held for thirty-two years had a lot to do with keeping him anchored in Houston, Mitchell also simply had little interest in traveling far from home. Thus, even as he aged, until his death he maintained his status as the unofficial king of Houston zydeco. As Rick Mitchell (no relation) observed in a 1992 article, "Although he must sit down while he plays, he says he's not yet ready to retire," adding the accordionist's quip, "I think I'll play music till my fingers don't work no more. I just love it. And I love to see people enjoying themselves."

The length and consistency of his commitment to the music (and to the local folks who enjoy it) make Lonnie Mitchell an especially important figure in the evolution of zydeco in southeast Texas. Though generally unknown to much of the zydeco world at large, he served a key role, one that some might argue was as necessary as that of more commercially successful role models. Lorenzo Thomas, for example, asserts in *Juneteenth Texas*:

Indeed, Chenier's innovative virtuosity in blending Louisiana heritage and blues sung in English propelled the form into the modern entertainment industry; but it is a musician like Lonnie Mitchell who helped keep the source of the music alive. Zydeco—as a folk music—could only survive by being transmitted through the family band, master musicians such as Mitchell, and a devoted audience.

Texas zydeco, particularly as it has evolved and thrived in the state's largest city, probably never had a native-born player more devoted to the tradition, its past and its future, than Lonnie Mitchell.

THE EMERGENCE AND SURVIVAL OF THE SPELLING z-y-d-e-c-o is a story, like that of the Continental Zydeco Ballroom, rooted in the social changes of Frenchtown in the mid-twentieth century. As the hottest point in the cauldron in which la-la was slowly fusing with urban blues, the Creole neighborhood in Fifth Ward was a logical place for the standard spelling to originate. Up till then, this blended music was being labeled—on posters for dances, record labels, promotional chalkboards, and such—in different forms ("zodico," "zordico," "zarico," "zadacoe," "zologo," and other variants). In Frenchtown such terms existed as a means of distinguishing this vibrant synthesis of musical influences from the more purely traditional la-la, from Louisiana. Within the larger black community of Houston, numerous manifestations of that orally transmitted z-word were already established as a potent force, despite the indeterminate orthography. But a white man who was closely observing and documenting that scene would be the one, through the power of publishing, to establish its ultimate spelling.

As most sources (including Ancelet, Sandmel, Thomas, Tisserand, and others) concur, Houston resident Robert Burton "Mack" McCormick is the person who created the new way to write the word that city blacks already were utilizing to describe a dynamic style of music. As a young jazz enthusiast and record collector, McCormick had, by the late 1940s, become the Texas correspondent for *Downbeat* magazine. This position encouraged his impulse to seek out and experience live performances of jazz and blues, an insatiable search that regularly took him deep into the black neighborhoods of segregated Houston. Such journeys were facilitated in part by McCormick's primary means of making a living at the time—as a driver for a local taxicab service. As he explains,

It's all mixed in with me driving a cab. I used to, when I was driving, take advantage of being in different places to get acquainted with things. And in that area [near Frenchtown], the Liberty Road area, the part that fronts the railroad tracks, that parallels it, the Settegast area . . . they had Mexican, black, and the French-speaking Creole black. The clubs just were all there. . . . I heard zydeco there.

And also when I was driving a cab, I would frequently just go to some place like that. Wherever I was, I'd go to some location where I could basically listen to music while sitting in the car or just get out and be close by until I got a radio call. . . . I think maybe the first time I went out looking for it, I went to Johnson's. . . . See, Johnson's used to have non-zydeco music too. They would have a night of blues and so on.

And that's one of the things that I don't think has ever been emphasized enough about zydeco. It's heavily blues influenced, and it was essentially what you might expect to happen, you know, a fusion of one group's traditions with another group's traditions—and the result being something that's new, or not entirely the same.

Frenchtown is just an amazingly good example of people coming together. . . . In Houston, white people were barely aware of Frenchtown and had no idea of these gradations between these communities. I mean, I first heard the word "zydeco" not from people in Frenchtown but from others [blacks] talking about Frenchtown, "where they have that funny zydeco." . . .

And by the way, the word "zydeco" did not necessarily mean the music; it meant the dance and the occasion. It's "a zydeco." "Let's go to a zydeco!" People would say they're going to go "to a zydeco," much like they'd say "to a circus" or "to a picnic": "We're going to go to the zydeco." That

would be Texans, not French-speaking, Texans going out to this special occasion that they liked to participate in.

Though the pronunciation of the term as it was transmitted vocally was fairly consistent to McCormick's hearing, the folklorist also noticed area signs, formal and informal, on which a hodgepodge of unstable spellings of the word appeared. At first it was merely a curiosity to him. But as he began to produce his own field recordings of the different styles of music he was encountering in southeast Texas, he eventually needed to settle on a single spelling for his written documentation of that work. He continues the account:

I had done some recording of what was known as zydeco music, and I had seen a number of post-ers—and had, in fact, begun to photograph some posters, because the variations of the spelling were so wide. And none of them sounded like the word. "Z-I-D-I-C-O," I think, was the closest thing. It just would be all over the place. I think one poster was . . . "Z-O-R-D-I-C-O" . . . "Z-A-R-I-C-O" . . . and so on. . . .

I was going to issue some material, so I needed to come up with a spelling that sounded like the word. See, the pronunciation of the word has never varied very much. I mean, when I first heard it, the way it's said commonly now is pretty much the same way. So I came up with that.

McCormick first formally published the now-common orthography in his transcription of lyrics for one track included on the double LP *A Treasury of Field Recordings*, which he produced and which was released in 1960 by the British label 77 Records. This two-volume set offered samples of the different types of folk music McCormick was documenting during the late 1950s in and around Houston. One performance was by Dudley Alexander, a black Creole who first came to the city from south Louisiana in the 1940s. Playing a small type of accordion called a concertina, and accompanied only by fiddle and washboard, Alexander sings in both English and French. His bilingual treatment of the 1930s-era blues classic "Baby, Please Don't Go" incorporates a spoken introduction that includes this commentary: "*Le zydeco,* that means snap beans in English, but in French, *on dit zydeco* [i.e., one says 'zydeco']."

Faced with having to transcribe Alexander's use of that slippery *z*-word, McCormick set-tled on the evidently unprecedented "z-y" spelling in part because of its consonance with the spoken proliferation he was hearing, but also for another reason, purely personal and eccen-tric. The best explanation comes from McCormick himself:

That z-y combination makes an interesting symbol. At some point in my youth, I used to look at the back of the dictionary. I don't know why, but I still can remember a lot of those words, like

"zymurgy" and "zygote" . . . Because there's only a page and a half, and you can read them all, it's not hard to master the Zs. [laughs] . . . And now one of them is "zydeco." . . .

The spelling, I mean, I didn't sit down and agonize about it. It seemed obvious to me that the way to get the proper accents was the way it's now spelled. And so I spelled it that way.

. . . It's an exotic-looking series of lines and patterns, you see. And it therefore kind of calls attention to itself a little bit in print. And if it's new to you, it especially calls attention to itself.

So I think what happened with the stuff that I wrote in the '50s was, you know, there's a lot of people that, if they see a new word, their eye just stops. You know, what is this? What is this all about? So it immediately registered on a lot of people. And it was within a year I kept seeing it everywhere, in terms of the writers in music and so on. At that time they were mostly commenting because there was no widespread zydeco music that was known. It was about another year or two before it really started to get recorded. But the word attracted people, just all by itself.

The name for this newly synthesized form of music alluded, of course, to the old Creole folk expression about beans: *"Les haricots sont pas salés."* But McCormick also had observed a Frenchtown dancing ritual that called to mind the act of snapping open the pods of such vegetables. This unusual dance step is perhaps somehow related to Ancelet's description (in *Creoles of Color*) of a folk custom among natives of the Indian Ocean island of Rodrigue, in which an elaborate dance "re-enacts the planting of beans." However, McCormick interpreted the Frenchtown dancers to be symbolically suggesting the postharvest breaking of beans into segments—the act from which the colloquial "snap beans" moniker derived. As he recalls the sight,

The dance that typically would be seen, people would leave their hands very loose. And as they danced, the hands would make a pattern. That pattern resembled . . . people breaking snap beans. So that, to me, has always been a perfectly good explanation of the term. [laughs] Some people like to bring in the song with "the snap beans aren't salty." But, to me, the essence is just that the snap-bean motion is part of a dance.

In addition to writing the word according to his new spelling in the liner notes for *A Treasury of Field Recordings* (which remains the first citation for "zydeco" in the authoritative *Oxford English Dictionary*) and in articles—and seeing other music pundits follow suit— McCormick eventually noticed something even more important. It offered verification that the quirky orthography was being adopted by the popular culture:

This local printer . . . Fred Marshall, he came across it somewhere. I think some people had started using it, you know, on the handwritten posters. . . . But anyhow, he came across it. So . . . then the

I·L·A·HALL
27th - MARKET
FRI., OCT. 7
9:00 UNTIL 1:00   PRE-SALE $1.50   AT DOOR $1.75
LOVELY LADIES SOCIAL - CHARITY CLUB
Sponsors A
BIG ZORDICO DANCE
IN PERSON
The EXCITING
CLIFTON
"EVERYTHING
IS ALL RIGHT"
"LOUISIANA BLUES"
CHENIER
RED HOT LOUISIANA BAN
FRED MARSHALL PRESS — Poster Printers — Houston, Texas

OPPOSITE PAGE: *Mack McCormick (with poster from the Fred Marshall Press showing an earlier variant spelling of "zydeco") at home, Houston, Texas, 2003.*
ABOVE: *Zydeco dancers, The Silver Slipper, Houston, Texas, 2003.*

phenomenon became something that I am somewhat proud of. On the one hand, the music writers, the scholars started using the word. And then the community itself started using the word. Now it's just used everywhere. . . . I'm talking about using the spelling; the orthography is what I invented. But the community adopted it, and that is something that I never would have expected to be true. But Fred Marshall was largely responsible for that, because he just used it everywhere. . . . He was the poster man in town, for everybody.

As the word and its ultimate spelling became more commonly recognized in Texas, it soon crossed back into Louisiana, where it came to signify practically all modern black Creole music. This development dismayed McCormick, who had never intended for "zydeco" to replace the older term "la-la." Instead he had hoped that "zydeco" would serve to differentiate the doubly syncretized urban music of Frenchtown from the traditional canon of Louisiana Creole songs. As Tisserand observes in *The Kingdom of Zydeco*, the Houston folklorist had intended for "zydeco" "to apply to the local alloy of Texas blues and French Creole music . . . and he was horrified when the word was sucked backed across the Louisiana border."

McCormick retrospectively still insists that the word should have been understood to denote this fundamental difference:

Zydeco is not anybody else's music. You know, it's Frenchtown's music. The world and Louisiana have usurped the term to fit what they have, and what they have has become a lot like [Frenchtown music]. . . .

Basically the music that was called zydeco was heavily blues influenced, and that's why that first thing I recorded was a blues, a bilingual blues. That seems to be the essence of the matter. The music from Louisiana that has not changed, that's come into Houston, is Louisiana music. Zydeco is Frenchtown music, you know. And it's gone through these different acculturations, changes.

And that's zydeco, and I liked it in that very limited sense, because that was the way the community gave me to understand that it was applied. They would talk about music from Louisiana and call it la-la or by these other terms . . . "that old-time music."

But it was always understood that zydeco was a combination of Louisianans and Texans. You had to have them, even though there might not be any Texans in the actual group; they somehow had been altered. And it's that thing of being altered that is so fascinating.

Having birthed a catchy new mode for spelling what for many was an obscure foreign term, McCormick thus played a crucial behind-the-scenes role in naming a postwar American musical form. But the full acceptance of zydeco (both the word and the music) would require regal sanction. And in the 1960s it would get it, compliments of the king.

Clifton Chenier's accordion, at C. J. Chenier's home, Houston, Texas, 2004.

Three

THE KING AND HIS
WESTERN KINGDOM

Among the thousands of black Creole immigrants who moved west of the Sabine River in the late 1940s was a singing accordion player who would ultimately become, especially during his lengthy tenure in Texas, the defining force in modern zydeco. By the time of his death in 1987, he would be internationally recognized as the z-word incarnate—its embodiment and its primary ambassador. More so than anyone else, past or present, he defined, maintained, and disseminated its fundamental sound. And during his prime phase of doing so, he was a longtime resident of the Lone Star State's largest city. As progressive Cajun bandleader Zachary Richard stated during a 1990 interview on NBC's *Tonight Show* (as cited by Thomas in *Juneteenth Texas*), the unique characteristics of contemporary zydeco emanate mainly from a single source: "a musician named Clifton Chenier, down in Houston."

Born in 1925 in rural southwest Louisiana, Chenier started playing the accordion in his late teens. But by his early twenties he had moved briefly to Lake Charles, then on to Texas. The two key cities in his intermediate and advanced development, as both a versatile musician and a professional showman, were Port Arthur and Houston. While residing, performing, and recording in southeast Texas through much of the late 1940s, '50s, and '60s, Chenier emerged as the great innovator of a new genre of music. It was there that he and his brother invented the now standard version of one of the two essential zydeco instruments.

It was there that he first fused electric blues with la-la and developed a strong following beyond the Creole population (a feat made possible by playing in urban nightclubs and auditoriums to general African American audiences). It was there too that he found some of his most noted sidemen and collaborators, and there that he made many of his greatest recordings—including the one that confirmed forever the word itself. And although the zydeco monarch is undeniably a product of the Louisiana homeland where he was born, raised, and died, he first established his kingdom on the western edge of a region where black Creoles had lived and made music for decades.

Though he has been gone from the scene for many years now, the legacy of Clifton Chenier lives on in Texas, just as it does in Louisiana. Even after he moved back to reside full-time in Lafayette for the final decade or so of his life, the king remained a regular presence along the Gulf Coast zydeco corridor that he helped create. Whichever side of the river he was on, he had many devoted fans and friends, some dating back to his childhood. And generally speaking, his people adored him. As Doris McClendon, the matriarch of Frenchtown's former Continental Zydeco Ballroom, put it in a 1993 interview:

Clifton Chenier originated the zydeco, and he played his last dance [in Texas] at the Continental Ballroom before he died. He's a Grammy Award winner, been all over the world. But his last dance in Houston was played at the Continental. . . . He was the king! It was his birthday party. When you say "Clifton Chenier," the people put the evening gowns on. He was truly the king of zydeco . . . [and] he was one of our own.

As a young man growing up near Opelousas, in an area described (by a relative named Mary Thomas) as "in the country, a little old place called Prairie Laurent," Chenier heard accordion music all the time. His father, Joseph, played the single-row button accordion and probably introduced him to basic instrument technique. And in the evenings after fieldwork, especially on Saturdays, the sound of the diatonic squeezebox was common at neighbors' houses throughout the area. Yet despite growing up in the heartland of country la-la (and for reasons that, as Tisserand and others have noted, are unclear), Chenier apparently first owned and regularly played the larger, fully chromatic piano-key type of accordion. This point of contrast with almost all the other black Creole accordion players of the time is crucial, for it laid the foundation for the potent musical synthesis Chenier would later achieve in urban Texas—the results of which he would then transport back to Louisiana and ultimately to the world at large.

Mary Thomas, Chenier's cousin by birth and a longtime resident of Houston, relates some of her memories of those early days in the development of the musician:

Mary Thomas, Houston, Texas, 1995.

I am Clifton's adopted sister. I grew up in the house with him. . . . I'm younger . . . but he was there when I was brought into the house.

I think he might have been about eighteen [when he started playing accordion]. . . . I remember that very well. Well, when he first started playing the accordion, it was a cousin—this guy [Isaie Blasa, who] said he was kin to us. . . . He came over and, I think, gave Clifton an accordion, or loaned it to him. . . . Clifton started rehearsing on it, playing it. It was like an every night thing, you know. Once he got his hand on the accordion, it was like, every night.

By her own account, the youthful Thomas often served as a facilitator of sorts for Chenier's practicing on the instrument:

Clifton was scared of the dark, you know, like to go outside where it was no light. . . . And we had this old barn, where we kept sweet potatoes and corn and what have you. So he would always ask one of us kids to go out there with him . . . so I would go out there with him, and he would sit on the inside, right by the door, and play the accordion. And I would sit on the outside of the door. . . . So he would play and play and play. . . . He never stopped playing until our mama would stick her head out the door and say it's time to come in. . . . It was zydeco then, but I don't think they were really calling it that then. . . . He played traditional.

. . . He started off on the big [i.e., piano-key] accordion. He never—I read something where somebody was saying something about him playing the little accordion—but he never played it, never. He started off on the big accordion. This accordion that I told you about that our cousin gave him, that was a big accordion. He never played the little one. He didn't know how to play it.

While some music historians have speculated that Chenier must have initially played the smaller and far more common button accordion, his own statements on that matter are consistent with Thomas's firsthand account. For instance, Tisserand says in *The Kingdom of Zydeco*, "When he was asked, Chenier would always report that his first accordion was a piano-key that an Opelousas house dance player named Isaie Blasa gave him," noting also that the instrument may have been a loan (that was later retrieved by Blasa), not an outright gift. One of Chenier's lifelong friends, and ultimately a fellow immigrant to Houston, the musician Willie Davis, offers his own observations on the matter:

I've been knowing Clif every since I've been knowing myself. He's the one that coached me on that piano accordion, you know. He had that piano accordion early on, yeah, yes indeed. . . . Most of them played button accordion, but he was the first one who played the big one. . . . The first time I seen him with an accordion, he had that piano accordion. Because you'd pass right in front of his

house to go to town, to Opelousas—we was in the country. And there he was on that porch with that piano accordion.

However, despite such oral-historical evidence that he possessed and at least experimented with his piano-key instrument while still living in his parents' home, Chenier himself often stated that he did not learn to play until he left the countryside and moved to the city. For instance, Ann Allen Savoy's book includes Chenier's interview with Ben Sandmel, and it contains the following assertion: "I left Opelousas way back there in 1946, and went on to Texas. And I learned how to play the accordion in 1947 and '48. From there, I played all around Texas and everywhere." Moreover, in a separate interview in Alan Govenar's book, Chenier says, "I learned to play in Lake Charles and in Texas, Houston mostly. . . . I never picked up an accordion until 1947."

How to account for such a discrepancy? Chenier may have simply meant that he *played with* but did not fully understand *how to play* his instrument until sometime after he moved. In other words, he might not have considered himself a true musician until he had gained full knowledge of what it could do. It can be assumed that he had minimal understanding of the keyboard accordion when he first acquired one. To complicate matters, practically every Creole player he knew at the time used only a diatonic squeezebox, a smaller machine that functions according to different principles. (For example, the piano-style instrument plays the same note whether it is pushed or pulled, whereas the smaller button models make different notes with the expansion or contraction of the bellows.) Thus, it may have been almost impossible for Chenier to watch others and learn, or to ask questions or get advice, isolated as he was in a rural area dominated by old-style la-la players. However, once he relocated to a city environment, he would have been far more likely to encounter musicians who could introduce him, directly or indirectly, to basic theory and demonstrate for him the full range of chromatic possibilities of his instrument.

Whatever the case, the fact that he chose to play the more musically versatile type of accordion was fortunate. For once he migrated to urban centers west of his prairie of origin, that unusual piano-key model would enable him to expand his repertoire beyond basic la-la and play modern blues and R&B. Unlike the single-row diatonic models, which were locked in a fixed pattern of musical intervals, the chromatic accordion made it possible for him to perform any song in any key and to play sharps and flats—a necessity, since he would begin to collaborate with city-dwelling players on other instruments (such as electric guitar and saxophone), as well as with singers from beyond the Creole tradition.

One such knowledgeable musician is Houston drummer Robert Murphy, who played and recorded with Chenier in the early 1960s. A college graduate with a degree in music education, Murphy first performed professionally on the trumpet (before suffering an auto-

OPPOSITE PAGE: *Piano-key accordion.*

mobile crash that seriously injured his mouth), and could well appreciate the musical contrast between Chenier and other Creole accordion players. As he explains,

That's the difference between Clif and all those early wind-jammers. You know they called the little ones [i.e., button accordions] wind-jammers, but the big one, that was the piano accordion. . . . Clifton Chenier, as far as my memory serves me, was the first man to play the piano accordion with zydeco, la-la, whatever you want to call it. . . .

Clif knew most [chord] changes. But la-la music wasn't like a regular twelve-bar blues . . . He did know some blues and twelve-bar changes. But when I started working with him, we started working with more blues and jazz numbers. And I'd teach him the changes, when to change. And he'd catch on just like that. Clif was smart. Clif was a good musician.

Back in the postwar '40s, Chenier had not necessarily chosen to move to Texas as a way of expanding his musical horizons and becoming a star, though that would be the eventual result. Instead, like so many others from Louisiana, he had been motivated by the good pay-checks available there for doing industrial work. As Tisserand documents in his book, after a brief period in Lake Charles, Chenier had settled in Port Arthur with his bride, Margaret, "and was making a living pumping gas and driving trucks for the Gulf Oil Refinery." Mary Thomas recalls, "I think his wife wanted to move to Port Arthur," but adds that he was also following the example of his older brother: "Cleveland moved to Lake Charles first, then moved on up to Texas . . . and Clifton followed him to find a good job."

Reunited in Texas, the Chenier brothers were soon performing together, Cleveland (1921–1991) providing percussion with the traditional la-la washboard. At the end of a typical work-day, they would station themselves outside the gates of the petroleum factory, where throngs of fellow laborers would pass with each shift change and sometimes reward them with tips. Before long they were also making music, still mainly as a duo, in icehouses and clubs across the Port Arthur-Beaumont-Orange region of southeast Texas. Even then the zydeco corridor was taking shape as musicians shuttled back and forth in both directions, for the Cheniers also played weekend gigs from time to time back across the state line in southwestern Louisiana towns. Soon they were also regularly traveling west to the larger city of Houston.

During this period of his earliest residency in Texas, Chenier's public persona metamorphosed too. Gone were the modest sharecropper clothes and the closely trimmed hairstyle of his rural Creole upbringing, replaced forever with a new manner of self-presentation, one that conveyed the essence of urban fashion and a cool demeanor. It consequently could cause quite a stir back in Acadiana whenever the transformed native son would return in all his citi-fied glory. Tisserand, for instance, quotes one of Chenier's old friends from Opelousas, Wilbert Guillory, in *The Kingdom of Zydeco*: "He came back from Texas, he was a changed man. . . . He had all kinds of colored clothes, and he had his conked hair. Gold teeth, talked nice, talked proper." The same source offers a series of pertinent observations from another Louisiana acquaintance, Frank Marlbrough:

He brought in a new style, that's what I think it was. Texas was always ahead in fashion. . . . Remember when he started wearing that conk. That was new to us, a black guy with straight hair, you know. . . . So we'd sit and watch him. . . . And we'd talk about everything. The color of his shirt, and the accordion, all that blue and that red and that white. Before that we had only seen the old French accordion, that these people had in the sack. They had no color to it, no chrome or nothing. But his accordion, it had glow into the color, man. And we'd go back home and tell people about what we had seen.

After settling in Houston for the duration of his Texas residency, Chenier eventually met a young immigrant accordion builder who became one of his main sources for those shiny multicolored instruments that could attract such attention back home. Known for his impeccably detailed craftsmanship and for having perfect pitch, Gianfranco "John" Gabbanelli (1937–2003), a native of the Italian town of Castelfidardo, was the owner and founder of Gabbanelli Accordions and Imports, a Houston family-owned-and-operated institution that still caters to players of the many forms of accordion-centric ethnic music that coexist in Texas (especially polka, Tejano, conjunto, Cajun, and zydeco). In Gabbanelli, Chenier found an expert technician capable of salvaging, repairing, and modifying old worn-out piano accordions that had been discarded as junk (especially the Italian models that the Creole musician came to prefer). Their relationship thus initially made it easier for Chenier to afford additional instruments, since he could purchase rebuilt models at discounted prices. And whenever one of his accordions required maintenance or repair, Gabbanelli could usually handle the task.

But the many changes Clifton Chenier would adopt in Texas went well beyond superficial details such as his fine wardrobe, processed hairstyle, or those brilliantly decorated accordions. The most crucial transformations would occur in the very sound of the music itself.

DURING THEIR EARLIEST YEARS IN TEXAS, Clifton and Cleveland Chenier accomplished something rare in the history of American music. First, assisted by a fellow immigrant from Louisiana, Clifton designed and commissioned the custom manufacture of a completely original musical instrument. Then Cleveland premiered it on area stages and, over the course of the rest of his career, set the standard for how to play it. Just as Clifton, by utilizing the piano-note model and incorporating urban influences, would revolutionize the concept of Creole-style accordion playing, he would also change forever the very form of its primary percussion accompaniment. His brother, in turn, would become the first master of

Gabbanelli Accordions on display, Gabbanelli Accordions and Imports, Houston, Texas, 2004.

Mike Gabbanelli at work, Gabbanelli Accordions and Imports, Houston, Texas, 2004.

that new instrument and define the wider range of sonic effects it was capable of producing. Together, as inventor and musician, they created the modern zydeco rubboard vest.

While living in Port Arthur around 1947, Clifton first had the idea to abandon the household utensil, the humble washboard, which had been co-opted for years by Creoles like his brother to produce rhythmic accompaniment for la-la. Chenier's friend and fellow accordion player Lonnie Mitchell explains the old tradition:

When I was a youngster coming up and first started playing, they would just take a regular old washboard that people used to wash their clothes with, and they'd cut the legs off, and they'd take a string and two nails and tack 'em on the washboard . . . and put a string hanging in there . . . If they didn't do that, they would just hold with one hand and rub with just one hand. That's the way it first started, rub with just one hand.

Cleveland, of course, had inherited this folk custom, and initially performed by simply scraping a spoon across the surface of one of those clothes-washing devices.

Then one day his younger brother envisioned a whole new possibility—an actual musical instrument inspired by the common washboard but improving on it in several ways. Because he was employed at Port Arthur's Gulf Oil plant, he easily located a metalworker who could bring that concept into being. As Clifton relates in a videotaped interview with Chris Strachwitz:

They used to tie a string around it, you know, and play it around the neck. So I went on to a white fellow down there at the Gulf Refinery. I told him, I said, "You got some tin?"
    He say, "Yeah." So I got down on the ground, in the sand, and I drawed that rubboard.
    And I said, "Can you make one like that? You know, with a collar plate?"
    He say, "Sure, I can make one like that." And he made one.

Thus, he conceived a customized musical instrument that would eventually become a signature presence in every zydeco band.

Fabricated from a single piece of metal by a Cajun welder named Willie Landry (the "white man" of the preceding anecdote), it featured two smooth tabs designed to curve over each shoulder—what Chenier calls the "collar plate." Supported in this fashion, the large corrugated rectangle that formed the main playing surface could hang freely over the entire front of the torso. Such an innovation offered a wider and longer board on which the percussionist could improvise his rhythmic strokes. It also liberated him from having to use one hand to grip the washboard or to steady it as it hung awkwardly from a string. Therefore, he could fully engage himself, using both his hands to scrape the board while he danced and weaved with the music.

Martin Chevis, Houston, Texas, 2004.

This instrumental innovation also significantly enriched the texture and range of musical effects a good percussionist could bring forth. In his essay for the CD *Zydeco: Volume One, the Early Years*, Chris Strachwitz notes, for instance, "The amount of air the player leaves in back of the instrument (by either standing up straight or bending forward) determines the brightness of the sound." Cleveland Chenier established this technique and ingeniously explored others. C. J. Chenier, who performed on stage with Cleveland for several years in his father's Red Hot Louisiana Band, recalls one of his uncle's many tricks: "Cleveland was natural . . . He would bend over, and his leg would kind of lift it up a little bit and then jam his knee back there and kind of dampen it a little bit."

Not only did Cleveland expertly play the very first rubboard ever designed to be a musical instrument, but he also innovatively experimented with the type and number of implements used for striking the surface of his brother's invention. In lieu of holding one or two spoons or forks to function like drumsticks, as others had typically done with the old-style washboards, he developed an unprecedented technique, incorporating a total of twelve so-called "church key" bottle openers. Holding six in or between the fingers of each hand, he consequently scraped the board in an entirely new manner that produced a far richer and more rhythmically complex sound. C. J. Chenier continues with his memories of his uncle's unique expertise:

I don't think I've heard maybe but one or two washboard players in my whole career of zydeco that could even come close to doing what Cleveland did. . . . Cleveland played the washboard—now a lot of people play with forks or spoons—but Cleveland played with six bottle openers on each hand. And he'd fan 'em out. You know, that way he got an amazing sound. . . . A lot of guys get on that washboard and think if you scratch fast, scratch hard, and scratch loud, jump around and do some flips, you know, do the splits and all that stuff, then you're the man. But it's a musical instrument . . . with different tones and colors. And the way he'd spread those things out! My dad would say, "I want you to roll with it," taught him how to do it.

Mack McCormick, a firsthand observer of the evolution of Creole music in postwar urban Texas, recalls his surprise at seeing this newfangled rubboard vest when it initially began to be adopted by other players on stages across the region:

I remember being aware at that time [1950s] of this rubboard phenomenon . . . and this had just recently happened. They had gone from the actual washboard to these manufactured—I'm not quite sure what the right word for it is—vests, almost. . . . And I got to thinking, who manufactures these things? It's clearly a highly specialized item. . . .

You could always go down to the store, or you could at that time, and get . . . those things they used to hang around their necks, and play with either spoons or bottle openers. Now that's not that unusual. A lot of musicians from all over this country used to use those kind of rubboards, like zydeco, in the same way. But the zydeco people had a certain flair about it.

. . . And then they invented this vest.

McCormick's curiosity concerning the source from which those early players were acquiring this revolutionary new rubboard brings up a significant point. In retrospect, it is now clearly established that Clifton Chenier and Willie Landry had collaborated in Port Arthur to create the original prototype. As a pragmatist who could surely then not have foreseen the impact his invention would ultimately have on the world of music, Chenier likely never even considered patenting the concept. As a consequence, there were soon many imitators. Inspired by Cleveland's dynamic performances at venues all along the upper Gulf Coast, other Creole percussionists began drafting the services of regional metalworkers to fabricate their own copies of the instrument.

Though the son of Willie Landry, the Port Arthur–born "Tee" Don Landry, now living in Lafayette, has since 1996 marketed his own trademarked version ("Key of Z Rubboards"), no single source has ever controlled the production of these musical devices. While they may vary in size or the gauge of the metal, rubboards otherwise essentially identical to the one the Chenier brothers introduced are now custom designed or even mass-produced around the world. Small ones or comically modified versions—such as those that include pointed female breast cups or the patented washboard necktie—are manufactured in bulk (in the latter case, made in China) and sold mainly as novelties. Others are fashioned by a variety of expert craftsmen, occasionally as custom orders, or else to stock regularly as retail merchandise in music shops catering to professionals and serious amateurs. And while the instrument is now ubiquitous wherever zydeco is played, not many folks realize that it originated with Clifton Chenier. As his son C. J. wistfully remarks, "It's something—because he actually created an instrument, but he got no recognition or nothing. . . . If my dad had just known at the time. But to him, he just wanted something easy for Cleveland to play, instead of tying the string on the washboard."

The metal percussion vest is one of the very few musical instruments of any type to have originated completely in the United States. As such, it is appropriate that, as the Key of Z Rubboards Web site states, a replica of the instrument Willie Landry first crafted is now housed "in the permanent collections of the Smithsonian Institution National Museum of American History." And although most zydeco fans are likely oblivious of the fact that it was invented by Clifton Chenier, even more fail to realize that this quintessential zydeco instrument first emerged in southeast Texas.

SET APART AND INVIGORATED BY THE MUSICAL DEXTERITY of the nontraditional chromatic accordion and the new rubboard vest, the dynamic music of Clifton Chenier pro-

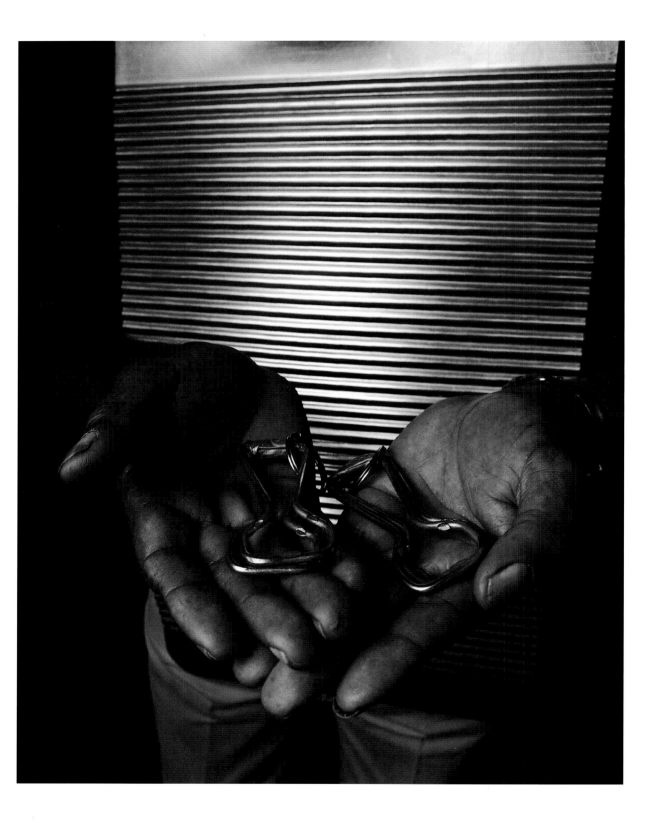

foundly altered, informed, and invigorated the subsequent course of zydeco history. Though he sometimes could spend long stints out on the road, throughout most of the 1950s and '60s and into the '70s Chenier's main base of operations was Houston—the city where he first fully realized the unique syncretism of la-la, blues, and R&B that is his most significant legacy.

After quitting his refinery work in Port Arthur and moving to Houston, he would never hold a day job again. Instead, as a full-time professional musician, he devoted himself to playing gigs at a wide variety of venues in what was quickly becoming one of the nation's largest cities. He also spent much time in automobiles, traveling back and forth on the highway that ran to Lafayette, working regularly in smaller towns and cities along the zydeco corridor. During this period, he emerged too as a recording artist, and from 1964 through 1970 he created many of his classic tracks at Houston studios such as Gold Star (the place where Bill Quinn had previously taped Lightnin' Hopkins performing "Zolo Go"). Depending on the ebb and flow of his commercial appeal, Chenier sometimes toured widely beyond the region—a practice that would continue and increase after he moved back to Louisiana in the late 1970s (and zydeco began to cross over into popular culture, establishing a larger, non–African American fan base well beyond the Gulf Coast). Yet during those decades of his Texas residency, Chenier had already achieved a level of success that was extraordinary, utterly without precedent, for a black Creole accordionist.

Nevertheless, in Houston today Chenier is often remembered as much for the many gigs he once played in obscure working-class joints and gritty neighborhood cafés as he is for having also been a frequent headliner at prestigious venues such as the grand Eldorado Ballroom. Similarly, some early eyewitness accounts of his local performances recall him mainly playing solo or with starkly minimalist accompaniment (in the tradition of la-la), and others recollect him as the leader of a blues-style four-piece combo or an even larger stage band. It all depends on where and when the memory was registered.

Texas-born zydeco bandleader Dan Rubit offers one such example:

The first places, the small places, he'd have just a drum. I had a brother-in-law used to blow harmonica with him sometimes, Allan Roberts. He was good . . . Sometimes Clifton would play just a rubboard and an accordion, which I did too, you know. You had to play a lot of accordion, though, if you were just going to use less instruments.

In a 1993 interview, Wilbert Thibodeaux remembers, with some measure of awe, Chenier's acumen and power as a solo performer:

I moved from Opelousas to Houston in 1951. . . . When I first moved to Houston, zydeco wasn't really very powerful at that time. There was a few zydeco people around—people like Clifton Chenier, and a guy by the name of Willie Green, and another guy by the name of Ernest Fox. . . .

OPPOSITE PAGE: *Rubboard scrapers (used by Martin Chevis), Houston, Texas, 2004.*

But when I came here to Houston, I soon met Clifton Chenier. . . . I seen him play by himself, without anything. He was playing at a club, and one night I went in there. And you know, he didn't have anything, anything but himself. Didn't have a drum, a lead or bass guitar, anything . . . a club out there in the west end they used to call the Dixie Grill . . . right off of Patterson [Street]. . . . And people was having a good time! . . . That's just how good a musician he was. He could make plenty of music by himself.

One of the musicians who played in Houston and on the road with Chenier in both formats—as part of a stripped-to-the-essence duo as well as a member of the full-force stage band—was drummer Robert Murphy. He recalls the typical arrangements for both types of gigs:

When I met Clif and I started playing with him, it was just the two of us . . . just accordion and drums. . . . We'd play in a joint, and if the dance lasted from eight to twelve, we'd take intermission from eight to eight-thirty, and then play from eight-thirty straight to twelve. . . . That's the first thing we did, take intermission. And then we'd play the rest of the night. . . .

At that time, if you made five bucks a night, you were doing pretty good. Clif charged twenty-five bucks a night [for the duo]. He'd take fifteen and give me ten. I was one of the highest paid drummers in town—when I played with Clif.

When he had a big job, he had a group in Beaumont, out of Port Arthur, that he picked up. And we would go on to Louisiana or wherever we had to go . . . We'd go down and spend the weekend. In fact, when I first teamed up with Clif, we rode in my car. . . . Now when Clifton put the whole band together . . . and when we had the electric guitars and horns and all that, it was a different sound.

Of course, that "different sound" is the fully orchestrated zydeco that most people are familiar with today. It is the same style of popular music (sometimes accented with horns, and regularly featuring lots of blues and rock licks on electric guitar) that, by the 1980s, Chenier and his five- or six-piece supporting ensemble were disseminating on festival stages around the world.

Murphy's affiliation with Chenier during the early phase of the king's ascent to the throne prompted him to bring up another point of history regarding the evolution of the stage band's name. During a visit in 2004 to Murphy's North Houston home, the now retired drummer displayed an old poster he has saved, an advertisement for a "July 4th Zodico Blowout" in Breaux Bridge, Louisiana, featuring "Clifton Chenier and his Hot Bayou Band." The text reveals, just as Murphy had previously recollected, that the gig lasted for an entire weekend (i.e., Friday and Saturday night, plus a matinee on Sunday). Regarding the band's moniker, Murphy points out,

Robert Murphy at home, Houston, Texas, 2004.

When he was working out of Houston in the early days, he first called it his Hot Sizzling Band and then his Hot Bayou Band—because of the Bayou City, and all the bayous between here and Port Arthur, the land of bayous. That's why he did that. But later on, he started calling it the Red Hot Louisiana Band [the name now most commonly associated with Chenier].

Whatever he may have called his group of supporting musicians during his Texas years, Chenier sometimes employed them to perform at one of the finest African-American-owned-and-operated venues in the South. Consider, for instance, an October 1955 item from the Houston *Informer* that includes a photograph of a smiling Chenier, decked out in suit and tie and holding a large piano-key accordion. The accompanying text offers clues to the high level of elegance at the establishment where the Creole musician was booked to perform—far removed, socioeconomically speaking, from the little joints where he might have played solo or with only a drummer. It reads in part:

Clifton "Hey-Tee-Fee" Chenier and his orchestra is the town's top attraction this week and he is doing his attracting at the spacious Eldorado Ballroom, best dance floor in the business. Preceding the aggregation is that sparkling rhythm of the Buddy Hiles saxophone and his orchestra on Saturday night. The fashionable nitery is launching its Fall dance season with nothing but the nation's best bands.

Likewise, in Alan Govenar's *Meeting the Blues*, an illustration of a photocopied newspaper article (undated, but given its mention of Chenier as "the Argo Records star," likely to be circa 1956) proclaims via a headline: "Clifton Chenier's Big Wheel Rolls to Eldorado." The text promotes Chenier's June 16th appearance at the Eldorado Ballroom, describing him as a rising star who "seems destined to break into the private echelon of big blues musicians with his magic accordion."

To appreciate more fully the implications of Chenier's headlining presence at the Eldorado Ballroom, a place where he is known to have performed many times in the 1950s, consider this excerpt from one of my entries in *The Handbook of Texas Music*:

Throughout the middle part of the twentieth century, Houston's Eldorado Ballroom reigned as one of the finest showcases in Texas for the live performance of black secular music—mostly blues, jazz, and R&B, but occasionally also pop and zydeco. This African-American owned-and-operated venue occupied the entire second floor of the Eldorado Building, located (across from historic Emancipation Park) on the southwest quadrant of the intersection of Elgin and Dowling Streets in Third Ward, home to the city's largest and most diverse black population.

From the late 1930s till the early 1970s this club was the venue of choice for upscale blues and jazz performances featuring touring stars and local talent. . . . The Ballroom was the centerpiece of several profitable enterprises owned by African-American businesswoman (and philanthropist) Anna Dupree (1891–1977) . . . [and] her husband Clarence Dupree. . . . Together they had created the Eldorado Ballroom in order to establish what they called a "class" venue for black social clubs and general entertainment.

To put it another way, as Mack McCormick once told me about the Eldorado Ballroom (an establishment he first visited in the late 1940s and '50s to see jazz icons such as Count Basie and Duke Ellington), "It was where the *royalty* came." As that comment suggests, the Eldorado Ballroom was once the ultimate performance venue of its type in Houston—the palace, as it were, for the local reception of visiting aristocrats of black popular music. Chenier's appearances there in the 1950s might therefore be understood to indicate that he too was proving his worthiness, which would eventually be universally recognized, of a regal title of his own. (After closing in 1973, the Eldorado Ballroom—now owned and operated by a Third Ward–based nonprofit organization called Project Row Houses—opened again in 2003 as a venue for special events.)

During the period of Chenier's emergence at the Eldorado Ballroom, the Houston resident also gained his first extensive touring experience by performing his hit single "Boppin' the Rock" (which he had recorded in 1955 for Los Angeles–based Specialty Records) as part of a multiartist R&B revue that played theater dates nationwide. Mack McCormick describes the phenomenon as "a road show, with four or five people put together in a package, and they'd travel. Sometimes they used to do that locally over a three- or four-state area. . . . I worked with Rausaw on booking these packages." The once prominent Houston-based promoter that he refers to is R. J. Rausaw, who "used to book traveling groups into the City Auditorium," among other venues. Observing such road shows, McCormick witnessed a gathering of diverse talents and a cross-genre musical synthesis in the making:

There again there were, well, mutual influences going on, because [singer] Etta James was blues and pop. . . . [guitarist-singer] Lowell Fulsom was blues . . . and Clifton, and [R&B pianist-singer] Amos Milburn might be on it too. There were usually five or six people who had recently had a hit record, whose names were known, plus one or two others who maybe were not that familiar. And Rausaw used to package those things for twenty cities in, you know, this area. Lafayette and Orange, cities like that.

As a featured performer on such professionally organized tours or as a headliner for his own show, Chenier by 1955 had graced the stages of at least two of Houston's most prominent venues for a black entertainer, the spacious City Auditorium and the first-class Eldorado Ballroom. He and his unique accordion-based blues music were suddenly popular, permit-

Juneteenth Dance (with Step Rideau and the Zydeco Outlaws),
Eldorado Ballroom, Houston, Texas, 2003.

ting him the newfound luxury of regular work and the financial rewards that it could offer. Locally, he reigned, at least for a while, as one of the city's most commercially successful African American musicians. Mack McCormick observes,

He worked regularly, three or four nights a week, and did quite well. I mean, he was a money-maker and an established record artist. . . . I wasn't that aware of how many records he'd made, and all that, or how successful he was, when I first went to see him. And he kind of had it pointed out to me. He wanted me to know he wasn't like a lot of these other guys who were scuffling for jobs—that he had all the work he needed, and he didn't work every night because he could make enough money in a few nights, and so on. . . .

And then on some particular occasion I went out to his house [on] . . . Mystic Street. I think it's 1610 Mystic. . . . He owned the house, I remember that.

McCormick's recollection that Chenier made a special point of highlighting his ownership of the Fifth Ward property where he (and reportedly several of his relatives) resided indicates just how profitable music-making had become for this former farmhand and refinery laborer.

Those high-profile package shows surely provided him with invaluable exposure and some infusion of income, but they ultimately offered only a limited series of one-night stands, and in those multifaceted productions Chenier was only one briefly featured artist among several others. Moreover, as many veterans of such mid-twentieth-century R&B revues can attest, the various expenses of life on the road could sometimes almost negate any profits that one might pocket at the end of the tour. Thus, the key to Chenier's financial achievement (rare for a full-time black musician at the time) was that there were plenty of fans of his updated and urbanized Creole music living not far from that piece of Houston real estate he so proudly possessed. As McCormick sums it up, "But . . . he was no distance from his primary audience. I mean, he played often just in this Houston, Beaumont, Galveston area. A little bit of Louisiana. Mostly he could stick to the near vicinity."

Another factor that professionally anchored Chenier in Houston during this era was his union membership in the local chapter of the American Federation of Musicians—a side effect of the commercial success he had begun to achieve in the mid-1950s. Unlike most black Creole accordionists before and after him—and for that matter, most southern blues musicians of his generation—Chenier was considered by the local union establishment to be especially worthy of recruitment into what was, regionally at least, often an exclusive group.

Yet again, McCormick provides valuable historical background:

Clifton was one of the earlier guys to get mixed up with the union. . . . Most local unions, musicians unions, their steadiest and largest membership in a city like Houston or Memphis is the symphony.

And so because they're this big voting bloc with regular jobs, they encourage rules like this: "Let's don't have any of those scuzzy, nonreading, inventive musicians in our organization." [laughs] But then at a certain point, those "scuzzy" musicians start making money, or build up an audience, or making records, or whatever, and so they become somebody who [officials consider] should be in the union—because they're taking jobs away from union musicians . . . getting on radio programs, doing all kinds of things that the symphony musicians were not doing, getting popular, getting well known . . .

Clifton was in the union fairly early—and trying to follow the rules. These acts from these package shows, most of those people were in the union somewhere, because they were beginning to get the kind of work, and with a nationwide record company. . . . So they'd get entrapped into union contracts, which they would not necessarily follow. But at least they were somewhere contractually obligated. . . . Clifton had to be in the union. He was getting those jobs . . . and there were advantages to being in the union. . . .

Earlier there was no black union. There was only, in Houston, Local 65. Then they formed Local 699 [for black musicians], and to the present day, the current local is called "65, dash, 699." . . . A swing bandleader named Skeets Tolbert came to Houston . . . and started the black union. And I worked with him in getting guys into his union. . . . And I suspect Skeets went to [Clifton], you know, as a local guy who was making records, and said, "We need you at the union." And it wasn't as complicated as getting into the other union, which always had an . . . attitude of exclusion.

Hence, union membership was one more indicator—along with his emerging prominence on urban stages, his early recordings, and his relative financial success—that Chenier had become a full-fledged professional during his Texas years. His achievement, however, had implications that extended well beyond his own career. As record producer Chris Strachwitz notes in his liner-note essay for *Zydeco: Volume One, the Early Years,* "Clifton's success gave all the other Zydeco musicians the impetus to put more blues or rock and roll (as they called it) into Creole Zydeco music, especially in the Houston area."

Various black musicians in the vicinity of Houston were inspired by Chenier's high-profile example, and soon began to imitate his lead by blending elements of Creole folk music with urban blues and R&B. In a 1993 interview, Louisiana-born Wilbert Thibodeaux, in many respects still a traditionalist well into the twenty-first century, summarizes the evolution of la-la into modern zydeco that was sparked by Chenier's uncanny success:

Zydeco sounds different now than what it did when I first was coming up. . . . You know, zydeco started out with the people playing the accordion and the spoons. Then somebody somewhere down the line decided they'd add the washboard to the durn thing. . . . That's how it really got started. Then later on they started putting the guitar and the drums and everything else in it, and it really

LEFT TO RIGHT: *Ashton Savoy and Wilbert Thibodeaux,*
The Big Easy Social and Pleasure Club, Houston, Texas, 1996.

enhanced the zydeco music by putting that in there. It's so much easier to play zydeco when you've got a band, you know. When you have a band, if you've got a good drummer, once you start off and he takes that beat, it's so easy to play when you're playing behind a band. . . .

[The change in the music occurred] when they left Louisiana and started moving to Texas . . . especially Clifton Chenier. . . . I think Clif had went to Port Arthur at one time and stayed there a long time . . . and then Houston. . . . That's where he really got going with that music.

. . . Mine done changed up some too. You know, I play a whole lot of this new stuff they got going on now. . . . It's zydeco, but it's got a different beat to it, what I'm playing now.

Another former Houston zydeco stalwart was Willie Stout (ca. 1920–1995), an accordion player and bandleader who, after experiencing a stroke in his final years as an active musician, switched instruments and played rubboard on local stages. He relates his introduction to, and indoctrination into, Chenier's style of music as follows: "I'm from Opelousas, Louisiana. . . . I came here in about 1956. . . . I wasn't in zydeco when I came here. I learned to play zydeco here. I learned it all from Clifton. I'm his cousin. . . . He taught me zydeco, that French music . . . and how to mix it good with the blues."

Wilfred Chevis, also a former protégé of Chenier's, says, "Clifton was the first one to mix it up. Everything was strictly straight Cajun-style music or la-la before him." That basic theme is echoed by many admirers, including Willie Davis, a man who had followed Chenier's accordion-playing career since the early days near Opelousas. He adds:

Back in the old times, mostly they was playing that old la-la. That chak-a-chank, chak-a-chank, all day and all night. When he start playing and bring that music out, he started getting that other stuff and putting it in that zydeco. Like Fats Domino . . . he'd get his music and play it in the zydeco style. Blues . . . he'd get it and play it in the zydeco style. So this is what changed the music. . . . He turned it around.

The Chenier-led fusion of Creole tradition and urban black music of the era was a bold experiment; as such, it could have failed. But the innovative blending of styles caught the attention of the African American public in big cities, as well as back in the Creole homeland. And as Davis puts it, "them people went crazy over that stuff."

Despite the fact that by the early 1960s Chenier had already toured nationally in an R&B revue and had recorded singles for several small record labels in Louisiana (Elko, Zynn), California (Specialty, Argo), and Chicago (Checker), it was not until he began to make records in Houston that he truly entered what most music historians now consider his major phase as an artist. In early 1964 at a Fifth Ward establishment, Chenier met roots-music aficionado and record producer Chris Strachwitz, a California resident who had been making regular field trips to the Houston area since 1959. It was there that, with the collaboration of Mack McCormick, he had first recorded the guitar-picking songster Mance Lipscomb (1895–1976), the artist who launched his Arhoolie Records label. The great blues singer who had initially attracted Strachwitz to the Bayou City, Lightnin' Hopkins, was also the inadvertent catalyst for bringing Chenier to Arhoolie Records. In his subsequently lengthy affiliation with that label, Chenier issued the majority of tracks by which posterity now judges him to be most worthy of his title as the king of zydeco.

In a 1998 interview previously published in part in my book *Down in Houston*, Strachwitz explains how his close relationship with Chenier began:

When I met up with Lightnin' Hopkins one night later on, he said, "Let's just go hear my cousin."
And so he took me over to this little beer joint in Houston in an area they call Frenchtown. And here
was this black man with a huge accordion on his chest and playing the most unbelievable low-down
blues I'd ever heard in my life—and singing it in this bizarre French patois! His name was Clifton
Chenier. . . . I don't think the place had a name. It was just a beer joint. And since Houston has no
zoning laws, you could build a beer joint anywhere you feel like, as long as the neighbors don't shoot
you down. I remember it was called Frenchtown, in Fifth Ward.

So as soon as Lightnin' introduced me, [Chenier] said, "Oh you're a record man. I want to make
a record tomorrow."

Having observed Chenier performing with only a drummer (Robert Murphy) and liking what he heard, Strachwitz eagerly made quick arrangements to book a session at the Gold Star Studio for the very next day. However, things did not unfold as the visiting record producer had expected. As Strachwitz writes in his liner-note essay for *The Best of Clifton Chenier*, "I had hoped to see him at the studio with just the drummer I had heard the night before— but I didn't know Clifton yet! He showed up with a full band: piano, guitar, bass, drums, and of course himself on accordion." Nevertheless, because of some technical problems with the amplifiers, neither the guitar nor the bass were utilized on that very first session (to the glee of Strachwitz). Instead, the resulting 45 rpm single, "Ay, Ai, Ai," featured only three players: Chenier on accordion, Murphy on drums, and Houston's Elmore Nixon (1933–1973) on piano; Chenier sang lead, and the other two provided background vocals.

While all the producers for whom Chenier had previously recorded had sought to make R&B hits, Strachwitz preferred what he typically calls "down home" music. Consequently, Chenier was not initially prepared to accommodate Strachwitz's folk-music sensibility when the Arhoolie producer returned to Houston a year later to record an entire LP worth of material. As Strachwitz told me for *Down in Houston*:

When I first heard Clif I heard him singing in Creole patois. That was his first language. And I didn't think his phrasing in English was nearly as good. So it was a battle, then and every time we recorded. Clif would say, "I've got to make rock-and-roll records—that's what sells." And I begged him to sing in French. So he said, "OK Chris, I'll make you a deal: If you let me cut one side of the album rock and roll"—as he called it, [but] it was really R&B—"I'll make the other side French for you."

And from that session, we did have a regional hit, but it was the French one that sold. It was a low-down blues, "Tous les Jours la Même Chose," something like that. I said, "How do you spell that?" And he said, "Spell it any way you want to." Then I asked if I could just call it "Louisiana Blues," and he said, "Okay." So that's what I put on the label—and it sold.

Chenier's long association with Arhoolie resulted in an outpouring of classic tracks (enough to fill at least fourteen CDs in a recent catalogue for the company). And though Chenier went on to record for a few other labels from time to time (including Huey Meaux's Houston-based Crazy Cajun Records), the artistry that qualified him to be acclaimed the king of zydeco is, most people would agree, best documented by Arhoolie. For not only did he issue the bulk of his classic material there, but because of Strachwitz's desire to document the accordionist performing songs in French, Chenier also was prompted to rediscover his Creole roots. As Strachwitz related to me in 1998, "So he said, 'Maybe this French stuff is OK and people'd like to hear this.' . . . And he really became proud of his heritage."

Of the seventeen tracks of music Strachwitz compiled for *The Best of Clifton Chenier* (Arhoolie, 2003), ten were recorded between 1964 and 1970 in Houston. This fact alone suggests that Chenier's tenure there marked what was arguably the prime period of his creative productivity. Moreover, it was there, during a 1965 recording session for Arhoolie, that Chenier first cut the track most responsible for disseminating the word "zydeco" itself. While Mack McCormick had originated and begun to popularize that unique spelling of the Creole term, Strachwitz's decision to use it on the title of an essential Chenier recording provided a sort of royal confirmation that, from this point on, the name of this music would be zydeco.

A decade earlier, before his lengthy affiliation with Arhoolie, Chenier had recorded a number entitled "Zodico Stomp" for Specialty Records. But his May 1965 session at Houston's Gold Star Studio yielded a song that Strachwitz, following McCormick's precedent, wrote down as "Zydeco Sont Pas Salé." Soon fans were not only hearing this vibrant reinvention of an old Creole folk song, but also seeing the new orthography on jukebox listings or on the printed label affixed to the disc. As Clarence Gallien, a Houston-based promoter and Chenier's close friend, once told Alan Govenar for *Meeting the Blues*, this circumstance made all the difference. "The name changed from la-la to zydeco when Clifton made the record," he says. "Clifton is the man who got credit for changing the name."

Nevertheless, while the king's example ultimately prevailed, the universal adaptation of the new spelling happened gradually, especially in older Creole communities in southeast Texas and southwest Louisiana. Among some folks, previous versions of the word persisted well into the 1990s—sometimes because of reliance on old signs containing variant spellings, and other times because of obliviousness or deliberate defiance of the popular norm.

For example, a Robert Damora photograph that accompanies his article in *Living Blues* shows Brian Terry, Mickey Guillory, proprietor Doris McClendon, Wilbert Thibodeaux, and Lonnie Mitchell posed in front of Frenchtown's most famous Creole nightclub. While the caption identifies the place and date as "Continental Zydeco Ballroom, 1994," the overhead façade of the building features the following words in large lettering: "Continental Zodico." Similarly, a photograph by Rick Olivier (in *Zydeco!*, the book written by Ben Sandmel) shows a Houston-based musician, large accordion strapped across his chest, standing beside his van; the hand-painted writing on the side of the vehicle advertises the artist and his group as "Willie Davis and the Zordico Hitch Hikers." (While this photograph is undated, it was surely taken in the 1980s or '90s, the only decades in which Davis performed professionally.) Another residual orthographic variation occurs in Rick Mitchell's 1986 *Houston Chronicle* article previewing the Texas Folklife Festival in San Antonio: he writes of a scheduled appearance by "performers from Houston's Frenchtown area, including Alcide L. C. Donatto and the Slippers Zoddico Band." While the spelling of the band name likely originated with Donatto and not Mitchell, it illustrates yet again that the hegemony of z-y-d-e-c-o was still incomplete at the time within the Creole community at large.

Moreover, some academically trained folklorists from beyond that community have occasionally chosen to avoid the most common form of the word as a way of making a political point. For instance, as Ancelet points out in his essay in Dorman's anthology, "Québecois filmmaker André Gladu drew criticism from Strachwitz for entitling his 1984 film on Louisiana black Creole music *Zarico*"; Gladu considered the now standard spelling to be a "colonialistic foul . . . based on superimposed English phonetics."

"Zodico," "zordico," "zoddico," "zarico": through the 1980s and '90s such spellings continued to surface here and there. But among mainstream audiences discovering the music for the first time, as well as for the black Creoles who have heard it all their lives, most people have simply accepted and propagated the term as "zydeco." In doing so, they are adhering, consciously or not, to a codification that emanates from the only undisputed king that music has ever known. And whether they realize it or not, that crucial connection between the now ubiquitous form of the word and the powerful influence of Clifton Chenier did not originate in Louisiana, but was first established in a recording studio on the southeast side of Houston.

SOME OF THE TEXAS-BASED MUSICIANS who collaborated with Chenier also played a direct role in helping him define and expand his ongoing syncretism of different styles. One such example comes from drummer Robert Murphy, who brought a sophisticated grasp of jazz rhythms (in his own words, "a lot of color") to zydeco percussion:

At first, I really was just taken back with that zydeco because, oh man, that was something brand new to me! . . . Oh yeah, the beat! . . . I wasn't used to just a backbeat. I was used to playing, you know, jazz and stuff, and it took us a while to feel each other out, but once we did . . . I created my own style.

I'd play with brushes too, and I'd see people staring at me like that, and they'd wonder what I was doing. [laughs] . . . I never saw a full set of drums [in a zydeco band] before I started with Clif. . . . Whenever they would see me set up, I'd have all this stuff here. [He points to a full drum kit in his room.] And usually they [the other zydeco drummers] would just have three pieces: bass drum, sock cymbal—or if they didn't have a sock cymbal, just a plain ride cymbal—and a snare drum. That was it. . . . But very seldom did they have a high-hat and a ride cymbal. And no tom-toms. . . .

Nobody had the sound with Clif that I did. Everybody wanted to play some sort of Louisiana stomp beat, zydeco beat, if you want to call it that. But I mixed the zydeco beat with a jazz beat, with a Cuban beat. That's why I had the bongos on top of my drums. I used all of that—even with just the two of us.

Murphy's fundamentally urban musicianship surely influenced Chenier's style in other ways too. For instance, as the multi-instrumentalist once told me (for the *Living Blues* article "Houston's Blues Teachers"), "I met Clifton Chenier here in Houston. . . . He taught me how to play zydeco, and I taught him how to play [the music of jazz organist] Jimmy Smith on his accordion."

In addition to Houston-based drummers such as Murphy and the frequently utilized Robert St. Julien (aka St. Judy), Chenier procured the services of some top-notch blues guitarists who—like the king himself—were Louisiana-born Creoles that had become longtime residents of Texas. Two of the most prominent were Phillip Walker (b. 1937) and Sherman Robertson, both of whom eventually graduated to star status as internationally recognized touring and recording artists. Despite having worked with Chenier during different eras, both Walker and Robertson share similar accounts of how they came to be drafted into the band and how they learned to be true professionals under Chenier's tutelage.

In his interview (conducted by John Anthony Brisbin) published in 1997 in *Living Blues* magazine, Walker first explains how in 1945 his Creole family moved from Welsh, Louisiana, to southeast Texas while he was still a child. Unlike most such Creole migrants, however, Walker's father did not relocate to procure a job in industry, but instead to work on a

1,800-acre farm located on the coastal plains between Beaumont and Port Arthur. By the time Walker was in his late teens, however, he had left his father's farm and was employed, like Chenier before him, at the Gulf Oil refinery in Port Arthur. A self-taught guitar player, during his time off he had also begun gigging occasionally in area clubs. Then one day in 1954, to his intense surprise, Chenier suddenly showed up, offered him an opportunity, and changed his life forever:

He heard about this young kid playin' the guitar around there. So he come lookin' for me. . . . He said, "Well, would you like to be a musician? Would you like to come go with me?" I'd heard of the King of the South, this great accordion player, but I never dreamed he would come lookin' for me. . . . So I went to be a musician.

Cliff put me in his car and took me to Houston, Texas, with him—and bought me my first guitar, a real one. I got a Gibson amp and a Black Rose guitar. And bought me a suit of clothes for a uniform.

Playing Chenier's blues-and-la-la fusion, the now nattily dressed Walker immediately found himself performing extensively across the Lone Star State, not only in the southeast region that was the zydeco bandleader's base, but also in major cities to the north and west:

When Cliff and us started out in '54, we were playin' regular little bars and nightclubs. Then we expanded out. We would start out in Houston, Texas, double back into Galveston. Go into Beaumont and play that stuff right there in my hometown, the Club Raven. Leave there and go to Houston and play the Eldorado Ballroom there. Leave Houston and go to Dallas to play the Empire Room. We'd go up to El Paso, play a little place called the Black and Tan up there.

However, during this era of Chenier's initial popularity, his hot new band featuring the teenage Walker on guitar was also soon playing one-night stands in other cities nationwide. In particular, Walker recalls early gigs in Phoenix, Los Angeles (at "a big famous bar there by the name of the Five-Four Ballroom"), and New York City (at the ultimate entertainment venue for a black performer of the time, the Apollo Theater). Walker says these urban audiences, far removed from the Gulf Coast, responded to Chenier's unique sound with loving enthusiasm "because there was nobody out there but him playin' the blues accordion." And though he has gone on to make a name for himself as a guitar slinger fronting his own blues band, Walker credits those early experiences with the king of zydeco as the key to his success. "Clifton Chenier made a good side musician out of me," he says, adding, "He made leader potential out of me."

The same holds true for another widely acclaimed blues guitarist and bandleader,

Sherman Robertson, who says of the approximately three-year term he spent working with Chenier in the 1980s:

Clifton Chenier gave me the privilege of being a sideman. . . . So I know the both ends of it. I know how a cat feels standing behind the front man. One night he told me, "You really want to play that guitar tonight, don't you?" He said, "You don't want to play Clifton tonight. You want to play Sherman tonight." And boy, he read me up and down. He said, "I tell you what you going to do. . . . You step your butt out here. Let's hear that first number. Let's go!" And that's how I started opening up for him.

He actually sat back that night . . . got on the mic and said, "My guitar player say he hot tonight. Say he want to show his grits. So let's see what he got. C'mon, boy! Step up here. Let's see what you've got." And man, I just pulled something out of my hat and jammed. He looked at me and said, "You're learning." He was taking me to school. He knew I hadn't planned it, how I was going to kick it off or anything. I just had to do it right there. And I was ready—didn't know I was ready, but he knew I was ready. . . . He was showing me how to maneuver on the moment.

That band was so tight. But we had so much fun, off the bandstand. That experience taught me how to get along with the guys. Because when you're a front man, a lot of times there's a bit of friction. It's kind of a management-labor thing, you know. Being with Clifton let me be just one of the band for a while—and then trained me to emerge as a more polished front man. It was like going to college for me.

Robertson, like Phillip Walker before him, had never imagined being a key part of Chenier's famous band until the day it suddenly happened. Before the phone call that made him an instant member of the Chenier touring unit, Robertson had been mainly performing in the Houston area with his own group, the Crosstown Blues Band. His local popularity had earned him a reputation that attracted the attention of the organizers of what was then the city's largest and most prestigious annual blues event, the SumArts Juneteenth Blues Festival at Miller Outdoor Theatre in Houston's centrally located Hermann Park. At that event in 1982, where he was booked to perform as the opening act on the main stage, Robertson unwittingly laid the foundation for his subsequent close relationship with Chenier:

I came and played. And the lucky thing was Big Mama Thornton's band didn't show up. So she said, "Get that little fat-assed boy out there—the one that just got through playing that guitar. Tell him he's got to play behind Big Mama Thornton."

They came to ask me . . . and I already had the guitar in my hand. . . . Then we looked around, and Clifton Chenier was coming on. . . . So his driver told me, said "Clifton say, when you get through playing, he wants to talk with you."

OPPOSITE PAGE: *Phillip Walker, Chicago Blues Festival, 1996.*

When I met him, he say, "Hey boy, you from Louisiana, you?" You know, he was a real French-man. . . . He say, "You ever travel?"

I said, "No, I'd like to, but I've never really traveled." I said, "I've got a wife and a kid. I'm a mechanic, and I play on the weekends."

Cliff say, "Where did you learn how to play the guitar?" . . . And then he say, "What part of Louisiana you from?"

When Robertson responded that he had been born in Breaux Bridge, Chenier followed with other questions that led him to conclude that he remembered the young guitar player's father, John "Choo-Choo" Robertson, as a childhood friend with whom he had once worked chopping sugarcane. That connection immediately established a special bond between the two, and Chenier told his flattered new acquaintance that he wanted to stay in touch. Robertson continues the narrative:

So he say, "You got a telephone?" . . . and wrote my telephone number down on a piece of paper. . . . He said, "Charles, put that in your book. Give it to the driver" . . .

About a month later, the phone rang. I had just got in from a gig. . . . He say, "Hey boy, you that guitar player? . . . This is Clifton Chenier." Now it's about three o'clock in the morning. . . . He said, "How you like to tour, to go on a tour? . . . Right now. I'm on my way to California, and I need a good guitar player. You the one—if you want it. I like the way you play. I need you to do something for me." That's how he said it.

I turned and looked at my wife, and I could see she wanted to say no. But she said, "There's your break. Go."

So I said, "How much time I've got to get ready?"

He said, "I'm parked in front of your house." [laughs] Actually they was at the public telephone about a block down the street. So, sure enough, I looked out the window, and I'm wiping my eyes. I went to the bathroom and looked—and there's the truck and the trailer pulled up on the side of the street. So I packed in a hurry, and . . . they loaded me up, put my amp and guitar in the truck. I kissed my old lady goodbye. So we turned the corner and were getting on [Highway] 59 when I said, "Oh no, what have I done here?" . . .

Then I got out there, and I started liking it. . . . It was so much fun to see places I hadn't seen—and not to have to front the band. It was fun to be a sideman and just to enjoy myself.

Robertson worked consistently with Chenier's Red Hot Louisiana Band till he left some time in 1985, intending to devote himself exclusively to promoting his own career as a blues bandleader. However, he has never fully abandoned his connection to zydeco. Having grown up in Frenchtown (after his Creole parents moved to Houston while he was still a baby), and

Sherman Robertson, Eldorado Ballroom (before renovation), Houston, Texas, 2000.

having played with the seminal figure who put the urban blues sound in zydeco, Robertson can naturally move with ease between the two related genres. Thus, though intending to focus on his own blues band, he soon found that other zydeco artists were requesting his services. As I once wrote of him in a 2000 *Living Blues* cover story:

His decision to part with Chenier happened to coincide with the mid-80s zenith of zydeco's break-through into popular culture. Various bands . . . were suddenly looking for dynamic musicians to join them on international tours. The pay was good, especially for skilled guitarists (who were in demand because they played an instrument that mainstream fans could easily relate to, bridging the gap between rock and Creole dance music).

As a result, Robertson soon worked also with Louisiana-based zydeco groups such as Terrence Simien and the Mallet Playboys, and Good Rockin' Dopsie and the Twisters (with whom he also performed on Paul Simon's popular *Graceland*, the 1986 Grammy Award–winning Album of the Year). More recently Robertson has continued to dabble as a zydeco side-man during breaks in his blues touring. For example, he contributed his considerable guitar talents to the 2004 release *Right Now Is Prime Time* by Houston's Leroy Thomas and the Zydeco Roadrunners.

Regardless of the style of music he may be playing at any given time, however, Robertson steadfastly points to Clifton Chenier as his primary inspiration as a showman:

The thing I took from Clifton, I learned how to work a crowd. He would never miss. I don't care where we went. It was not the thing where he played the same show every night—because he didn't, like most guys do. He didn't have a set show. He'd say, "I know what will work tonight," and that's what we'd do. He could feel the people. . . . Whatever it was, it was right on the target. . . . He taught me. . . . And I loved that, because it kept the whole experience, the whole band, fresh. . . . He was just an original. And believe it or not, he blessed me with it too.

Perhaps the most personally significant Texas-based protégé that Chenier ever recruited into his band was the world famous musician who still carries his name, his son C. J. Chenier. Now an established accordion-wielding recording artist and the leader of the Red Hot Louisiana Band that he inherited, the younger Chenier was originally just as startled as Phillip Walker and Sherman Robertson to discover that the king of zydeco wanted him to join the royal entourage on stage. In the fall of 1978, while still a resident of his native Port Arthur, C. J. first learned of his father's plan for him to take over the role of saxophone player for the band:

It was a shock to me when my dad called my mom and told her, "Get him ready; I want him to come out on the road." . . .

See, I was twenty years old. I was playing in a funk band, keyboards at the time. And we were playing a Catholic bazaar, and my friend came over and said, "Man, your momma say come call her."

So I called her up, and she said, "You need to come home. Your daddy wants you to go on the road with him." . . . He called me from Louisiana and said he was going to pick me up on his way through. . . . I was in Port Arthur one day, and the next day I was cruising down the highway in the van with my dad and his band! And I thought, Oh man, what's going on here?

And those guys, when I got in that band, I thought I was going to be just like on the road with a bunch of old cats. Well, we took off and went to Austin, Texas, and did Antone's [nightclub] for a week. I made twenty-one at Antone's, on Sixth Street. . . . Clifford Antone [club founder] told me, "Man, when I first opened my club there wasn't but one person I wanted to come in here, and that was Clifton Chenier." . . . You know, Antone is from Port Arthur. . . .

And then we took off from Antone's and went up to California and up to Oregon and Washington and Canada and back down. And I got back home and it was the best tour I ever had in my whole career, to this very day. My very first one, it was so exciting.

Despite his initial reticence about being drafted to work with musicians a generation older than himself (including his uncle, Cleveland Chenier), C. J. says his underlying fears were mainly tied to his sense of his own musical limitations. Yet he soon learned and adapted:

And I didn't know nothing, no songs. I didn't know anything. I hadn't played my saxophone for about six months before I got in the band. I was really kind of rusty on it. And I didn't know those blues songs. I didn't know none of that stuff. I had to learn everything from scratch. And those guys didn't give me a hard time; they just hung in there with me.

This was the band with Robert St. Julien, Little Buck [Senegal], Jumpin' Joe Morris, you know. . . .People were used to John Hart on saxophone. He was great, just great. I thought he was going to be there, to tell you the truth. But he wasn't there. And I found myself there by myself. I thought, like, man, I don't know none of these songs . . . so I learned those songs. We'd go to certain clubs, and they'd have the blues and stuff playing [on recordings over the PA], and I said, "Oh, that's the way it goes." Because I had never heard that stuff before. That's how I learned, just hearing some of the songs [on recordings] when we went to the club.

Not only did C. J. elevate his grasp of his father's style of music during that first major road trip with him, but he also discovered a new basis for respecting the venerable showman:

C. J. Chenier at home, Houston, Texas, 2004.

It was just great to me. You know, I had never experienced that kind of feeling from an audience, like it felt from when you got on stage. It was my daddy, that's true, and he was the king of zydeco, that's true, but I didn't really know how people reacted to him, you know.

I had [previously] seen him at the Sparkled Paradise in Bridge City [Texas] and . . . the Satellite Club in Port Arthur a couple of times. But, you know, people would dance all night back home. But I didn't expect people to react like they did when we went to California. They was going crazy out there, man! Like, wow!

C. J. performed with his father, on saxophone and keyboards, from 1978 until the king died in 1987. Before his death, however, the elder Chenier had insisted on tutoring his son in how to play the signature instrument of a zydeco bandleader—preparing the prince, as it were, to succeed to the throne. C. J. explains the process:

When he got sick, his exact words to me were, [imitating his father's voice] "You know, son, the old hog's not going to always be here." He called himself the hog. "You've got to learn how to play that a-cah-jin because"—that's what he called it; he didn't call it an accordion; it's an a-cah-jin—"you got to learn how to play that a-cah-jin because you've got to take over for me one day." . . .

So when he started getting sick, I, in the beginning I tried on his big accordion, and it just seemed like it was a little too much for me. But then I got my hands on his little one, and—it was a little piano accordion—and I started beginning to figure out the buttons a little better because there wasn't so many to start off with. And I got used to playing up and down instead of across, like you do a piano. After I played that little one about five or six months, you know, just pressing and playing around with it, I picked his up again, and it felt a whole lot better to me. . . .

When I first started trying to play the accordion . . . back then he would say [again imitating his father's voice], "Mon garçon"—that's "my son," you know—say, "Mon garçon, C. J., hit 'em a scale, hit 'em a scale." And I'd have to get the accordion and play. . . . And he was proud that I was trying. . . .

So, you know, he got sick, man, and the first night I played that accordion on a gig, was at Tipitina's [nightclub] in New Orleans. And I had never played [accordion] with the band. Actually I had never played except just messing around. So my first experience was like, boom! in front of a crowd on the stage at Tipitina's, man. He would let me start the show off. . . .

I didn't really know any songs to play. And "Hot Rod" was like my favorite song of my daddy's. . . . It was a cool instrumental. So that was about the first song I learned how to play. So I went on the bandstand, and I played my "Hot Rod," and I tried to play a little boogie. I just didn't know nothing.

In addition to learning to play the accordion and beginning to open the shows for his father, C. J. also soon was being instructed in things he would need to know when it came his time to take over the band:

As far as the singing, I had never been a vocalist. I had always been in the background, playing saxo-phone and being just a background vocalist. But as for getting out in front of people and being a lead vocalist, I had never done that. It was all just overwhelming for a little while. . . . But Daddy made me do it.

. . . After that . . . he would let me take over a little bit. . . . And we would go out [without him]. He'd let me use the trailer and the instruments, and we'd go out and play a small gig here and there, not too many, mostly just small clubs for the door. . . .

So when he passed, it was just like a natural thing for me to keep going. You know, I had no other thought in my mind other than just to keep going. Because by that time, not only was that what he asked me to do, but by that time, that's what I really wanted to do.

Most obviously in the case of his son C. J., but also with various other musicians he once employed, Clifton Chenier was more than a boss; he was also a valuable mentor.

In commentary on professional team sports, it is often observed that the greatest stars are the ones who bring out the best in their teammates—the ones whose influence causes their supporting personnel to perform on a higher level. Though not an athlete, Chenier seems to have been that kind of professional. Whether he was designing the rubboard vest for his brother to play or pushing a young guitarist into the spotlight or prodding his heir to master the essential zydeco instrument, Chenier facilitated growth among his subordinates. And so his influence goes beyond his seminal sound, his showmanship, his many record-ings, or his commercial success. For a select roster of fortunate players, he was that rare king who deigned also to teach.

CLIFTON CHENIER'S LEGACY IN TEXAS bridges the gap between secular venues and the Catholic Church, for he helped establish a robust Houston tradition that has solidified the link between zydeco and its cultural roots as family-oriented music. While it has long been common for Creole Catholics elsewhere to feature the music of their ethnic heritage at special church functions, like the occasional fund-raiser or the annual bazaar or Mardi Gras dance, in the heavily populated Houston metropolitan area it has been an almost weekly phenomenon. In short, there is usually a zydeco church dance happening somewhere in the city almost every Saturday night, year round, and it has been that way for well over four decades. Queries and firsthand observations suggest that such regularly scheduled church dances do not occur anywhere else along the zydeco corridor, including the cities of south-west Louisiana. However, it has been the norm in Houston for several generations, and Chenier played a key role in making it that way.

The local tradition originated through the inspiration and efforts of a church member named Clarence Gallien. In a 1993 interview, his son, Clarence Gallien Jr., explains that his parents left Opelousas in 1953 and settled in Frenchtown, where they were first affiliated with Our Mother of Mercy Catholic Church. About five years later the family transferred its membership to the neighboring St. Francis of Assisi, a larger church that nonetheless was desperate to raise some much-needed funds. When the senior Gallien, who had hosted la-la gatherings back home in Louisiana, proposed a church-sponsored dance featuring the kind of Creole music that most of the parishioners had grown up with, the pastor was initially reluctant to approve. As Gallien Jr., relates:

The church didn't allow them to have zydeco dances. . . . But my father kept talking and talking and talking until they finally seen. There was of course the money aspect of it too, at that time. So my daddy kept talking and talking, trying to get the priests to sponsor the dances. . . . And he kept convincing and talking to Father about starting zydeco, so they finally give him the OK to sponsor the dance, give a dance . . . and they finally let him start it. It went over big. . . . He was very successful with it. He had a knack for putting a dance together and putting some musicians together and doing a beautiful thing with it.

To the delight of the parish priest, the church profited nicely from that first zydeco dance, so he soon approved another one. Gallien then hired his fellow Houston resident and childhood friend Clifton Chenier to play, and this follow-up event drew an even larger crowd, which provided more income for church coffers. They repeated that success at regular intervals, and it caught the attention of other predominantly black Creole Catholic churches in Houston. In *The Kingdom of Zydeco*, Tisserand summarizes the result: "Soon a dozen other churches in the city started holding dances, and Gallien began training recruits for a new ecclesiastical position: dance chairman."

In a 1993 interview, Frenchtown nightclub owner Doris McClendon remembers the sudden popularity of this church-dance phenomenon, for it affected secular venues such as her grandfather's Johnson's Lounge. "Way back," she says, "the Catholic churches did not have it at all. But it got to be so popular that they went to building recreation halls, each parish, to have zydeco music on Saturday nights. . . . Any parish that's having a dance, their members support them."

Following the lead of St. Francis of Assisi, Houston churches such as Our Mother of Mercy, St. Peter Claver, St. Francis Xavier, St. Philip Neri, St. Mary's, and others began to capitalize on the popularity of zydeco dances. One key reason for their success was that they offered an alternative to adults-only nightclubs, providing venues where whole families could gather with friends and relatives to socialize to music that had evolved from the Creole culture that so many of the participants shared. It some respects, it was almost like attending a giant la-la party from the old days back in the Louisiana countryside. But this vibrantly

Zydeco dancers, St. Anne de Beaupre Catholic Church, Houston, Texas, 2004.

new form of the music reflected the life experience of so many of its most devoted fans. Like them, it had been transplanted to Texas, updated, and urbanized, yet it still managed to retain its fundamentally Creole identity, and both the music and the people celebrated that heritage proudly.

Of course, as more churches joined in the practice of staging their own zydeco dances, the events began to overlap. And with dances being staged independently, sometimes at multiple sites on the same night, it put the various Creole Catholic congregations in the awkward position of competing against one another—both for the paying customers and for the talent that would draw them. Gallien Jr., who later "took over the zydecos" at St. Francis of Assisi for a while, describes the situation:

My wife, she was president of the Family Club. That's an organization they formed with the zydeco, after they organized the zydeco. . . . We would sponsor all the dances . . . every fourth Saturday of the month. We used to give eleven and twelve dances a year. Then they formed a coalition, the ICA [Inter-Catholic Association], and they got together and split the dances up to the churches in the parish. And each one had seven dances apiece, I believe. Because we were cutting each other's throat so much [i.e., competing for audiences at the dances]. You know, you couldn't make any money. You'd give a dance, and you'd just have overhead, no profit. So that's why they formed the coalition, the ICA.

With the intervention of the Catholic leadership, the fund-raising dances thus began to rotate from church to church regularly, making each event the one big draw of its particular week. It also made each production more profitable for the sponsoring church, since the competition essentially disappeared. To keep people informed of where to find the dances, the diocese also began to publish schedules and updates in its semimonthly *Texas Catholic Herald* (a practice that continues in the "Around the Diocese" section of the Web site www. texascatholicherald.org).

From the late 1950s through the early 1980s, Clifton Chenier was the king of the church-dance scene in Houston. His former drummer Robert Murphy points out, however, that Chenier not only worked the urban church circuit but also performed at similar dances in small towns across southeast Texas. "Playing the church dances . . . he started that," Murphy says. "We helped build churches in Barrett Station . . . Ames, and Raywood. We'd play church dances all up in there. We helped build the church halls all in those areas."

Based on the sizable crowds Chenier (and later bandleaders such as Buckwheat Zydeco, Boozoo Chavis, John Delafose, and others) could consistently draw, some churches built large social centers to accommodate patrons and maximize fund-raising. St. Francis of Assisi, for instance, expanded its space to accommodate up to 750 people at a dance,

Zydeco dancers (with Jerome Batiste and the ZydeKo Players),
St. Francis of Assisi Catholic Church, Houston, Texas, 2004.

Billy Poullard, St. Pius Catholic Church, Beaumont, Texas, 2004.

and some newer churches, such as St. Mark the Evangelist, in the southwest suburbs, constructed and regularly filled even more spacious halls. These proved to be good investments. As Lonnie Mitchell once explained, "They pay the band, and all the rest of that money goes to the church," providing thousands of dollars for the ecclesiastical coffers. And as the church sponsors have pointed out, these regular, close-to-home gigs in front of large and appreciative audiences have certainly benefited the zydeco artists, too. Concerning his father's impact on their careers, Gallien Jr., asserts, "My daddy made 'em, even Buckwheat. He made 'em famous."

But it was Clifton Chenier who first helped make the Houston church dance scene so vital, and few other artists could regularly attract the crowds as the king did. Even after he became a world-recognized icon of zydeco, Chenier continued to appear at church dances—not only along the Gulf Coast but also in California. Such venues remained an important part of his career throughout his final years. His son C. J. recalls, "When I got with him [in 1978], the main thing in Houston was all the church halls. *Every* time we'd come to Houston we were playing at St. Philip's or St. Francis. Yeah, Saturday night at the church hall! And it'd be just rows of people in there having a good time." As Chris Strachwitz writes of such celebratory rituals (in the liner notes to *Zydeco: Volume One*), "entire families would attend and the Zydeco once again became a communal celebration having come full circle from the old community 'house dances.'"

Via the zydeco church-dance phenomenon that evolved from Clarence Gallien's original efforts for St. Francis of Assisi Catholic Church, black Creole artists and their dance patrons forged a way to reconnect with their Louisiana roots even while embracing life in Houston. Their experience at large thus mirrors that of their most famous musician, Clifton Chenier. For during his long residency in, and in subsequent visits to, the Bayou City—and whether he performed in ballrooms, cafés, or church halls—the king epitomized a cultural transformation. In leaving the birthplace of his la-la heritage, he helped create other ways and places for celebrating it anew.

DESPITE THE PRODUCTIVITY AND SUCCESS HE ACHIEVED during his long residency in Texas, Clifton Chenier lived mainly in his beloved Louisiana during the final decade of his life. By then, as he related to Ben Sandmel in a 1983 interview (reprinted in Ann Savoy's book), he had had enough of big city life: "I stay in Louisiana and Texas, but I'm more in Louisiana than I am in Texas. . . . Texas, man, is crowded; Houston is getting crowded." Chenier's move back to his home state also coincided with the culmination of his fame and worldwide renown. After revolutionizing the concept of Creole music in the late 1940s, '50s, and '60s, Chenier had finally obtained the stature of a widely acclaimed music legend—the kind of recognition that earned him many national and international tour-

OPPOSITE PAGE (LEFT TO RIGHT): *An aspiring zydeco player and Brian Jack, St. Anne de Beaupre Catholic Church, Houston, Texas, 2004.*

ing opportunities, Grammy Award nominations, and high-profile media appearances. Yet through this period of his most impressive success, he still took perhaps the greatest pride in the royal title he had long carried, for a role that he had always viewed quite seriously.

In the Sandmel interview cited above, Chenier offers the explanation that his status as "the king" originated in 1971, the result of a European contest in which he reportedly prevailed over "about 500 accordion players." As he puts it, "They had a lot accordion players but they couldn't capture my style. . . . that's how I walk out with the crown. I been havin' it ever since." Though the precise facts of that competition remain vague, the ornate crown that Chenier thereafter adopted became his personal symbol—an adornment he wore sometimes during photo shoots or musical performances onstage. It was in some respects perhaps his most prized possession, one that he guarded fiercely. "I tell you what, to get that crown, you have to roll me, oh yeah, they have to roll me," he adds. And in my 2004 interview, Chenier's son C. J. addresses the same subject: "I'll tell you what," he says (echoing his father's introductory clause), "That crown meant the world to him. It wasn't a gimmick. It was real. . . . It may seem like a gimmick to you, but that was real to my daddy."

Though he suffered from diabetes and kidney disease that required regular dialysis treatments, the king continued to tour until the week before his death on December 12, 1987, in Lafayette. News reports around the world typically proclaimed his regal stature while sadly announcing his demise. "'Zydeco King' Clifton Chenier Dies at Age 62" reads the headline of a widely circulated Associated Press story. In addition to summarizing Chenier's musical legacy, this unsigned article quotes Lynn Boutin as saying, "He was the king of zydeco. . . . Because of him, the movement is growing. . . . There are other bands starting up, playing what Chenier first played—black Cajun music." And although "black Cajun" is not the most accurate label for Chenier's uniquely syncretized sound, critics everywhere concur that the late king had not only defined the essence of zydeco but also, through his success, encouraged other musicians to follow its path.

Chenier died at the very time that zydeco was starting to experience its greatest crossover success, especially with mainstream white audiences throughout the Western world. By recording and touring into the 1980s, Chenier had spurred a major wave of interest and acceptance from mass music culture—a trend that would benefit those who emerged to popular prominence in his wake (such as his former band member Stanley "Buckwheat Zydeco" Dural). By the 1990s, bands playing variant or mutant forms of Chenier-inspired black Creole music began to emerge not only nationwide but also overseas. (For example, Chris Jagger—younger brother of Mick, the famous lead singer for the Rolling Stones—formed the British band Atcha! and released CDs such as 1995's *Rock the Zydeco* on Sequel Records.) Yet the impact of Chenier's life and death remains most significant along the plains of the upper Gulf Coast, the region he knew best, the land of the zydeco corridor.

Newspaper clipping (announcing the death of Clifton Chenier),
Gabbanelli Accordions and Imports, Houston, Texas, 2004.

Dan Rubit, Missouri City, Texas, 2004.

In Houston, the city where he lived for much of his adulthood, countless musicians still point to Chenier as their single greatest personal inspiration. To friends such as these, the late king lives on in special memories that animate their smiles and gestures when they share them aloud.

Robert Murphy, for example, radiates a deep sense of awe in recalling his former bandleader's personal charisma: "Clifton Chenier was an amazing man. He knew more people than anybody I know of," he says while spreading his arms far apart. "That's right. I never saw a man knew as many people! And he'd call them by name, and they'd call him by name," he remembers, shaking his bowed head in a gesture of amazement and then breaking into laughter that waters his eyes. Minutes later, with a devious grin and a whisper, Murphy confides, "Clifton was a ladies man. He was a stone ladies man! I don't care where we went, there were women waiting for him. They were always waiting for Clifton Chenier." Following a series of stream-of-consciousness recollections of some of their experiences playing music together, Murphy pauses, sighs, and then solemnly concludes, "Clifton Chenier was the greatest man I ever knew."

Fellow piano-style accordionist Dan Rubit especially treasures the personal encouragement his more famous mentor granted him over the years. Reflecting on his early attempts to master the instrument, he says, "I had two brother-in-laws in zydeco, so I messed around with it a little bit. But after Clif came to Houston, Clifton Chenier . . . I got with him a little bit, and then I really picked up." He goes on to recount his final conversation with the musician who influenced him the most:

He told me before he passed away, him and I were together one day, and he say, "Dan, I'm going to give you my right finger."

And I say, "Let me see it." And I looked at it, and that finger looked rough. So I say, "Well I don't want the finger. I'd like to do what you do with my finger [laughs] . . ." and we laughed about it. . . .

Yeah, Clif and I—he was an older guy than I was—but he, he say, "Dan, I don't like to hear these other guys play. They don't even know nothing about accordion." And he came over to The Silver Slipper, and he said, "I want to hear you play." I've got his style of music, you know. . . . He'd say, "Dan, you've got it. Look at the people you put on the [dance] floor!" And that made me satisfied, just to hear him say that.

C. J. Chenier ultimately defines his father's legacy in a global context:

To me, music is one of the few things we still can offer that other countries want. . . . And there's lots of groups over there [in Europe] that are starting to play zydeco. Because accordion here for a *long time was not considered a great instrument, but in Europe, accordion has been king for a long time. . . . And they know Clifton Chenier over there! They know him there, and they have this greater appreciation.*

His intense pride in his father's far-reaching musical achievements is countered by his sad assessment of the obliviousness prevalent among some members of the younger generation of zydeco players back on the Gulf Coast:

Then you come back home, where it all comes from, and the people that are supposed to really be into it have got the narrow mind, this tunnel vision, stylistically and historically speaking. . . . I'm just sorry that today some of them don't even have a clue where it came from or how it started, might not even know Clifton Chenier or anything about his music! . . . I'm glad zydeco is more known now; I'm glad. But [some zydeco musicians] don't have a clue where it came from, you know. I know my dad didn't exactly start it, but he took it out of the closet and brought it to a whole new level. . . . And then he gave it its name! How do you don't even know the man that named the music?

Mary Thomas, for one, is doing her part to make sure that people young and old respect the zydeco heritage that emanates from her family member Clifton Chenier. Not only does she cover some of his songs in her role as a bluesy vocalist, but she also regularly features recordings by Chenier on the weekly zydeco program she cohosts (with James B. Adams and others) on KPFT radio. Moreover, for eighteen years in a row (and counting), Thomas has more or less single-handedly produced an annual tribute concert to honor the memory of the late king. In a 2004 interview she explains the origins of that Houston tradition:

He passed away in December of 1987, and . . . in January of '88, a lady I didn't even know—she got my telephone number from a lady that knew me—she called me and asked me about doing a tribute. She knew Clifton pretty good because she would go to all of his dances, right here in Houston . . . But I hesitated because, you know, Clifton had a living wife. . . . So I called Margaret, and I told her what the lady had asked me. And I told her exactly how it was going to go down, what was going to be happening there and stuff. So she told me it was OK. And she said, "As long as you want to do it, you do it." . . . She said, "It's going to keep his music going. It's going to let people remember him. Because, you know, he was the king of zydeco. And then people won't forget him." . . . I guess that's still the reason why I do it.

One recent manifestation of this important event, which functions also as a yearly reunion of Creole old-timers and zydeco enthusiasts in the Houston area, took place in the historic Frenchtown neighborhood at The Silver Slipper. It is an old club that has been run by

Clifton Chenier's great-grandson, at C. J. Chenier's home, Houston, Texas, 2004.

several generations of the Cormier family for approximately half a century, and the king often performed there (located, as it is, close to his former home on Mystic Street). Thus, it made an especially appropriate venue for the 2004 Clifton Chenier Tribute. This four-hour concert and dance featured scores of different musicians, most of whom had personally known and performed with Chenier. The event ended with Mary Thomas taking the stage to talk passionately about the man she calls her "brother." Of her various recollections and declarations, one in particular provoked the most heartfelt response from the audience: "There wouldn't be no zydeco, like we know it and love it, if it wasn't for Clifton. And you *know* that's the truth!"

For the generation of Texas zydeco players represented by the likes of the late Lonnie Mitchell, such a judgment was beyond debate. "Clifton's the one that started it. He blazed the trail," Mitchell acknowledges in a 1993 interview, adding the awe-struck observation that "He's the [first] zydeco man playing in New York, at the Carnegie Hall." Though they were peers who sometimes shared regional stages together, the highly respected Mitchell ultimately insists that neither he nor anyone else had ever been Chenier's equal. When asked whether he might have taught his good friend anything about playing zydeco or working a crowd, Mitchell replies, "Naw, I ain't going to lie. He was *good*! When he passed, he was the best zydeco music there were, that I know of. You couldn't beat him!"

In truth, nobody ever did surpass Clifton Chenier during his lifetime. And though, in the years immediately following his death, a number of accordionists attempted to claim the preeminent title for themselves, nobody else has ever attained the people's full consensus of worthiness for royal stature. For Wilbert Thibodeaux, as for many other Texans along the western span of the zydeco corridor, one truth remains self-evident: "Clifton Chenier is the only zydeco man who ever really deserved to call himself the king."

Raymond Chavis, Eldorado Ballroom, Houston, Texas, 2004.

Four

Out of the Cradle, Rocking

he 1987 death of Clifton Chenier came at a time when the postwar music genre that he had helped create was experiencing perhaps its most significant and commercially successful phase of mainstream exposure. It was an era in which various bands from small towns and cities along the Louisiana-Texas zydeco corridor were suddenly being booked to perform on major stages, nationally and internationally, as well as gaining unprecedented media attention in the process. Moreover, zydeco had begun to surface in other previously unlikely places. As Lorenzo Thomas points out in "From Gumbo to Grammys," since the 1980s it has "contributed to the musical vocabulary of 'rock 'n' roll' which, in the late twentieth century, is nothing less than the popular music of the world." Thus, basic elements of the sound were gradually becoming more and more familiar to mass audiences—many of whom had never even heard of Clifton Chenier.

For instance, the 1986 Grammy Award for Album of the Year went to Paul Simon's phenomenally successful *Graceland*. This record introduced millions of listeners to Simon's formerly obscure guest collaborators—not only many South Africans playing their "township jive" (or *mbaqanga*) music but also a group of Gulf Coast Creoles performing zydeco. Though the former style had originated on a distant continent and the latter was homegrown in the United States, at the time they were both pretty much equally foreign to most of the American public. Yet Simon's album—which included a track recorded in Lafayette with

Good Rockin' Dopsie and the Twisters (featuring Houston's Sherman Robertson on guitar)—soon triggered interest in zydeco among an entirely new base of potential fans.

Another significant factor in the late-twentieth-century absorption of zydeco into popular culture involved Stanley Dural, a pianist and organist who had worked in Clifton Chenier's band in the late 1970s before taking up the accordion and forming his own group in 1979. Under the nickname Buckwheat Zydeco, Dural issued several successful albums in the 1980s, but one in particular played a key role in disseminating the zydeco sound to large numbers of consumers of rock and roll: 1987's *On a Night like This* (on Island Records). Though it included some updates of traditional material, such as "Ma 'Tit Fille" and Chenier's classic "Hot Tamale Baby," this enthusiastically received disc hooked a large segment of its audience with Buckwheat's unique zydeco treatments of songs originally written and performed by well-known rock artists such as the iconic Bob Dylan, Dave Alvin (of the Blasters), and Booker T. Jones (of Booker T and the MGs). Thus, Dural shrewdly appealed to the tastes of many baby-boomer-generation music fans, offering them familiar tunes transformed into a style that most of them probably viewed as new. As producer Ted Fox accurately observes in his liner notes on the LP jacket, "In the hot, steaming swath of country between New Orleans and Houston they have been dancing to zydeco music for decades, but until recently the music has been little heard outside of this realm."

The international success of *On a Night like This* soon led to opportunities for Dural to tour nationally and to record with British rock superstar Eric Clapton (who contributed a guest appearance on guitar and vocals on Buckwheat Zydeco's follow-up album, 1988's *Taking It Home*). This high-profile collaboration helped establish Buckwheat Zydeco as one of the most widely recognized black Creole musical acts actively performing through the end of the millennium. Perhaps the culminating moment in his fame occurred in 1996, when he played live on globally broadcast television during the concluding ceremonies of the Summer Olympics in Atlanta.

Beyond the most obvious manifestations of the music business (including Rockin' Sidney Simien's 1984 million-selling, Grammy Award–winning recording of "My Toot Toot"), other forms of media exposure also helped introduce zydeco to large numbers of people during the decade in which Chenier passed away. For example, one of the hit films of 1987 was director Jim McBride's *Big Easy*, a mystery-romance starring Dennis Quaid and Ellen Barkin. The fact that it included scenes of authentic zydeco in performance (and featured the music on the accompanying sound-track album) signaled yet another way that zydeco was working its way into popular consciousness. By the early 1990s the distinctive sound had begun to surface in other films, such as John Sayles's 1992 *Passion Fish*. Moreover, it even invaded some momentarily ubiquitous television advertising campaigns—for products ranging from

Toyota automobiles to Reese's Peanut Butter Cups to Nike athletic shoes—demonstrating irrefutably that this Creole-originated musical phenomenon had evolved into a commodity deemed palatable for the masses.

Meanwhile, back along the zydeco corridor, the impact of this apparent national awakening was both positive and negative. Some of the more established, professionally managed, and fortunate bands reaped the benefits of the expanded zydeco market by working at venues and for record companies far removed from the Gulf Coast. Though the media coverage of the rise of mainstream acceptance of zydeco typically lacked much insight regarding the black Creole culture that birthed the genre, it sometimes at least acknowledged the existence of this unique ethnic group (as distinct from Cajuns) and certain aspects of its musical traditions. To many black Creoles, such notice was generally interpreted as a sign of social progress.

However, as the most commercially successful zydeco bands spent more time in the national marketplace playing to non-Creole audiences, and as the price they could command therefore rose, the likelihood of them performing regularly back home (in the folksy southwest Louisiana and southeast Texas venues that had originally nurtured their talents) decreased. Also, at the very time that zydeco was becoming more integrated into pop culture, it was rapidly losing senior members of its core audience, denizens of the Gulf Coast, patriarchs and matriarchs who had grown up attending house parties and church dances but who now—like the departed king—had begun to succumb to various illnesses and conditions associated with aging. Moreover, as some of the new wave of younger zydeco artists assimilated various postmodern pop influences, many of the old-school zydeco loyalists grew less comfortable with the musical results; in short, what was now passing for zydeco did not always sound like the style they preferred. Not only were different artists stretching the range of the basic definition of the term, but there was also no longer a central figure to epitomize and propagate what many people considered the "true" zydeco sound.

Through the late 1980s and into the 1990s, Chenier's absence haunted the now-kingless zydeco realm. As Barry Jean Ancelet writes in *Creoles of Color of the Gulf South,*

Clifton Chenier dominated the world of zydeco, as his title implies. He was such a creative genius that he transformed anything he played into his own, including blues, country, rock, western swing, and big band tunes. He was so important to the tradition that he helped to define that, after his death in 1987, the zydeco community fell into disarray. There was a power vacuum at the top.

In response to this lack of an undisputed monarch, zydeco folks from Breaux Bridge to Houston debated the possibility of finding a worthy successor to the throne—and some opportunistic promoters staged contests that promised to establish the new king. Among some of the more prominent zydeco bandleaders and their most fervent supporters, there was much posturing and bluster over the rightful claim to the title.

The controversy had, in fact, begun even well before Chenier's death. In a chapter entitled "Coronation Blues" in *The Kingdom of Zydeco*, Michael Tisserand cites an August 1980 article in Houston's *Forward Times*, an African American weekly newspaper, which reported matter-of-factly that Stanley "Buckwheat Zydeco" Dural had been crowned the new king of zydeco, thus bringing the royal tenure of Clifton Chenier to an end. Tisserand goes on to explain that Dural had evidently been the focus of a crowning ceremony at a church dance in Houston—an act that reportedly proclaimed him to be the "Texas King of Zydeco." Despite his subsequent protestations that his participation in the Houston coronation had been reluctant, the public figure known as Buckwheat Zydeco did thereafter sometimes imply (in the phrasing of onstage introductions and in photographs of himself decked out in cape and crown) his belief in his own royal standing. To some people, Dural's actions may have suggested that he was impolitely attempting to usurp the title of king from Chenier (who, though slowed by illness, was still performing at the time).

The situation climaxed on the final weekend of October in 1982 with a Chenier-Dural showdown in Houston, a major event staged at the spacious sports-and-entertainment arena called The Summit (then also the home of the Houston Rockets of the National Basketball Association). In a concert billed as the first Texas-Louisiana Blues and Zydeco Festival, each of the zydeco bandleaders performed on stage in royal regalia. In Chenier's closing set, he reportedly flung his crown from his head and announced to the audience that he was the one and only true king of the whole zydeco world. Thereafter neither he nor Dural seemed to have raised the sensitive issue in public again.

However, in the aftermath of Chenier's funeral (where, as illustrated by a Michael P. Smith photograph published in *Living Blues* issue number 138, his crown was displayed on the edge of his open casket), the scramble of contenders hoping to seize the make-believe kingship ensued anew. This time Stanley Dural wisely declined to be drawn into the fray. But within three weeks of Chenier's burial, Alton "Rockin' Dopsie" Rubin had staged an event at which the mayor of Lafayette formally crowned him and proclaimed him to be the new king of zydeco. Many people, including Clifton Chenier's son C. J., were displeased—both with the bold presumption and the timing of the action. The resulting arguments and accusations among zydeco musicians and fans was a public-relations disaster for Rubin, one that troubled him repeatedly till his death in August 1993.

Nevertheless, not long after Rubin's demise, other figures resumed the public struggle to claim the mythic crown of zydeco. No single authority, of course, existed to settle the matter, so various organizations and events delivered declarations immediately ignored or denounced by others. Robert Mugge's 1994 film, *The Kingdom of Zydeco*, focuses primarily on one big event in particular, staged in Lake Charles, which pitted country-style zydeco traditionalist Boozoo Chavis against Beau Jocque, the master of a more progressive urban sound that was being called by some "zydeco nouveau." As Rick Mitchell writes in his *Houston Chronicle* film review, the ostensible purpose of this much-hyped concert was "to determine the line of royal succession following the death of Rockin' Dopsie." Though Chavis was alleged to have been Dopsie's designated choice to receive the honor, and had in fact received a crown in a public ceremony the day before the musical face-off, there was still heated debate. As the film documents, various zydeco promoters and insiders contended instead that the increasingly popular Beau Jocque deserved the crown. Ultimately, the contest was called a draw, and zydeco people have since then remained mostly divided over the notion of whether anyone would ever be truly worthy to assume Clifton Chenier's former title (one whose ambiguous origin may have been, after all, simply an act of self-proclamation on the part of the original "king"). For the most part, by the late 1990s the whole notion of establishing any consensus to resolve the squabbling over kingship had faded away.

The contrast (though perhaps not the adversarial relationship implied by Mugge's film) between Beau Jocque and Boozoo Chavis nonetheless represents a significant fact of post-Chenier zydeco through the end of the twentieth century. During that era (until their deaths in 1999 and 2001, respectively), these two button-accordion players were arguably the dominant figures in the actual zydeco corridor subculture—that is, the multifaceted southwest Louisiana–southeast Texas network of nightclubs, radio programs, regional festivals, church dances, trail rides, and related events at which zydeco has been nurtured for decades. Given their stature, their influence on the emerging younger generation of black Creole zydeco musicians from the upper Gulf Coast was profound. Yet though they both played the button accordion, they represented two conspicuously contrary ways of utilizing it to make late-twentieth-century zydeco.

In many respects, the elder Chavis offered a repertoire, technique, and self-presentation that looked backwards, so to speak, toward the rural experience from which Creole folk music had originated. On the other hand, the younger and hipper-looking Beau Jocque boldly embraced all manner of contemporary urban influences, including elements of funk, reggae, pop, and rock. Collectively, these two zydeco legends would inspire scores of zydeco-corridor-based players (especially those born in the 1970s and '80s) to take up the button accordion. Of those who did so, some would veer mainly toward the new traditionalism personified by Chavis; others would choose instead to experiment with the Beau Jocque model of progressive fusion; the most musically adventurous would mix both styles. But not many would choose to play the piano-key chromatic accordion, or the type of material, associated with the memory of Clifton Chenier.

That is not to say that there were no more piano-note accordionists in the region; however, those that continued to play tended to be older, and they dwindled in number and influence as members of the younger generation gravitated mainly toward the button model and the playing styles associated with its two most prominent practitioners of their time. Of course, the piano accordionist known as Buckwheat Zydeco was certainly widely famous and quite commercially successful during this era. But by the 1990s he had become primarily an internationally recognized zydeco celebrity, a show-business figure who mostly appeared at venues far removed, geographically and demographically, from the upper Gulf Coast cradle. Playing the same type of instrument as his former bandleader Clifton Chenier, Buckwheat Zydeco—like only a few other widely known piano accordionists, such as Texas-based C. J. Chenier and Brian Terry—often appealed broadly to relatively cosmopolitan (sometimes predominantly white) audiences possessing certain classic-rock sensibilities. As a result, even though Stanley "Buckwheat Zydeco" Dural has continued to make his home in southwest Louisiana, by the 1990s it was unusual for him to perform regularly in the kind of places where black Creole zydeco people most often congregate to hear music and dance.

Thus, Boozoo Chavis and Beau Jocque became established as the two highest-profile Louisiana-based role models most directly accessible to many young black Creole enthusiasts and budding musicians along the zydeco corridor. Therefore, their shared reliance on button accordions significantly shaped the instrumental preferences of the next generation. As Brian Terry relates in Tisserand's book, "It seemed that when Clifton Chenier died, the piano notes were wiped out for a while." Button accordions, being smaller, generally less expensive, and (particularly in the case of the old-style single-row models) less musically complex (hence, theoretically easier to learn to play), were important factors in this regard too. But apart from utilizing the nonchromatic button accordion, Chavis and Beau Jocque's essentially different styles highlighted a fundamental dichotomy inherent in late-twentieth-century zydeco: neotraditionalism versus neofusion. And as had been true since at least the 1940s, black Creoles residing in Texas played a key role in the evolution of both strains of music.

YEARS BEFORE AND UP TO THE TIME the phrase "zydeco nouveau" entered common parlance, a couple of youthful, innovative accordionists from metropolitan Houston were already leading bands that broke new ground and arguably allowed the concept to take root. Certainly, some zydeco players had been fusing the Creole musical tradition with contemporary sounds ever since Clifton Chenier moved to Texas and started showing them how to do it. Following his lead, black accordionists on both sides of the Sabine River, especially in the larger cities, conducted ongoing experiments in this process. "But it was two bands that emerged from Houston—one in the 1970s and the other in the 1990s—," Tisserand asserts

OPPOSITE PAGE: *Travis "Cowboy" Johnson, The Silver Slipper, Houston, Texas, 2003.*

in his authoritative tome, "that really answered Clifton Chenier's call to put new hinges on the old French music and update it for a new generation."

The earlier of these two pioneer neofusion bands, Sam Brothers Five, officially formed in Houston in 1974 and flourished through (and embodied many of the pop-cultural trends of) the rest of the '70s. Described by Tisserand as kind of like "the Jackson Five with an accordion," this group of teenage and preteen Texas-born black Creoles initiated the mainstream synthesis of zydeco with funk, disco, and other postmodern forms. The ensemble consisted of five sons of Herbert "Good Rocking" Sam (b. 1924), the same Opelousas-born immigrant to Houston that Chris Strachwitz had first recorded back in 1961 (see *Zydeco: Volume One, the Early Years*). Accordion prodigy and lead vocalist Leon Sam (b. 1964) fronted the group, capably supported by his older brothers Carl (b. 1961) and Rodney (b. 1963) on guitar and drums and younger brothers Glen (b. 1966) and Calvin (b. 1968) on bass and rubboard. They were an unusually fashionably dressed unit, typically performing in colorful matching outfits with bell-bottom pants. Most of the brothers also sported expansively Afro hairstyles, except for Leon; he wore his processed hair combed straight back, held in place by a headband—just like Clifton Chenier, the idol he had observed at Houston church dances since he was a toddler. Their repertoire mixed Chenier-penned classics such as "I'm a Hog for You" with innovations such as their signature number "S.A.M. (Get Down)" (based on "Le Freak" by the '70s disco sensation known as Chic).

Under the primary guidance of their father, a veteran of the Houston zydeco circuit since the 1950s, each of the brothers had started learning to play almost as soon as he was physically capable, and each was assigned a particular instrument so that collectively they would form a complete zydeco combo. Along the way, the boys also received moral support, occasional mentoring, and impromptu onstage performance opportunities from their father's many local musician friends. For example, the late Houston accordionist Lonnie Mitchell attests:

Their daddy and I used to play together, before they was even born, before their mother and daddy married. And when they was little and just learning how to play, they used to come in there to Johnson's, the Continental [Zydeco] Lounge, and I'd let 'em sit in. . . . That little one rubbing the board was only about five years old then.

Those early appearances at the venerable Frenchtown establishment best known as the Continental Zydeco Ballroom surely enhanced the youngsters' credibility, as did the implicit endorsement of the widely respected Lonnie Mitchell. With such exposure they earned a reputation that quickly opened other doors for them.

For instance, Dan Rubit, bandleader of the Zydeco Rockets, remembers the Sam Brothers Five soon being booked to play at Vada's Lounge, a popular southeast Houston zydeco venue during the 1970s. He speaks too of a special relationship with the family band. As a performer he shared stages with them not only at Vada's, but also on some of their first road trips. Rubit claims also to have been an early influence on Leon Sam's choice of instrument:

As a matter of fact, I started with them when they were very young. . . . I know the father real good. The Sam Five, it was five brothers.

. . . And we hooked up together a few times and traveled a little bit. . . .

I started Leon off with the piano accordion. I had a twelve-bass piano accordion, and I let him play it. He cried. He was at my house, and his dad say, "Well, let's go, kids." And he wanted to learn.

I said, "Sam," I told his dad, "Why don't you let him learn how to play that piano accordion?" He was playing [only] the double-note [button accordion] then. And I picked up the piano accordion . . . and took his two fingers and put it on that accordion. He still brags about it now. And he picked up that accordion, but it was too big for him, one like that. And I had a twelve-bass, so he picked it up. And I'd teach him, and man, he was hot on that accordion! Real hot.

As the brothers developed their instrumental skills and stage presence, their youthful exuberance and progressive approach to the music garnered attention on a larger scale. While the fundamental elements and the Sam family pedigree identified this music as zydeco, it was nonetheless a revolutionary manifestation of the form. As such, it reached out to a whole new realm of regional fans—young people who recognized familiar pop-cultural signifiers in the contemporary look and sound of the Sam Brothers Five, but who might have never previously considered zydeco (if they were aware of it at all) as "cool" music. Suddenly, however, it was being featured prominently at various youth-friendly venues around the city, as well as on local radio and television programs. As Tisserand writes, "the band took Houston by storm," performing at a wide variety of venues and opening for established blues and R&B performers at big shows.

After emerging and developing initially on the Houston scene, in 1977 the Sam family moved back to the ancestral Louisiana community where the parents were born. In so doing, they were following a pattern established by numerous black Creole musicians before them: that is, having modified the music of their ethnic heritage while residing in urban Texas, they now transported the newly synthesized results back to their cultural homeland. By 1979, the Sam Brothers Five had gained enough in-state notice to be invited to perform at the New Orleans Jazz and Heritage Festival. There they crossed paths with producer Chris Strachwitz, who promptly arranged for them to travel to California for a short tour and a recording session for his Arhoolie Records—the results of which are now available on a CD entitled *SAM (Get Down)*, issued in 2004.

Leon Sam, The Silver Slipper, Houston, Texas, 1998.

However, as the 1980s progressed and the brothers grew older, the novelty of their youth-infused (and essentially 1970s-style) zydeco began to fade, so the Sam Brothers Five eventually settled into periods of sporadic gigging interspersed with phases of musical inactivity. In time, they essentially disappeared. Then in 1996 they reemerged under the new moniker Leon Sam and the Sam Brothers with the comeback album *Leon's Boogie Is Back* (MTE Records). Before that year was over, though, this reassembled version of the band broke up. Undiminished in the desire to resurrect his career in music, but unwilling to work professionally with his brothers (at least for a while), Leon chose to move back to the Texas city where he was born and raised.

Leon Sam was fortunate in his timing, for he immediately found a job. The securely established Zydeco Dots had recently parted ways with Pierre Stoot (who had previously fronted the group as the replacement for its original accordionist, Pierre Blanchard). Now back in Houston without a band, Leon was available and eager to form a new affiliation that could capitalize on his talent as an experienced accordion player and singer. So for the first time in his career, he joined a band not composed of his family members, and this new relationship lasted for the next seven years. Because the Zydeco Dots were a popular group that performed regularly (at festivals, clubs, private parties, and corporate affairs), they could offer their new front man plenty of gigs. And Leon's ability to step right into a dominant leading role clearly energized and focused this multifaceted band. "The addition of Leon Sam gives the Dots a top-notch accordion player, one who favors a wide range of bluesy notes," wrote Aaron Howard in the *Houston Press* in 2000. "The group's sound is now more classic, less contemporary."

That same year, Leon Sam and the Zydeco Dots released a CD entitled *Tribute to Clif* (Klarity Music). As the title implies, it is a showcase of Leon's ability to sing (in French and in English) and play in the style of his artistic role model. Zydeco Dots cofounder and lead guitarist Thomas "Tee" Potter explains why: "Leon can do some Clifton Chenier–style songs that, if you close your eyes and know Clifton's stuff, you cannot tell the difference, he does them so well. It's incredible." Even though Lonnie Mitchell did not live long enough to hear and comment on this tribute recording, he had already formed a similar opinion years earlier. As he asserts in a 1993 interview, "Now them little Sam boys is just about as good as Clif, Sam Brothers Five. . . . That Leon, he damn near as good as Clif. . . . If he's inside and you're outside and you don't know who's playing, you'd listen there and you'd think it's Clif playing."

From 1996 through the first half of 2003, Leon worked mainly with the Houston-based Zydeco Dots. However, he also eventually resumed some level of intermittent professional collaboration with his fraternal siblings (who by now were living in various places in Louisiana and Texas), and they occasionally staged special appearances as the reunited Leon Sam and the Sam Brothers. Sometime near the midpoint of 2003, the Zydeco Dots and Leon elected to part ways, and he reportedly has now returned to full-time residency in the Lafayette area.

Leon Sam's impact on Texas zydeco is significant for more than one reason. Most recently it includes his turn-of-the-century tenure with one of the most active bands in the state's largest city; in that role, he particularly helped spark some renewal of interest in the rich legacy of Clifton Chenier. Yet in historical retrospect today, some thirty years after the Sam Brothers Five debuted in Houston, it is clear that Leon's fundamentally urban and youth-oriented group was a harbinger of stylistic fusions to come. Nobody really knew it at the time, but this band of Texas-born brothers arguably laid the foundation for what would later be known as zydeco nouveau.

OF COURSE, "ZYDECO NOUVEAU" is an elastic label that has sometimes been applied to performers that differ vastly from one another. The term became fairly common in the 1990s, and although it may suggest various things to different people, most seem now to use it to signify a kind of "zyde-rap" hybrid sound. In that case, its main characteristics usually include beat-dominant elements of hip-hop fused with repetitive accordion riffs and rubboard rhythms, as well as what Ben Sandmel aptly describes as "rap's staccato, declamatory vocals." In this music, the bass lines are thick and extra heavy, and the drum work is especially emphatic. Except for some occasional pyrotechnics on electric guitar, there is usually little emphasis on instrumental soloing. The tempo is often accelerated, and certain forms that have traditionally been associated with zydeco (such as waltzes and blues) are mostly ignored. As might be expected, the use of the French language is almost nonexistent (except for a few well-known exclamatory phrases).

To its detractors (and there have been many), in its worst form it seems to reduce itself mainly to nonmelodic shouting over a pounding beat, spiced with rudimentary looping phrases squeezed from the button accordion. Though intensely popular with many younger African Americans along the zydeco corridor through the start of the twenty-first century, this profoundly urbanized style has the capacity to alienate traditionalists and older Creole folks in general (particularly those on the church-dance circuit). Zydeco players and fans who are more inclined to appreciate Clifton Chenier's musical style (as well as jazz, blues, or classic rock influences) also often have viewed it with disdain.

C. J. Chenier, for one, objects to the narrow limits of much zydeco nouveau:

What they're doing right now, what I'm seeing, is that the accordion is not creating the music. The accordion is just like playing a riff. The band behind them [has] got to create all the music. But that's not the way it goes. The accordion is the main instrument out there. It's supposed to be the main focus. . . .

Today, you play a riff, you have a steady beat, you have a bass line, you have a rhythm, and you play a riff, and then you holler some stuff. [laughs] . . . To me, that's not what's supposed to carry zydeco. . . . I'm not a one-dimensional player, man. . . .

To what I'm hearing these days, guys now [are] trying to do zydeco and get some rapper to throw some rappin'. All that's great, you know.

. . . This nouveau zydeco thing came out, which everything has got to branch off. To me, that's fantastic because this music that my daddy started has branched off like this. But man, how can you forget where it came from? [laughs] Those branches got to be connected! That's right, just got to have a trunk, man! Do you know what the trunk is? Most of them don't.

Chenier's emphasis on the importance of respect for musicality as well as music history is reflected in his own career. The fact that he earned a scholarship to the jazz-studies program at Texas Southern University vouches for his sophisticated mastery of musical challenges, even at a young age. That he later recorded for national labels as diverse as Arhoolie and Slash before settling into his current long-running affiliation with Alligator speaks directly to his impressive versatility—as does the use of his accordion talents on Paul Simon's adventurous 1990 album, *The Rhythm of the Saints.* Yet even while expanding his command of musical idioms, C. J. Chenier has always retained some of the basic elements of the Clifton Chenier sound—and has recorded several of his father's songs over the years. As former *Houston Chronicle* music critic Rick Mitchell points out in a 1990 article, "Like Ziggy Marley or Hank Williams Jr., C. J. will forever be compared to an incomparable father." Yet C. J. employs a progressive, musically rich style that complements and respects but does not seek to imitate the patriarchal legacy. As Mitchell says, the younger Chenier "represents a living link to a vital regional tradition." Thus, the widespread obliviousness of that cultural legacy, which he perceives among some of the young practitioners of zydeco nouveau, clearly rankles this Houston-based bandleader.

As veteran Wilfred Chevis notes wistfully about the zydeco nouveau trends of the 1990s, "Now everybody's playing accordion, but they're playing a different style. It's not the same style. You know, putting kind of like a rap beat or new kind of rock-and-roll beat in it. . . . You know, the young generation is really into it." While some aficionados of the classic sound might wince at this development, Chevis himself accepts it as a continuation of a process, recognizing that from la-la to zyde-rap, black Creole music has never really been a static form. And though he most enjoys the now out-of-fashion style of his mentor, Clifton Chenier, Chevis recognizes that zydeco has been evolving organically for decades, reflecting changing environments and influences among its creators—especially among those residing in big cities.

For many young blacks and black Creoles living in urban centers of zydeco culture during the mid- to late 1990s, zydeco nouveau was or is part of the cultural sound track of their generation. Though the trend may have peaked in popularity at the turn of the century, it still retains a large following among fans of Houston groups such as J. Paul and the Zydeco NuBreedz or Nooney and the Zydeco Floaters. In clubs and on disc, they often mix it all up—funk, hip-hop, pop, R&B, and accordion-led zydeco—creating something new and uniquely their own. As is generally the case with many forms of specifically youth-oriented music, members of its target audience generally consider the fact that it sometimes bewilders the older generation to be a plus.

In a 1999 interview, for instance, a sixteen-year-old Houstonian enthusiastically told me (in a mishmash of profane hip-hop slang) how he's a "hard-core fan" of a local performer he identified only as "Big Mike," a zydeco rapper and accordionist who then played regularly at Club Classic on the north side of the city. When I inquired about the phenomenon with the owner of that now-closed Crosstimbers Road establishment (who volunteered "Redell" as the only moniker he was willing to share), he explained that he booked a lot of what he called "radical zydeco" specifically because the younger crowd could relate to it—and would turn out in large numbers to hear it performed live. Why? Because "it has more fire" and a really "heavy beat," he said. Meanwhile, at the nearby former Homestead Road club known as Buffalo Soldier, owner Eddie Moore was then concurrently reserving Thursday nights exclusively for youth-oriented progressive zydeco shows, naming J. Paul Jr. and the Zydeco NuBreedz as one of his main draws.

Since forming in 1997, that prolific group (having produced nine albums through 2005) in particular continues to attract a devoted hip-hop-savvy following through regular appearances at Houston clubs, particularly the one near Fifth Ward called Mr. A's, as well as at other venues around the metropolitan area and in other cities along the zydeco corridor. "Old-school zydeco is good. I need to give props to it, because that's where I come from," J. Paul tells Rick Mitchell in a 1999 *Houston Chronicle* article. "But when people get tired of hearing the same thing, they want something new." That same article quotes a record producer, Kerry Douglas, as saying, "What attracted me to sign J. Paul was that I saw him perform. He has a young audience. He's bringing in the Generation X rap fans. He has a lot of energy and a lot of style onstage."

The eruption of rap-influenced zydeco nouveau in the 1990s coincided with the emergence of a whole new generation of zydeco bands such as J. Paul Jr. and the Zydeco NuBreedz—and lots of them, especially in Houston. Usually led by players then in their teens or early twenties, for some of these performers the zyde-rap hybrid was and is their primary connection to zydeco culture at large. They identify, it seems, with hip-hop just as much as they do with zydeco. However, for some of this new breed of zydeco players, in the early twenty-first century the novelty of fusing '90s black urban sounds with their ancestral dance music has faded to some degree as they have grown older.

OPPOSITE PAGE: *J. Paul Jr., Original Zydeco Jamm Festival, Crosby, Texas, 2004.*

Today more and more of these young groups are moving on to explore other possibilities—including a few daring counterrevolutionaries who are starting to discover and appreciate the beauty of elements of traditional Creole folk music (such as the melodic interplay of fiddle and accordion), and are now incorporating such contrary influences into their more mature sound. In such cases, zydeco nouveau functioned as the introductory hook that pulled them into the music scene; it was the first step, but not necessarily the ultimately defining step, in their personal growth as serious musicians. From that perspective, zydeco nouveau (whether old-timers and cultural purists can relate to it or not) deserves some measure of appreciation, for it has served an important purpose in energizing the ongoing evolution of black Creole music in the region.

DURING THE EARLY 1990S perhaps no zydeco artist anywhere embraced change with more creative flair than did a young Texas-born accordionist and singer named Brian Terry, leader of the group Lil' Brian and the Zydeco Travelers—the second of those two Houston bands (after the Sam Brothers Five) that Tisserand credits with triggering seminal trends in the post–Clifton Chenier evolution of zydeco. The originator of a sound he calls "z-funk," Terry is appropriately noted in *The Kingdom of Zydeco* as the first artist to forge and record a musically and lyrically sophisticated link between zydeco and rap. Yet unlike some of the button accordionist–rappers who have since followed in his wake, Terry mainly (but not exclusively) plays the chromatic keyboard accordion; moreover, he is musically dexterous enough to avoid the monotony of repetitious riffs and nonmelodic song structures.

For Terry, the original fusion of Creole accordion dance music and an unapologetically hip-hop mentality came naturally. Around age thirteen he first started learning how to play the single-row squeezebox during visits with relatives back in Louisiana (his father and mother were originally from Ville Platte and Basile, respectively). Luckily for him, the large circle of Louisiana kinfolk included the legendary Delafose family, one of the major multigenerational sources of zydeco talent (including bandleaders John Delafose and Geno Delafose). From them he absorbed basic instrumental technique and tradition, as well as a deep love for the music of his ethnic heritage. Later, he formed his own band and start gigging at local venues back home in Houston:

I started off in a few clubs around in this area. The one that really got things started for me was the Continental [Zydeco] Ballroom. . . . That got things jumping for me in Houston; that was around '89 or '90; I was about sixteen or seventeen.

At that time I was basically playing straight-ahead zydeco. I had envisioned in my head that I wanted to do some different things with my music, but I was kind of sticking to the roots back then. . . . I was just trying to survive around here, basically playing what everybody else was doing—I mean, traditional as I can be, because I had to get the local gigs, and that's what they wanted. But at the same time, when we would go to rehearsals, that's when we would work on [the experimentally progressive] stuff. . . . I felt like we should try to raise the music and get it to more of a mainstream level.

For an intelligent teenager who says he also was then regularly absorbing lots of "Snoop Dogg rap and Tupac [Shakur]" hip-hop recordings, it wasn't long before he went public with his evolving syncretism of musical forms:

Growing up around [Houston], I was listening to a lot of different styles of music. And of course I had friends who were definitely not into zydeco. Into other stuff, you know, rap and hip-hop and R&B. So I began really trying to put some funky hip-hop grooves into what I was dealing, you know. Wasn't nobody doing it but me. . . . Rap and stuff like that—we were basically the only group at that time that did it.

Terry's early experimentation immediately set his band apart from every other zydeco outfit, young or old. It soon also caught the attention of producer Scott Billington during one of his talent-scouting field trips for Massachusetts-based Rounder Records. Their collaboration eventually resulted in the 1995 CD *Fresh*, which introduced the world to an unprecedented blend of zydeco, funk, and rap, a mixture that featured challenging arrangements far beyond the norm, especially for such a young artist. On the song entitled "FuNkABlUe-SaDeCo," for instance, heavy bass intertwines with pounding drums and the jingly funk of rhythm guitar. Tight accordion riffs lay down a groove that evokes the distinctive sound of a rap MC scratching a turntable. On this track and others Terry makes a major breakthrough, effectively processing hip-hop elements, both verbal and musical, through a zydeco filter. "I was raised up on zydeco. That's in the blood of my family from Louisiana," he explains. "But the rap and the hip-hop just give me some room to play around with other stuff, to make it my own thing and mess with the ideas I have going around in my head."

Terry's bold evolution continued on his second Rounder CD, 1997's *Z-Funk*, beginning with the opening song, "H-Town Zydeco," a tribute to the Houston music scene. Featuring some piercing blues-rock guitar by brother Patrick "Heavy P" Terry, the number climaxes with a bass jam reminiscent of those from the classic 1970s-era funk band Parliament Funkadelic. Meanwhile, the title track offers a swaying groove of hip-hop atmospherics fused seamlessly with an eerie accordion line. In a fiercely aggressive manner, Terry recites his rhymes. Near the end of each line, the crew shouts out each final phrase in gang-chorus fashion. The lyrics flow forth in rapid-fire sequence, culminating each time with the major theme: a vow that zydeco will always survive.

Brian Terry, Juneteenth Music Festival, Beaumont, Texas, 2003.

By 2000 Lil' Brian and the Zydeco Travelers had left Rounder Records and formed a multifaceted professional affiliation with Stanley "Buckwheat Zydeco" Dural, who had recently launched his own label called Tomorrow Recordings. The result was Terry's third major CD, *Funky Nation*, consisting of twelve original tracks composed by the bandleader and his brother Patrick. "Significantly, this album represents the first time Buck and I have produced another artist," writes Dural's longtime coproducer Ted Fox in the liner notes for *Funky Nation*. He points out that it is also "the first album by another artist to be released on Buck's own label," describing Terry's Houston-based group as "the most innovative and musically accomplished zydeco band on the scene . . . drawing upon contemporary urban black sounds while remaining respectful and true to their zydeco roots."

In some ways, however, the artist best known as Buckwheat Zydeco had been mentoring Terry, indirectly at least, for many years before they ever entered a recording studio together. As Terry told Michael D. Clark in a 2001 *Houston Chronicle* article, "Every time Buck would come to play churches around Houston, my father would bring me down to see him. . . . He had just gotten off the road with Eric Clapton and had been on David Letterman. I felt like I knew a superstar." Clark also notes Ted Fox's observation that "Buck would come to Houston to play, and Brian would just prop himself at the edge of the stage with his elbows and watch." The young Terry's studying of the star's technique ultimately paid off, for by 2000 he and his band were not only recording but also touring nationwide with the bandleader he had once scrutinized at local church dances. Barring any future releases, *Funky Nation* remains for the moment the crowning achievement of this Buckwheat–Lil' Brian relationship.

That album's title track repeatedly references "BST" as shorthand for "Barrett Station, Texas"—that small, historically African American community in the eastern part of Harris County near Crosby (and the family home of the Terry brothers). While electric guitar, bass, and drums dig a groove as deep as the nearby Trinity River, the front man works his accordion into a vibrating frenzy. Each chorus concludes with an emphatic couplet that rhymes "Barrett Station" with the album's title. Yet such obvious zydeco-nouveau moments are also balanced by more traditional tracks, such as the instrumental "Uncle Cliff," which pays appropriate musical tribute to the late great king of zydeco in the form of an upbeat shuffle that percolates with the power to pull even staunch purists onto the dance floor.

Those three CD releases on the Rounder and Tomorrow labels between 1995 and 2000, plus Terry's concurrent and subsequent appearances at festivals and major venues worldwide, have raised the profile of Lil' Brian and the Zydeco Travelers well beyond their southeast Texas home base. In particular, the band has proved to be especially popular on the East Coast college circuit and at venues such as the New Orleans Jazz and Heritage Festival. "Even if they've never even heard zydeco, they hear us and have a good time, tripping out because we [are] adding elements in an original mix. We're not just giving them a straight-up, repetitive zydeco thing all night long," Terry says. Indeed, in addition to rap-tinged interpretations, the crowd-pleasing concert repertoire of Lil' Brian and the Zydeco Travelers is known to include songs originated by artists as diverse as reggae icon Bob Marley or the seminal British rock band the Rolling Stones. Terry elaborates further on the fundamental philosophy underlying his success as a kind of zydeco crossover artist who caters particularly to the younger generation and fans of alternative music:

They really dig it because it's zydeco, but it connects with their own music culture too. So somebody [who is] into alternative, or hip-hop or rap, reggae, whatever it may be—when they hear my band, oh yeah, we can connect with them too. We lure them in and they can learn to like this music too. They learn not to be so judgmental about the music just because it's got an accordion and a scrub board.

You know, a lot of young people [when faced with a zydeco band] be like, "Oh shit no, I just can't get with that." But once they hear the funk of the band and also the character of zydeco as we mix it in my band, even with that scrub board and accordion, man, I mean they fall in love with that kind of stuff.

Despite his awareness of those who find zydeco nouveau to be an affront to their traditionalist sensibilities, Terry ultimately makes no apologies for being progressive. "We ain't scared to try to push this stuff mainstream, and get it off the back burner," he says. "Zydeco is definitely in the heart and in the blood. But I just feel like we must acknowledge rap. We must not box ourselves in. . . . Being versatile like that gives me freedom."

LONGTIME HOUSTON-BASED STEP RIDEAU, a native of southwest Louisiana, has occasionally, like Brian Terry, exercised his liberty to combine elements of zydeco nouveau with his relatively more traditional repertoire. Though he still performs and records many classic-sounding tracks and sometimes sings in French, Rideau also has experimented—at least briefly—with the melding of zydeco and rap. The best example is found on his fourth CD, the 1999 release *I'm So Glad*. On that disc Rideau, who does not play the chromatic keyboard-style accordion, delves most deeply into the interfusion of musical styles. Along with his band, the Zydeco Outlaws, he too breaks new ground.

Perhaps the most unusual track, as far as the wedding of old and new forms, is called "Bayou Swamp Thang," which combines the seemingly antithetical elements of waltz and hip-hop. It also features a chorus of vocal harmonies rarely encountered in zydeco, the kind of group singing one might expect to find in traditional gospel or R&B. (Such skillful multi-part singing is one of the most consistently strong characteristics of Rideau and his band, regardless of the type of material they perform.) The lyrics celebrate an idealized vision of the rural ancestral homeland, a cultural memory for thousands of Creoles who have settled in the urban magnet of Houston over the years. The softly flowing rap describes riding on tractors, feeding livestock, and other bucolic delights—especially the rituals of gathering and sharing food. For instance, one stanza tells of a bountiful fishing trip that leads to a feasting party for the whole community. Near the end of the track, the contrast between country and city living is succinctly communicated in a line that voices a preference for home-cooked étouffée over fast-food staples such as hamburgers and fries.

Rideau himself was born in the tiny Louisiana hamlet of Lebeau, and came to Houston on his own around 1986, motivated to do so by the faltering economy back home and the opportunity to work construction in the big city. Before that move he was a just another zydeco dancer and fan, regularly visiting venerable southwest Louisiana clubs such as Slim's Y-Ki-Ki and Richard's—but not yet an accordion player or a singer.

After settling in Texas, however, he became an almost weekly participant at the Saturday-night zydeco dances sponsored by local Creole Catholic churches. It was at such gatherings that Rideau's general fascination with the music focused itself into a compelling case of squeezebox fever. Eventually he decided he wanted to play. "So I went all over Houston, trying to find a cheap accordion in the pawnshops—just to see if I really could play it," Rideau says. "I eventually found one for forty-five dollars, an old Hohner accordion with holes all in the bellows and everything; a couple of the valves was broke off too. So I patched it up, man, and made it work and got to learning on it."

After a period of private experimentation, Rideau eventually had the nerve to take that raggedy instrument out in public, showing up at a dance hosted by local zydeco stalwart Wilfred Chevis at St. Monica's Catholic Church. "He let me sit in on his gig over there at the bazaar. I played and enjoyed it," says Rideau. "So I went and invested my money, got a single-note accordion out of Louisiana—the kind I play now—and started really practicing on it." In a 2003 interview, Chevis offers his perspective:

Step wanted that accordion real, real bad. He liked it. . . . He wanted to play. He said, "Man, if I get an accordion, do you think you could help me. Man, I want to learn to play!" And it didn't take him long. He would play that accordion every chance he get. He worked on it. . . . He'd go around Houston, everywhere they had zydeco, and people would let him play a couple of songs.

After subsequently sitting in at other Houston church dances (including impromptu appearances with well-respected artists such as Boozoo Chavis and Willis Prudhomme), Rideau formed his band and began playing his own gigs at places such as the Ebony Club. "Step also started at the Continental Club," Wilfred Chevis adds. "When he got him a band together, for two weeks in a row, I booked me and him together, and we split the money. We didn't make no big money, but then the people got to hear him, and he took off from there." When the late Frenchtown matron Doris McClendon hired Rideau to play her famous Continental Zydeco Ballroom, it was a sure sign to him that he was on the right track. "She gave me my big break over there," he says.

Starting in Houston and then shuttling back and forth to gigs along the zydeco corridor, Rideau quickly earned a reputation as one of the leading proponents of the youth-fueled button-accordion craze of the late twentieth century. His mentor Chevis, in fact, credits him with igniting that trend, at least in the Bayou City. He asserts, "Now he's the first one of the younger players in Houston, Texas, to start off with the little accordion. . . . Step started the whole youth thing with the button."

As he gained fans by proving his mastery of the instrument, Rideau also began to work more diligently at the craft of songwriting. "What I'd been doing in the past was real danceable music," he told me in a 1999 interview, noting that early on, he didn't really pay much attention to developing lyrics. But eventually the accordionist came to realize that "the best music is about telling stories."

In that respect *I'm So Glad* was truly a breakthrough for Rideau, who wrote or cowrote twelve of the fourteen tracks. Many of them have fairly traditional themes, celebrating elements of Creole folk life such as community barbecues ("Fire It Up") and horseback excursions ("Step's Trail Ride"). But they generally offer lyrical depth beyond the generic standard—and also include occasionally startling references to contemporary amenities such as cell phones and pagers.

However, the most daring compositions are those featuring guest rappers. On "If U Don't Use It, U Gonna Lose It" Rideau delivers some classic R&B-style testifying, complemented by the slick versification of a hip-hop poet known as Swiff Haywire, moniker for a Houstonian named Vonnie C. Dones III. Following two lengthy verse-chorus cycles led by Rideau, Haywire takes over, seamlessly building on the song's nostalgic theme of learning from the elders and holding on to what you've got. It is an energized yet mellow sequence highlighting the value of paternal wisdom.

Though he was initially a bit wary of the producer's suggestion to weave rap into the mix, Rideau now delights at the song's "inner message" as well as the impressive synthesis of disparate musical styles. "People don't understand what a lot of rappers be saying," Rideau says. "And then what they be saying is usually a lot of negative stuff." Dones, however, was up to the challenge of keeping it accessible and positive, and Rideau soon realized that "this is the key to the rest of the puzzle." On another track, "Keep On Doing It," rapper John Calvin Henry (aka Dirty Red) contributes an equally impressive series of verses. Without getting X-rated, he graphically praises the physical charms of a "pretty little girl" who has now developed into a "voluptuous lady." Rideau says, "We broke the music down and just

OPPOSITE PAGE: *Step Rideau, St. Mark the Evangelist Catholic Church, Houston, Texas, 1996.*

kept the drum beat going, let the guitar and bass do fillers. Red did the rest, and it fit right in the story."

However, Rideau also asserts that the hip-hop collaborations and funky beats are not the defining elements of his music. "Now I'm not fixing to go total rap," he says. "It's all about spice. That's how this rap thing got to be part of my work; it's just a spice that adds to the flavor of what I'm serving up," he explains. Then, he emphatically adds, "We're all for zydeco. But we're open-minded, and anything is possible. . . . This new way of music is just part of who we are, here and now."

Being true to "who we are, here and now" is arguably the subtext of all progressive zydeco history, and especially that sizable portion of it based in the Lone Star State—dating back at least to Clifton Chenier. However, as time changes, so does that truth. For as Rideau illustrates on his 2003 CD entitled *From: Step 2 U*, the previously indulged experimentation with zyde-rap is apparently now part of his past. This disc, for example, features less sophisticated storytelling than that on *I'm So Glad* and no guest rappers. As such, the lyrics offer few surprises—touching broadly on familiar themes such as dancing, partying, eating, loving, and traveling. But they sometimes do incorporate lines sung in French, and the band's danceable grooves are exceptionally tight. Though it maintains a vividly accentuated contemporary vibe, the supporting instrumentation also conjures up the perfect complement to the old-school glories of Rideau's deft command of the button accordion (particularly the triple-row type).

Thus, Step Rideau at various times in his career has participated in some nouveau experimentation as well as in a countermovement toward a sort of neotraditionalism. "There's something about Step's sound, no matter what he does, he kind of keeps things more traditional" says one of his younger peers and fellow zydeco bandleaders, Robert "Ra-Ra" Carter. "And you know, he sings some songs in French too. He has a sense of true zydeco—what zydeco should be." Rideau therefore serves as a relatively high-profile reminder that classifying younger artists according to any particular label is an inexact and necessarily fluid analytical process, subject to change. Rideau and many of his Texas-based contemporaries (such as Leroy Thomas or the younger Brian Jack, for instance) are still quite obviously growing as musicians: they are still learning about their instruments, their talents as singers and songwriters, and in some cases the larger scope of their Creole musical heritage. They are still absorbing different influences, creating new material, exploring the range of possibilities that will ultimately define their place in Texas zydeco history.

BETWEEN THAT GENERATION of Texas zydeco players born in the 1970s or '80s (represented by Brian Terry, Step Rideau, et al.) and the older generation born in or before the 1930s or '40s (such as Wilbert Thibodeaux, Willie Davis, Chester Papillion, Billy Poullard, et al.), there is a currently middle-aged group of artists who have also made their mark on the music, past and present. Members of this segment of the regional zydeco community perform in a range of styles, from the old-style Creole-fiddle-and-accordion music of Beaumont's Ed Poullard to the more mainstream zydeco sounds of bandleaders such as Houston's Willie T. York or Barrett Station's Charles "Lil' Reb" Wilson. However, during the 1980s and early '90s, perhaps no Texan from this particular generation achieved as much regional popularity as a musician who is best known as Jabo—a talented singer and accordionist once billed as "the Texas Prince of Zydeco."

This man, actually named Donald Glenn, was born in 1954 near Humble, Texas, just northeast of Houston. The son of an amateur country-blues guitarist and the grandson of a gospel singer, Glenn grew up first making the same kind of music that his non-Creole family patriarchs played. Early on, he discovered that he possessed a talent for soulful vocalizing, as well as a natural sense of timing on drums. Then, while still a child, his family moved from the nearby countryside to Houston's Fifth Ward, and he began performing at church. As he relates:

My dad, he was an old guitar player. He played guitar, but he played single. . . . just acoustic guitar—blues. . . . My grandfather was an old quartet singer. . . . He used to teach me a lot of old quartet songs and things, and I found out during that time that I was blessed to sing. So I would go out there and get on buckets and tubs. We had a tub we used to bathe in, so I would go out there and take that tub, get me a stick and just beat on it and start singing and then just making me some songs up. And I found a gift in that area.

After we moved to Houston, I finally got with a couple of old guys that was playing at church, doing gospel. . . . That's when I began to do a little drums. I started with the drums, playing gospel music.

However, when he was around the age of twelve, one day a relative carried him into a Fifth Ward club, stood him up on the pool table, and told him to sing for the people. He spontaneously performed an a cappella version of a blues song he had learned from his father—and was immediately showered with tips, earning more pocket change than he had ever previously possessed. The impact was immediate. "So I started singing the blues," he says with a laugh, before turning serious and asserting, "Actually, I *am* a blues man."

It was not long, however, before young Glenn became aware of, and eventually enchanted by, this music called zydeco. He had heard it here and there—on jukeboxes, on the porches of Creole neighbors in Fifth Ward, on his mother's high-fidelity phonograph, and in relatives' backyards on visits to Louisiana. His personal discovery of this strange style of music served also as his introduction to its seminal musician, the figure who would be his ultimate zydeco role model:

Not long after we moved to Fifth Ward, my mother, Wanda Towers, she would always be playing [recordings by] the king of zydeco, Clifton Chenier. And I loved it all. . . . I loved "Hey 'Tite Fille." We would just burn that record up, and it really inspired me. I really loved Clifton's accordion playing. It amazed me hearing an accordion man playing the blues! I give him all the credit. I give Clif all the credit for exposing zydeco across the country and across the world. Before Clif come out with the zydeco, no one in Texas that I knew of knew anything much about zydeco, except for those that came out of Louisiana.

I had relatives in Louisiana, and later I'd go back and find there was some old zydeco players, but they was playing in the house, outside in the yard—that's right, la-la. And they would entertain each other, neighbors and one another. Get out there and dance and play and hit on the rubboard and play the accordion and make a noise, you know. . . . But Clif I give credit to, because he took that early zydeco and mixed it in with the blues, and rhythm and blues, and then that's what they started calling it zydeco.

Once he was hooked on the music, he began to emulate the bluesy singing style and repertoire of Clifton Chenier and to spend more and more time among Creole people. In particular, he gravitated toward a core group of Houston musicians that often congregated or performed (in the Sunnyside neighborhood south of Third Ward) at a 1970s-era club called Vada's Lounge. There he met and eventually played drums for one of Houston's late Creole accordion masters—the man who would later introduce him to basic technique on the instrument. "I picked up an accordion through a guy called Willie Stout. He's out of Opelousas, but he was living in Houston at the time," Glenn recalls. "Willie Stout introduced me to L. C. Donatto, Wilbert Thibodeaux, Ashton Savoy, and all them. So I got to being friends with those guys, and started singing and drumming with those guys, and before you know it, I done got off into the zydeco field."

Glenn's older friend Stout, a cousin of Clifton Chenier, unfortunately had experienced a partial stroke that left him unable to manipulate his keyboard accordion effectively. As a result, Stout no longer could lead his own band and had reemerged as a sideman playing the rubboard. However, his change of status also meant that he had the opportunity to take on a new role, that of Glenn's informal tutor on the accordion. In a 1993 interview, Stout confirms the account:

I taught Jabo after I caught my stroke. I met Jabo at Vada's. He was playing drums for me. So he wanted to learn how to play the accordion. So I taught him how. I remembered the keys enough to do that, you know. . . . I used to play the accordion, but then I couldn't play. So I played rubboard after then. . . . But I could still teach him to do it like I used to.

One of the musicians who also then frequented the stage at Vada's was the veteran bass-guitar player Joseph Charles (b. 1937), best known in zydeco circles simply as "Tee June." Also a native of Opelousas, Louisiana, Charles had arrived in Houston at the age of three when his parents relocated there to find work. He grew up on the east side of the city near the ship channel, and in his teens gained notice as both a high school basketball star and a budding guitarist; however, both of those careers were cut short when he suffered a hand injury in a shop-class accident. After graduating from Fidelity Manor High School in the early 1950s, Charles gradually regained use of the hand and began learning to play bass. Eventually he was good enough to work regularly with local blues musicians such as Johnny Copeland (1937–1997) and Big Roger Collins (1935–2001) as well as with zydeco bandleaders such as Wilbert Thibodeaux, Lonnie Mitchell, Herbert Sam, and (most recently) Mickey Guillory (aka Bon Ton Mickey). Glenn summarizes Charles's credentials with a pronounced sense of gratitude: "He's the one who helped make me, him and Willie Stout. . . . He's from that old school, man, you know . . . old-school zydeco. That's where it really started from." For his part, the bass player recalls,

Jabo first started down there at Vada's. . . . I was playing there before Jabo got there, with Willie Stout. . . . Willie Stout got old Jabo started, got Jabo to playing. And Jabo was doing nothing but just a drummer then. And he learned how to play accordion, and man, he could sing. He sure could sing!

Under Stout's tutelage, as well as from the influence of Clifton Chenier (whom he had observed occasionally on local stages and whose recordings he treasured), Glenn was interested in playing only the large, fully chromatic piano-key accordion. "I never have played the button accordion," he says firmly. "I was only a piano-note accordion player." He goes on to explain how and why he came to possess and play such an instrument.

Willie Stout, he awarded me my first accordion. We went over to a little pawnshop, there off McCarty Drive. And we purchased my first accordion there, cost about two hundred and something dollars. . . . It was missing a few keys on it, but I took that accordion and we worked on it, and that's when I started. . . .

The king of zydeco, and the original accordion, was the piano-note accordion. . . . I mean it makes some pretty music. And it's not taking away nothing from the little [button] accordions, but the piano-note accordion, you can play a variety of music on it. And you can make different [chord] changes. . . . It's just like a regular piano. . . . You can play the blues. You can really play good waltzes on it. You can even play jazz on it.

After initially mastering the accordion, Glenn formed his own band, Jabo and the Southside Playboys. After first gigging at Vada's Lounge, the group gained enough positive notice to be booked at other venues in the region, eventually landing a long-running affiliation with the city's most prominent zydeco dance hall. "I believe I played my first dance at the Continental [Zydeco] Ballroom like about, I would say, 1982, somewhere along in then," Glenn says. "When I wasn't out of town traveling, I was there quite frequently, at the Continental Ballroom. Doris [McClendon, the proprietor] and I came to be very good friends."

Over the next fourteen years, the artist known to most people only as Jabo would perform at practically every major zydeco club and festival in Texas and Louisiana. Along the way he gained a large following of fans for his bluesy, R&B-based zydeco. His son, known as Jabo Jr. (or Lil' Jabo), also gained attention by performing occasionally with the group on rubboard and accordion. Then in 1990 the Louisiana-based Maison de Soul label issued Jabo's debut album, *Texas Prince of Zydeco* (based on a royal nickname he says originated in the hype for his 1988 performance at the New Orleans Jazz and Heritage Festival). A few years later Jabo followed up with *Love Is for the Birds*, another album of mostly original songs, on Sea Ell Records. Through the mid-1990s, Jabo and the Southside Playboys did reign, it seemed, as southeast Texas zydeco royalty of sorts.

Then in 1996 it all abruptly ended when Donald Glenn was forced to leave the music business because of a personal crisis. Though they had once rated as one of the most popular zydeco bands on the upper Gulf Coast, Jabo and the Southside Playboys suddenly were no more.

However, in 2004 Donald Glenn reemerged on Houston stages of a different sort. Though his old friends and acquaintances still refer to him as Jabo, this talented singer and musician is also known today as the Reverend Glenn, having served as an associate pastor at First Morning Star Baptist Church in the Kashmere Gardens neighborhood near old Frenchtown. He has served in a similar capacity also on the ministerial staff of the nondenominational Crusader Church on the northeast side of the city. He says he is now devoting himself mainly to Christian ministry.

Although performing zydeco in secular venues is no longer his major focus, Glenn has not forsaken the accordion or the opportunity to sing:

Since I'm now going into the ministry, I'm not looking at [playing zydeco] right now. . . . But now the Lord has been speaking to me, and I'm going to get back on the accordion and start that same kind of music, zydeco style, but I'm going to be doing gospel. . . . I'm planning on taking that accordion and doing something original in the church.

Indeed, on a July 2004 visit to First Morning Star Baptist Church, I witnessed Glenn treating the Reverend Carl E. Isaac and members of the congregation to his solo interpreta-

Joseph "Tee June" Charles, Houston, Texas, 2004.

tion of several gospel numbers (such as "I'm Going to Keep On Walking with the Lord" and "He's My Everything") rendered in the testimonial style of a slow blues—and accompanying himself fluently all the while on piano-key accordion. The audience responded with fervent shouts of "Thank you, Jesus!" and "Yes, Lord!" as Glenn walked around the front of the small sanctuary, singing and playing without microphone or amplification. When he shifted to a zydeco two-step beat for "This Little Light of Mine," the church folks clapped along with the brisk rhythms and sang out enthusiastically. The performance ended with much applause, loud cries of "Amen!" and people in the pews smiling broadly and nodding their heads in delight. As one small-framed elderly lady leaned over and whispered to me, "I ain't never heard no 'ccordion in the church-house before today. And he sure plays it right!"

Though Jabo is now not defining himself exclusively as the secular bandleader and recording artist he once was, the onetime "Texas prince of zydeco" still cares deeply about the music that made him regionally famous. In particular, he expresses concern that zydeco has veered too far away from the sound established by its premier royal figure:

I look at zydeco today, and I'm really not as happy with the new generation of zydeco as I was with the zydeco that we was playing. . . . When you don't recognize a person as the king of zydeco, Clifton Chenier—when you don't look into your history as deep as that—well then, to me, in your music you've got a problem. . . . I love Clif. Clifton is the man. When you say "zydeco," Clifton Chenier is all I think of.

Glenn, of course, is not alone in these views, especially among his generational peers. Many of them bemoan the dearth of blues, waltzes, French lyrics, and other characteristics of classic zydeco in the accordion-based music of the majority of younger black Creoles. Moreover, a significant part of the Chenier legacy cherished by Glenn and others lies in the particular sonic qualities and musical versatility of the piano-key accordion. To them, this larger, full-sounding instrument epitomizes zydeco. As one lifelong fan, Doris McClendon, the late matron of the Continental Zydeco Ballroom, put it in a 1989 *Houston Chronicle* article by Marty Racine, "I think when you play the big accordion, that's Creole, which is zydeco." And her good friend Jabo still concurs.

AMONG ACTIVE TEXAS ZYDECO BANDLEADERS who still commit themselves exclusively to the keyboard accordion, C. J. Chenier is the best known, both as a live performer and a recording artist. However, there remain various other accordionists—such as Wilfred Chevis, Raymond Chavis, Charles Wilson, Chester Papillion, Dan Rubit, Willie Davis, Otha Sanchez, and others—who persist in being true to the type of instrument played by Clifton Chenier. Granted, chromatic-keyboard-accordion devotees such as these are clearly in the

OPPOSITE PAGE: *Jabo (Donald Glenn), First Morning Star Baptist Church, Houston, Texas, 2004.*

LEFT TO RIGHT: *Larry Citizen and Otha Sanchez, The Silver Slipper, Houston, Texas, 2005.*

minority among zydeco players in the Lone Star State today. While a few of the younger Texas musicians (such as Brian Terry) regularly perform on the piano-key, and others (such as Leroy Thomas and Corey Ledet) alternate between it and the button accordion, they are rare.

Charles Wilson (b. 1949), a longtime resident of Barrett Station and the leader of Lil' Reb and the Zydeco Hucklebucks, is one of the steadfast proponents of the fully chromatic accordion. After first gigging professionally as a bass player and drummer in various Texas blues and soul bands of the 1960s and '70s—and performing in groups that toured with such notables as Al "TNT" Braggs (1934–2003) and Tyrone Davis (1938–2005)—he left the music business for most of the 1980s. Then around 1988 he returned as a drummer with a zydeco band. That fledgling unit was the initial incarnation of what would become Lil' Brian and the Zydeco Travelers—led by Wilson's much younger fellow resident of eastern Harris County, the then sixteen-year-old Brian Terry.

Over the next couple of years, as Wilson directly witnessed Terry's development on the chromatic accordion, he too fell in love with the sound of the instrument and experimented with figuring out how it was properly played. So when the first version of the Zydeco Travelers broke up, Wilson decided to study it for himself. He recounts the initial phase of the process leading to that breakthrough:

When I got with Brian Terry, he wasn't playing the piano accordion then; he was playing just the single-note [button accordion]. . . . Brian was just getting going. . . . Then one day his daddy picked up for him one of these things right here [points to his own piano-key accordion]. . . . And he messed with it awhile. . . . As we went on, he started rocking with it, and really rocking with it! Then we got off into a little groove with it. And, wow! And we shot from nine to two, you know, in the rate [of skill]. And we really went big from there, uh-huh. We started to getting a little more recognized and stuff.

. . . When I left the band, he asked me: "What you going to do, Charles?" I hadn't even started playing it then, but I said, "Well, I guess I'll start playing accordion now." So he was laughing and say, "Hey, OK, all right!" So I picked this thing up. . . .

I started only with the piano-note. . . . I just like that full, rich sound. And the button-note, it can't turn over; it can't make changes. It stays in one spot, and you can't move it.

Though he was devoted to the sound of the keyboard accordion, Wilson learned slowly at first. Then, like most self-taught players, he found a more experienced musician who helped show him the way:

I would play that thing so much, I think I must have worried everybody to death. Everybody'd yell, "Hey! Will you please cut that noise out!" [laughs] You know, I went to bed with that thing. I stuck with that thing. I just stayed with it! . . .

Charles "Lil' Reb" Wilson, Barrett, Texas, 2004.

Then a guy [Houston zydeco bandleader] named Paul Richard—he died a few years back—well, he came around and wanted me to play the drums with him. I told him, "Man, I'm on to something else now, you know. [laughs] I ain't playing the drums no more." . . .

And he said, "Well, OK, I'm going to show you something." And he showed me a little riff [he makes the sound of a basic riff] . . . and then another and another. . . . So I took that, and I started going around and sitting in with bands.

After gaining self-confidence on his new instrument and learning from other musicians whom he watched and performed with at jam sessions, Wilson took the final step and launched his own group. In doing so, he unwittingly initiated what has since become something of a minitrend in late-twentieth-century Houston-area zydeco—that is, a former zydeco drummer learning to play accordion and becoming a front man, leading his own unit. "Now, if you notice, all the drummers want to play accordion," Wilson points out. "I'm the one that started all that. When they seen me done that, that's when the rest of them started coming out of the closet." Yet while the younger drummers who have followed his lead (such as J. Paul Jr., who formerly drummed for Step Rideau) typically choose to play button accordion, Wilson remains a disciple of the chromatic instrument. To offer yet another explanation for that decision, he shrugs and says, "Basically I listened to a whole lot of Clifton's music."

By late 1992 Wilson was ready to present himself professionally as the accordion-wielding musician he had become—and the zydeco bandleader he envisioned himself to be. So he went on to assemble the Hucklebucks and to gig regularly on southeast Texas stages. Though that unit has undergone various personnel changes over the years, his longest-running musical partnership is with his female rubboard player, Jerri Hunter:

So I learned and learned, and then I formed a group of my own. . . . And from that point on, it was Lil' Reb and the Zydeco Hucklebucks for me.

. . . And I don't want to play no more drum or bass, 'cause I'm an accordion man. . . . Jerri's been with me now for over twelve years, and sometimes we just play as a duo, for small gigs. But mostly it's a full band. . . . We play Texas zydeco-blues.

As for that last comment, a similar self-definition is offered by one of Wilson's peers on the southeast Texas circuit, Willie T. York (b. 1950). Speaking of the group he formed (after first apprenticing on keyboard accordion under the guidance of Wilfred Chevis, Jabo, Bon Ton Mickey, and various others), York says:

When I first organized my own band, I called it Willie T and the ZydeBlues Band. . . . Then about three years later I changed it to Willie T and the Zydeco Posse Band, and that name has stuck

Jerri Hunter and Charles "Lil' Reb" Wilson, Barrett, Texas, 2004.

Willie T (William T. York), Houston, Texas, 2004.

ever since. . . . I do more of a traditional style of zydeco. I do follow some of Beau Jocque's style, Buckwheat's style, and a little bit of Boozoo's style. . . . But I mix it all in with the blues, like Clifton Chenier. We even do a little country and western and jazz. But I got started with the blues, and that's how zydeco sounds best to me.

Born in Houston to parents who had recently migrated to Texas from New Iberia, Louisiana, York joined his first band while still in high school, a blues and soul group for which he played lead guitar. After graduating, getting married, and devoting himself to full-time employment and family, York began to make music again around the age of thirty-eight. It was a newfound fascination with the accordion that lured him back. "Zydeco music is music that gets to your heart," he explains. "I heard zydeco music growing up, but didn't appreciate it till I got older. . . . And for me, it was just a natural way to play the blues."

York's wife of over thirty years, Rita, spent her childhood in southwest Louisiana, and was exposed to a lot of Creole accordion music in the process, but she understands Willie T's style of Texas zydeco to be significantly different from the dominant sound track of her early years. "I'm from Lafayette, Louisiana," she says. "Oh yeah, I love zydeco. But it wasn't really so much zydeco at that time, though. In Louisiana it was more like Cajun music. . . . I didn't learn about blues-zydeco until I came here [in 1967]."

As one might expect of a bandleader of his age and stylistic inclination, York originally approached zydeco as did Clifton Chenier—that is, through the large, fully chromatic keyboard accordion. However, in recent years York has increasingly utilized the smaller button-style versions of the instrument. The explanation has less to do with any evolution in his musical tastes or aesthetic preferences than with his physical health. As he sums up the situation, "Well, I once played piano accordion all the time, but now I've got a couple of discs messed up in my back, and I really can't play those big accordions no more. . . . It's just too much strain." Thus, York has made a necessary transition, yet he still presents a more classic style of blues-infused zydeco than most of the younger button-accordion players on the scene today. And so, in many respects, he appeals to a different audience from theirs.

As Pierre Stoot (b. 1966), one of the former front men for the Houston-based Zydeco Dots, puts it regarding the recent dominance of button accordions in zydeco, "To be honest with you, it's a younger crowd that's listening to it, and it's a younger *black* crowd that's onto the little button. Now the white crowd, and the older black crowd, they like the piano accordion—because the piano is a more bluesy sound." A native of Lafayette, Stoot comes from a musical Creole family that includes his father, singer Lionel Stoot, and his paternal grandmother, Ophelia Stoot, a fiddler who reportedly played at house parties back in Lebeau, Louisiana. When Pierre was approximately six years old, his father moved the family to Texas. "Everybody shot down here for a better job, and we've been here ever since," he relates, adding, "I was raised in Barrett Station and Crosby."

After developing his fundamental grasp of music theory in high school band and then serving in the short-lived original version of the Zydeco Travelers as a piano and organ player, Stoot began to experiment with the piano-note accordion around age twenty-two. Working with his father, he formed the Zydeco Two-Steps and recorded on Louisiana-based Bad Weather Records. But today he is best remembered for his mid-1990s tenure with the consistently popular Zydeco Dots.

In fact, when Stoot joined that band in 1993, it was already billing itself as Pierre and the Zydeco Dots—because its former accordionist had also been named Pierre. As John Minton points out in his *American Music* article, that first Pierre was born Jean-Pierre Blanchard, and he is truly French, "but neither Creole nor Cajun. Born in Nice, Blanchard came to Houston at age fourteen, first taking up blues harmonica and later accordion." Blanchard had affiliated with the Dots' founding members, guitarist Tom Potter (b. 1955) and the original drummer (now the rubboard man), known mainly as Mike Vee (the stage name of Mike Vowell, b. 1956), at the time when their previous group was being reconstructed and reborn as a zydeco unit. After Blanchard departed and Stoot, a genuine Creole, took his place, the band conveniently retained its original moniker. "Pierre and the Zydeco Dots," Stoot recalls, "Blanchard left, and I was the second Pierre. Of course, they didn't even have to change the name."

Now known simply as the Zydeco Dots, this group has prospered over the years despite several personnel changes involving the singer-accordionist role. The unlikely origins and evolution of this Houston zydeco band reflect the multicultural realities of recent social history. The predecessor of the Zydeco Dots had actually been formed by three Caucasian roots-rock musicians who had met in the mid-1970s while attending Murray State University in Kentucky (where they were all on athletic scholarships for track and field). When, by 1980, they all happened to end up residing in Houston, they reunited, drafted other players, and around 1981 began to appear on local stages as Ted and the Polka Dots—a name reflecting the polka-music background of their accordion player, Ted Pacholick (though the band played mostly classic rock). However, even then, being located as they were in the Bayou City, the musicians soon began incorporating some crowd-pleasing zydeco numbers into their accordion-based repertoire. Thus, by the time Pacholick left the band in 1987, the other two founding members, Potter and Vee, began to explore the possibility of committing themselves more fully to zydeco music. Fortuitously, a *Houston Chronicle* music writer, Marty Racine, recommended they talk to Pierre Blanchard, since the blues band he had been leading (Pierre and the Nightcats) was also in the processing of breaking up.

The timing of this big change just so happened to occur during the heyday of zydeco's larger breakthrough into pop cultural consciousness (that is, in the era of Paul Simon's

Graceland, Buckwheat Zydeco's touring with Eric Clapton, etc.). As a result, local interest in zydeco among general fans of live music was unusually high. When Potter and Vee approached Blanchard about the possibility of uniting forces to play zydeco, the latter accepted, for he too had been absorbing and learning this music in the various clubs where it was played on the Houston blues circuit. Thus, the Dots were transformed from Polka to Zydeco.

From 1987 through 1993, this original manifestation of Pierre and the Zydeco Dots established itself as a favorite among mainstream Houston audiences. Eventually, however, Blanchard decided to relocate to Austin (where he continues to reside and to perform with his new band, Jean-Pierre and the Zydeco Angels). Even after Blanchard's departure, the Zydeco Dots did not falter, continuing successfully with Stoot at the helm through 1995. Next there was an approximately one-year stint when Donald Glenn's son, known as Jabo Jr. or Lil' Jabo, performed with the unit. Then from 1996 until 2003, the dynamic Leon Sam fronted the group, helping it earn an even higher profile along the upper Gulf Coast. Following Sam's decision to end his affiliation, Raymond "Ray-Ray" Chavis, took over. Through all these changes, the Zydeco Dots have consistently featured accordion players who are versatile enough to sing and perform not only Clifton Chenier–style zydeco but also some of the classic R&B and rock cover tunes (rendered zydeco style) that also appeal to their diverse fan base.

The most recent incarnation of the band still includes the two original members, the New Jersey–born guitarist Potter as well as his longtime collaborator, the Indiana-raised rubboard man called Vee (who gave up the drummer's role after the first eight years). Though neither of these players hails from the Gulf Coast, they have now assembled a group otherwise composed of black Creole natives of Texas and Louisiana, men who grew up immersed in zydeco culture. In addition to Chavis, there is bassist Thurman Hurst and drummer Joe Rossyion.

Chavis, for instance, was born and raised in a rural area near Lafayette, and he is a cousin and boyhood companion of fellow Houston-based accordionist Wilfred Chevis (whose family has long spelled the Creole surname differently). By marriage he is also related to the Herbert Sam family, as well as to other folks who have traditionally played zydeco or la-la, both professionally and otherwise. Though Chavis had heard, enjoyed, and danced to accordion music for most of his life, his original instrument was the upright piano that had been a fixture in the family home. However, in the 1990s, after he was well into middle age, he began to experiment with making music on the accordion. Naturally, being already familiar with the keyboard of a regular piano, he utilized the piano-note accordion; it was also the same type played by relatives, such as Leon Sam and Wilfred Chevis, both of whom would serve informally as his teachers. Also a capable vocalist who can perform some songs in French, Chavis eventually began to sit in and jam with various zydeco bands around Houston. As his accordion skills developed, Chevis gained enough confidence in his musical protégé to recommend him to Potter and Vee when they began searching for a replacement for Leon Sam.

Four members of the Zydeco Dots (left to right: Mike Vowell, Raymond Chavis, Joseph Rossyion, and Tom Potter), The Big Easy Social and Pleasure Club, Houston, Texas, 2004.

Raymond Chavis, The Big Easy Social and Pleasure Club, Houston, Texas, 2003.

Though he had never worked professionally in music before, Chavis considered the proposal for a while and then ultimately decided to join the Zydeco Dots. "I knew about the guys. I knew they were good musicians and everything," he explains. "I just wondered, you know, can I fit with them?" As it has turned out, the fit has been a good one.

With Chavis and Rossyion handling most of the singing, the high-energy quintet continues to draw strong fan support along the upper Texas coast, especially in Houston. Except for Chavis, most of the band has been together for well over a decade now. Their onstage familiarity with one another is evident in the nimble manner in which they perform, deftly improvising among selections from their deep repertoire. Rossyion, the son of veteran Creole guitarist Joseph "Black" Rossyion Sr., describes the Dots' blend of music as "zydeco with some blues, rock, and jazz." Having drummed also in groups led by artists such as C. J. Chenier and Brian Terry, Rossyion is accustomed to collaborating with players who freely incorporate such influences while maintaining a foundation in Clifton Chenier–inspired zydeco, and so are his current bandmates. "Our strength is we can do traditional zydeco very well," says Potter, "and we can also get away from that. We have the ability and diversification to do that."

Since the late 1980s the Zydeco Dots have remained one of the most widely recognized and generally popular zydeco bands regularly gigging in metropolitan Houston. And though much of their predominantly white audience approaches zydeco music from a mainstream perspective, the Zydeco Dots have also earned the respect of many in the city's sizable black Creole community. After all, the band members have shared not only many stages but also close friendships with respected Creole accordionists such as Wilbert Thibodeaux, Wilfred Chevis, and C. J. Chenier. Moreover, the Zydeco Dots are regular participants in special functions such as the annual Clifton Chenier Tribute produced by Mary Thomas, as well as other benefits and gatherings in traditional venues. And though Raymond Chavis sometimes now also utilizes the single-row button accordion for certain songs, the fact that he (like most of his predecessors in the Zydeco Dots) is fundamentally a piano-note player accounts for a portion of the band's appeal too, especially among the older generation that came of age hearing Clifton Chenier. For in the button-accordion-dominated zydeco youth culture of recent years, that large chromatic instrument still evokes, to some folks, the truest sound of the music they love best.

ONE FACTOR IN THE FAIRLY RECENT widening popularity of zydeco among general audiences in Texas goes well beyond the impact of any particular band or trend in commercial music. Since 1990 a phenomenon known mainly as the Accordion Kings, a production of the nonprofit organization Texas Folklife Resources (TFR), has united fans from a variety of ethnic groups that all cherish their own accordion-based music traditions. At annual gatherings at Houston's spacious Miller Outdoor Theatre, tens of thousands of people have celebrated and learned about the many forms of folk music prevalent in the Lone Star State in which the accordion indeed has reigned supreme. As a result, enthusiasts for styles as diverse as conjunto, polka, and vallenato (i.e., Afro-Caribbean music from Colombia) have intermingled with zydeco people, and generally speaking, they have found common ground for enjoying one another's distinct forms of musical expression. Moreover, because the events are both free and located in the most prominent venue in the city's premiere public green space (Hermann Park), they also have drawn a large number of people with little previous knowledge of any of these styles of music or the ethnic subcultures that spawned them—curious onlookers who sometimes experience epiphanies that alter forever their musical tastes.

The Accordion Kings series came into being through the efforts and vision of Pat Jasper, the cofounder and former director of the Austin-based TFR. As she relates, this unusual undertaking evolved organically and unexpectedly:

In 1989 Betsy Peterson and I did the fieldwork and research for an event at Miller Outdoor Theatre called Dance Traditions. It looked at the range of dance and movement styles that existed in a wide range of (mostly) Houston-based cultural communities. . . . In the middle of this fairly lengthy program[,] we curated a segment that at the time we referred to as "ethnic varieties of the Texas two[-]step."

. . . We hired two small bands—a little country band and Wilfred Chevis. The first played western swing and then maybe added an accordion to demonstrate polka. Wilfred played a Cajun tune for Cajun dancers, and then we finished with a zydeco tune and dancers. It was a great success.

. . . [After the event] I started expounding on how accordion-driven many of the truly traditional and extant dance forms of Texas are. From there I realized that there were these very coherent and distinctive communities that used music to knit themselves together—and that the accordion was at the center of these musics. My initial focus was Czech and German polka, Cajun music, Creole zydeco and Texas Mexican conjunto.

The more I thought about it and, of course, the more research I did, the more I realized that these seemingly disparate and, in many ways, mutually alienated communities and their musics had an enormous amount in common: mostly rural, largely Catholic, a non-English repertoire of songs, dance oriented, family identified and so on. It was a natural way to look at significant and substantial continuities across cultural communities that had little history of interaction.

Inspired by the insights triggered by a folk-dance event (which had only incidentally featured accordion accompaniment), Jasper and TFR soon acquired additional funding and other support that led to the creation of the Accordion Kings enterprise. Eventually the organization would expand that concept to include programs that toured to other venues around the state, as well as a radio series. Meanwhile, in southeast Texas the annual gathering each

Les Amis Creole (seated, left to right: Cedric Watson, Ed Poullard, and James B. Adams),
Accordion Kings concert, Miller Outdoor Theatre, Houston, Texas, 2005.

summer at Miller Outdoor Theatre has remained the primary focus, especially as more and more urbanites have developed an appreciation for the dynamic forms of roots music, including zydeco, that are regularly highlighted by the festival. Jasper offers additional insights on the now established popularity of the Accordion Kings phenomenon:

I think [it] has been successful because of the very cultural continuities that we identified at the outset and because along the way artists and their audiences came to understand that intimately through the performances. For audiences that are not connected to the music through, say, membership in one of the above-mentioned communities, there was the ever-increasing hip factor of Cajun or zydeco or conjunto to propel them into closer examination of other forms. Our non-community-based audience has always had a very large aficionado quotient.

In addition to her crucial role in launching the long-running Accordion Kings programming (which continues in the twenty-first century under the leadership of current TFR director Nancy Bless), Jasper also created and helps organize the widely acclaimed International Accordion Festival in San Antonio. The success of this annual production is yet another factor in raising consciousness in Texas (and beyond) about the cultural significance of zydeco and several other typically marginalized music genres. Jasper credits her colleagues Eduardo Diaz and Juan Tejeda in particular for the success and growth of this event, which began operations in 2000 with the assistance of TFR and has now evolved into its own independent non-profit organization. Expanding on the Accordion Kings concept, this yearly gathering reaches beyond the borders of Texas to bring together an even wider range of accordion-based folk-music forms from all over the world. Since its inception it has also regularly featured zydeco from the upper Gulf Coast, and the headliner for the 2004 series of concerts and workshops was none other than C. J. Chenier, the son of zydeco's late and legendary king.

Cultural series such as the Accordion Kings and the International Accordion Festival have obviously played a key role in documenting and encouraging the vitality of Texas zydeco. In addition to the important recognition such high-profile events have provided to many of the region's zydeco musicians, they have also introduced the genre to a large body of new fans. Moreover, as they have grown, such programs have reflected the ongoing evolution of the form, as the 2004 production by Texas Folklife Resources illustrates. For what was once billed succinctly as Accordion Kings carried a revised and expanded title for 2004: Accordion Kings and Queens. And therein lies another important facet of recent zydeco history in the Lone Star State.

WHILE MALES HAVE BEEN MAKING black Creole dance music since the early days of Amédé Ardoin, female zydeco performers have historically been exceedingly rare—at least

Ms. T (Tiffany Jackson), The Big Easy Social and Pleasure Club, Houston, Texas, 2003.

until recent years. In contrast, since first crossing over into popular culture in the 1920s, the African American blues tradition has consistently featured female singers, songwriters, and instrumentalists—dating back to seminal figures such as Gertrude "Ma" Rainey (1886–1939), Bessie Smith (1894–1937), and Lizzie "Memphis Minnie" Douglas (1897–1973). Granted, some multifaceted contemporary Gulf Coast blues women—such as Houston-born Katie Webster (1939–1999, the performer known as "The Swamp Boogie Queen") or Louisiana native Carol Fran (b. 1933)—have occasionally incorporated elements of zydeco into some of their songs. And in the Houston area, as elsewhere, there are certain female vocalists—such as Mary Thomas and Annette Metoyer—who are best known for singing with zydeco bands. However, from the early days of la-la through the 1990s, female accordionists scarcely ever performed widely or recorded—with the California-based Ida "Queen Ida" Guillory being the primary exception.

Nevertheless, the final decade of the twentieth century gave rise to a new generation of zydeco women, who are defying the gender stereotype long associated with this male-dominated field. Among established bandleaders, there are still yet only a few women, even halfway through the first decade of the new millennium. The most well known of these today is probably Rosie Ledet (b. 1971) from Louisiana—which is also home to Donna Angelle (1951) and Ann Goodly (1971), the two other best-known examples from east of the Sabine River. But some accordion-playing women based on the west side of that waterway have also been actively engaged in redefining zydeco for a new era. Along with female collaborators on other instruments, particularly the rubboard, they personify perhaps the most dramatic change in the sociology of zydeco culture since black Creoles first began migrating to urban Texas.

For national visibility that now almost rivals that of Ledet, one Texas woman in particular has distinguished herself in recent years. Houston native and relative newcomer Dora Jenkins (b. 1966) has proved her credentials not only by appearing regularly—as the leader of Dora and the Zydeco Badboyz—at venues all along the zydeco corridor, but also by playing to acclaim at many of the largest zydeco-related festivals across the country.

Following her first appearance at a Houston nightclub, in November 1996—a life-changing moment when the novice accordionist was coaxed onstage for a brief performance—Jenkins has risen from total obscurity to become a major player. Within a few months of that impromptu initiation, she organized and developed her own band; within a few years, that unit played numerous stages nationwide. By 2004 Jenkins had also released two well-received Dora and the Zydeco Badboyz CDs: 2001's *Feels So Good* and 2004's *Dora's Time*. It is noteworthy that Louisiana zydeco kingpin Keith Frank (perhaps the most popular regional performer in the genre since the death of Boozoo Chavis) produced and performed on the more recent of the two. Frank's decision to collaborate with Jenkins is yet another measure of her widely acknowledged status as a rising star.

However, until she was in her late twenties, Jenkins had never imagined herself to be a zydeco musician; in fact, though she had sung in the church choir, she had never even played any kind of musical instrument. After graduating from Barbara Jordan High School in the Fifth Ward neighborhood where she was born and raised, Jenkins was dutifully pursuing a career in a Houston office, rhythmically pushing keys on typewriters and computers but not accordions. Then a close friendship with a professional colleague from Louisiana led to a weekend trip and her own remarkable zydeco conversion:

A coworker from Opelousas . . . she and I would go to Louisiana in the summer sometimes, on the weekends. I would always hear the Cajun music and mostly the older type of Creole music there. . . . So she invited me out to a couple of festivals. . . . Then we went over to the Breaux Bridge festival, and I lost my mind. I totally lost it! When I saw the bands, I totally lost it. I kept looking at everything and thinking, "I can do that. I can do that! I don't know why, but I can do that!" It was weird, but that's what happened.

Jenkins tells her story with a pronounced sense of awe, testifying repeatedly that her intense reaction was unanticipated, inexplicable, but likewise an absolute certainty. She says she just suddenly *knew* she needed to try to play the accordion, an instrument she then believed she had never even previously touched. Yet as she followed her instinct and began scrutinizing the squeezebox more closely, she discovered a buried memory:

The reminder was, when I finally went to one of the shows here in Houston, and one of the bands allowed me to pick up the accordion, just to look at. Well, the smell on the bellows caught my attention. And I said, "I remember this smell from somewhere." It was like déjà vu. . . .

So I couldn't play the accordion, but I bought me an accordion anyway. . . . And then one of my aunts called me, and she said, "Do you remember when you were a little girl, catching a spanking from picking up an old accordion on the trash pile?" . . . And I remembered that! The smell got all over my clothes because it was on the trash pile, and the bellows had gotten wet from being out in the dew.

She said, "That was an accordion that you were playing with then. . . . It had belonged to your great-grandfather." . . . Of course, when I picked up an accordion later, I had no direction at all. But that's actually how the memory of it came back, of ever having previously had any type of relationship with an accordion.

Inspired by the unlikely realization, Jenkins began to work diligently to achieve basic competency on the musical instrument. But it did not come easily. Having boldly purchased a button accordion for herself, and having possessed such a strong conviction that she was simply fated to make music with it, she nonetheless grew discouraged by the complexities of the challenge and her lack of mentorship. Yet her self-reliant persistence finally led to a breakthrough moment.

It was a single-row; it was a [key of] C accordion. I bought it from Gabbanelli [the Italian American accordion craftsman long based in Houston]. Again, it was nothing like I thought. It was just difficult to play, and I didn't realize that when you pull out one way and then push in the other way, there were two different tunes. I just had no direction. But I was determined.

And I kept asking accordion players, "How do you play one of these accordions?" But no one had time. Everybody was gigging at the time. I'd be out at dances trying to talk to the band and learn. . . .

So I just stayed at it, and it finally started coming to me. And I got excited! And I listened to the [instructional] tapes, and started playing an entire song and thought, "I'm getting it! I'm getting it! I'm getting it!"

Though still a beginner, Jenkins soon learned a few other simple songs. With each step forward, no matter how minor, she confirmed again the trust she had placed in her inner muse. So when one of the veteran local players (whom she had queried for advice) observed her improved musicianship, he invited her to come sit in with his band at an upcoming show. Jenkins consented—even though she knew her skills were limited:

I did eventually get on stage, thanks to Step Rideau, at Sugar's Hideaway. . . . It was Thanksgiving, and he invited me to come and perform. He said, "You are good. I know you don't think it, but you're a female, and there are no females doing like this. So you need to just come and just see how the people accept you. I'll let you on the stage."

That night, of course, I was nervous, but I did it. That was the first time I had gotten onstage. And it wasn't as easy as I thought it was, since I'd never played up against a live band. I had been playing only with records . . . so it was just totally different, but I did it.

And I felt good about it because I did such a good job. I mean, they all clapped and screamed.

The crowd's favorable reaction ignited Jenkins's sense that she ultimately belonged on stage. Most importantly, not only did she draw compliments from male and female zydeco fans, but she also suddenly found herself meeting a host of other musicians who were eager to offer their services to accompany her. This surprising development facilitated her quick decision to go ahead, even though she was still learning her instrument, and form her own band:

OPPOSITE PAGE: *Dora Jenkins, Houston, Texas, 2004.*

And people would say, "Dora, we didn't know you played an accordion," because, you know, I had kind of kept it undercover until I actually got on stage that night. . . .

And then after that, everybody was asking me, "Do you have a band?" And there were so many musicians in the place that night! And they were all coming up to me and saying, "I play this" and "I play that" and "I want to get in a band with you" and "If you need a band, here's my number." And I had so many telephone numbers when I left that time—like three scrub board players, two bass players, and so on. [laughs] . . . So I ended up forming a band.

Though the personnel has changed several times since the 1997 premiere of Dora and the Zydeco Badboyz, the band name has remained the same—even after Jenkins's cast of supporting musicians ceased to be exclusively male. In particular, Jenkins has featured at least two women in the prominent role of rubboard player, most recently (since 2001) Montanya Charles (b. 1976), who is better known as Me-me. Whether the result of a conscious strategy or a mere coincidence, Jenkins's decision to incorporate a female colleague into the group has likely attracted extra attention from a curious zydeco public. For while it is still quite rare to see a woman leading a zydeco band, it is even more of a wonder to witness two women (in particular, two tall and strikingly attractive ones) playing, singing, and dancing together at the front of the stage.

Me-me Charles was born and raised in Houston, where she first attended Yates High School in Third Ward before moving to the west side of the city and earning her diploma at Elsik in Alief. Though she has been a vocalist all her life (having grown up singing in church), Charles, like Jenkins, had never played any type of instrument until the late 1990s, when she suddenly experienced a strong compulsion to get involved with zydeco. After high school, Charles studied for awhile at the historically African American institution in Austin known as Huston-Tillotson College (now Huston-Tillotson University). While there she continued to enjoy singing in both gospel and secular styles. However, during a series of weekend trips back to her hometown, she suddenly and unexpectedly developed a new taste in music. As she explains:

It was a total, total accident! I grew up listening to my mom; on Saturdays, she used to clean up, and she used to play the zydeco music [on the radio]. And I didn't really understand what it was. I've always been a dancer, but I didn't understand what the music was saying, and the music was just too, too fast . . . not my kind of music at the time.

Then I came home from college one weekend, and my mother she was telling me that my Aunt Sandra wanted me to go with her to a zydeco show. And I had no real idea of what a zydeco was.

. . . And I'll never forget, we went to a Keith Frank show, over there on Anderson Road, and when I say I danced, I danced all night long! . . . I loved it.

And the next time I came back home, it was for the Crosby Fairgrounds show [that is, the annual Original Zydeco Jamm Festival]. And the year that I went was the last year that Beau Jocque played. And he was great. And that was the first time I ever heard of Dora; her band played there too, and I loved them. And again I danced all day long. . . . The music was fantastic. . . . And that's pretty much how I got off into zydeco.

After moving back to Houston and transferring to Texas Southern University, Charles began attending zydeco events more regularly. Originally, her enthusiasm was focused mainly on the music and the powerful dance experience it could provoke. However, like many single people who patronize social gatherings, she and her friends could not help but observing—and sometimes scheming to make the acquaintance of—members of the opposite sex. Such a natural instinct, combined with her newfound passion for zydeco music, inadvertently led Charles to her first thoughts of becoming a percussionist:

I used to have a crush on this one particular guy who used to play the rubboard. And so I always was too afraid to ask him, to just, like, go up and talk to him. . . . And so I figured if I asked him to teach me how to play the rubboard, he would have to talk to me. But I could never get enough mustard up to ask him to teach me how to play.

Although that ploy failed, it nonetheless triggered a notion that began to dominate Charles's thoughts when she watched other zydeco bands. In short, she started to imagine herself actually being a rubboard player—an identity she envisioned as an artistic extension of her dancing. Though she had no experience whatsoever with this unique instrument, her improvised ability to impersonate someone playing it eventually attracted attention and advice:

So I had started going to the Buffalo Soldier [a former nightclub]. . . . J. Paul [leader of the Zydeco NuBreedz] was really hot there back then, and I used to always watch Jon-Jon [his rubboard man] play. . . . It was like he was just having too much fun! And I wanted to have that kind of fun. . . . So I would always sit facing the stage, and I would mimic Jon-Jon playing the rubboard.

So one day he really caught what I was doing, and he actually walked off the stage and came and got me and put me on the stage. And I had never done it before, never touched a rubboard before! I didn't even know for sure what it was called. He said, "Well, all you do, is just do what I'm doing." . . . And I thought like, you know, I can't do it. I can't do it. So my friends that I was with, they all said, "Go ahead! Go ahead, girl! You know you want to do it!"

However, no miracle occurred. As Charles relates, when J. Paul and his band started to play, expecting her to join in, she found herself unable to respond, paralyzed as she was with

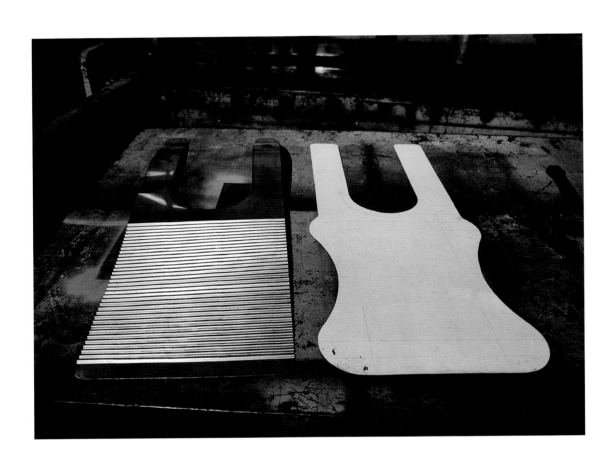

Rubboard and template, Metal Craft shop, Jacinto City, Texas, 2004.

confusion and fear. Then she suddenly broke down in tears and departed the stage to snickers and stares from the audience; she was totally humiliated, having never contributed even one stroke of metallic rhythm to the song. She says the situation made her feel "like a fool."

For many people, such an awkward and discomforting experience would likely make them too embarrassed to dare stepping onstage again for fear of another disgrace. But Charles reacted with a strong-willed determination to prove herself worthy of that spotlight she had so ingloriously abandoned. "And so from that moment on, I went and asked around about where could I get a rubboard," she says. "And I learned that if you're going to get one, it's best to get one made to your certain specifications. And so I ended up hooking up with Jon-Jon, and he told me to go to Metal Craft."

At this Jacinto City shop, located near the ship channel, on the east side of Houston (1309 Akron Street), Charles conferred with a legendary metalworker named Roger Reid. He is a man well known among certain local zydeco musicians for his ability (and until his recent retirement, his availability) to make first-rate customized rubboards at a reasonable price. Such projects had originated as something of a hobby for Reid, merely a sideline to his regular work, but over the years he earned great respect as a serious rubboard outfitter. When the old craftsman announced his plans to retire around 1999, there was such an outcry among zydeco players who had come to depend on his services that Reid decided to maintain the Metal Craft tradition by transferring his rubboard templates and knowledge of fabrication techniques to a younger employee. That man, Edward Gonzalez, still designs and produces custom instruments there today. Thus, when Charles followed Jon-Jon's suggestion and visited the Metal Craft shop, she unwittingly tapped into what is probably the city's best source (unadvertised though it is) for high-quality zydeco rubboards.

Of course, after eagerly picking up her order from the fabricator, Charles, like Dora Jenkins before her, now owned a serious zydeco instrument for which she had no training. Yet Charles proceeded to teach herself by trial and error. She says she would drape the board over her shoulders and scrape out beats whenever she could find time and space around the house, a habit that quickly aggravated her family and next-door neighbors. "I even had the police called on me one time," she quips. Eventually she figured out how to make some metal-on-metal music. The next step was to showcase her newly acquired skills by daring to return to the stage:

So then I went to Mr. A's [a nightclub near Fifth Ward] . . . And J. Paul remembered me. He didn't know my name or anything, but he knew me from that disaster at Buffalo Soldier. So Jon-Jon asked me, "Are you ready?" And I'm thinking, like, no, I'm not ready. I'm not ready. . . .

And so they called me up on stage, and I put the board on. And they were kind of looking at *each other like, "Yeah, We're going to do her the same way." So what Paul did, he picked this super-duper fast song—a real, real fast song.*

. . . And Jon says, "You'd better play!" So I just closed my eyes, and I just started playing. . . . And I don't even remember the music stopping. I just kept going on. And I kept hearing the crowd, which was screaming and yelling and everything. And so when I opened up my eyes, the crowd response was incredible. . . . So he started another song, and every time he would do a different song, I was right there with him. And so Jon-Jon says, "You've got it! You've got it!"

So from then on, I used to fill in, like when someone needed a rubboard player because someone couldn't make the gig, or someone needed to take a break. . . . Because now everybody knew, and I knew, that I really could play.

Following her unannounced debut with J. Paul and the Zydeco NuBreedz and the subsequent opportunities to serve as an occasional substitute with various bands, Charles eventually was asked to join other groups as a regular member. She sums up some of those early experiences:

The first band I ever really played with is called Weasel and the Zydeco Clan. I was Weasel's first rubboard player. . . . And I played like two shows with Weasel [the stage name of Ronald W. Lewis Jr.].

But then when I really got my break, I started playing with a fellow by the name of Kid Reece. That's Maurice Johnson, and I was really lucky that he had given me a chance. . . . Out of all the people that Kid Reece could have had to come and play the rubboard, he called and asked me. . . . So I was with Kid Reece for about two and a half, maybe three years. . . . Kid Reece opened up a lot of doors for me.

Not only did her tenure with Maurice Johnson's Houston-based band, known as Kid Reece and Mo' Live Zydeco, provide Charles with valuable early professional experience as a musician, but it also introduced her to a new area of personal interest: riding (and ultimately owning) a horse. "Playing with Maurice pretty much changed my whole outlook because I got into the horses and the cows," she explains, "because we always played a majority of the trail rides." This zydeco music that Charles had grown to enjoy and perform was now leading her into something else—the thriving black cowboy-trail-ride scene.

As some readers may know, throughout southeast Texas and southwest Louisiana, countless private clubs and associations exist to promote the enjoyment of horses in general and the large group activity known as trail riding in particular. Many of these organizations also feature live zydeco music as the sound track to the dancing and socializing that typically mark the culmination of each big event. Charles elaborates further:

OPPOSITE PAGE: *Me-me Charles, Houston, Texas, 2004.*

We normally would do a lot of the trail rides, which I love. . . . Here in Houston, I know there's at least about fifteen or sixteen various associations, and normally when they have a trail ride, they hire a zydeco band. . . . Pretty much every other weekend, you can find a trail ride—like, anywhere from February till, like, around the middle of the summer, there's a trail ride going on somewhere . . . up in East Texas and over in Louisiana too.

Though the band she plays in now does not work the trail-ride circuit, Charles still satisfies her equestrian urges by keeping her own horse. She admits that she does sometimes miss the trail-ride gigs, but says that as a member of Dora and the Zydeco Badboyz, she is also happy to be affiliated with one of the highest-profile women in contemporary zydeco. In fact, she sees her collaboration with Jenkins as having implications that extend well beyond their own careers—particularly in terms of the message she believes it sends to young females. As she states in a 2004 interview,

When the opportunity came available for me to play with Dora, it just kind of stuck. I had always wanted to play with Dora, but, you know, the timing wasn't just right before. So suddenly, it's, like, the time is right. So we've been together now for the last three and a half years. And we've been going full speed ever since. . . .

I think Dora and I are really changing the face of zydeco. Because whenever we go to places like San Diego, Fort Lauderdale, you know, we get a lot of little girls saying they're thinking about trying to play that rubboard, and wanting to learn how to play the accordion. . . . They really look up to us. . . . They say, "Y'all are like the Beyoncés of zydeco," you know.

As the allusion to the Houston-born pop superstar Beyoncé Knowles might suggest, prominently featured female players such as Dora Jenkins and Me-me Charles have brought a powerful element of feminine glamour to the sometimes gritty and historically mostly all-male realm of the zydeco bandstand. Yet if longevity and prominence in the state's largest city are factored in, the now-veteran accordionist and bandleader Diane "Lady D" Weatherall (b. 1952—and not to be confused with Texas blues singer Donna "Lady D" McIntyre) is arguably, as she often refers to herself, the reigning "diva of Houston zydeco."

As the leader since 1994 of Lady D and the Zydeco Tornadoes, Weatherall has developed into one of the most well-known zydeco figures appearing regularly at mainstream venues and festivals around Houston. In fact, in 2003 she and her group of all-male accompanists pulled off a surprising coup when they won the Best Zydeco Band category in the annual readers' poll for the Houston Press Music Awards, dethroning the otherwise perennial champions, the Zydeco Dots. In *The Kingdom of Zydeco*, Tisserand acknowledges Weatherall as a potentially significant female artist, noting that she took first place in a zydeco accordion contest in Lafayette. And though she was born in Opelousas and did not start playing her instrument until she was already in her forties, Weatherall is perhaps the first female accordionist and bandleader to establish herself in the history of Texas zydeco—and one of the few anywhere.

"Females, there's not that many in zydeco. Like Rosie [Ledet], she's been out there for at least eleven years. And Donna Angelle, who started with the bass, and now she's playing accordion. That's in Louisiana—nobody else in Louisiana to speak of," she says in a 2004 interview. "And over here in Texas we've got Dora [Jenkins], yeah, and me, and that's about it."

The story of how Weatherall came to be a Texas zydeco pioneer of sorts involves some episodes of gender-based adversity. In fact, this feisty and independent woman now credits the initial backlash and harassment that she experienced (as a female who dared to strap on an accordion and try to play) as one of her primary motivations for achieving the status she currently enjoys as a local zydeco favorite.

After graduating from high school in Louisiana and moving to Houston in 1971, for the next two decades Weatherall worked a variety of jobs and enjoyed the big-city nightlife of dancing in discos and R&B clubs—avoiding for the most part the zydeco scene that she associated with her parents' generation back home. But eventually she found a reason to reconnect with some of her cultural roots. As she explains:

I did a lot of different things before I even thought about playing zydeco. In fact, I didn't like zydeco, couldn't stand it. . . . I was into soul, disco, and pop. . . . But as I got older, I got tired of the disco clubs—the same old thing. So I said, "Well, let me start going to the church zydeco, and maybe I'll find me a boyfriend."

After visiting several church dances around the metropolitan area, she saw Beau Jocque and the Zydeco Hi-Rollers perform at a Knights of Columbus Hall in Baytown, and she became a confirmed zydeco fanatic. But something else occurred that truly altered her life: for the first time she began to relate to zydeco as something more than just a sound track for dancing; she grew curious about actually making the music herself. So when a Louisiana-based zydeco bandleader (whom she prefers to remain nameless in this account) spotted her dancing enthusiastically at one of his Houston shows, and then stepped into the audience to dance back-to-back with her, she figured she may have found not only a new boyfriend but also a potential music teacher.

At first, she confided to him that she was interested in playing the rubboard, so he bought her one in Louisiana, presented it to her as a gift, and showed her the basic technique. Later, when he came back to Houston to play a church dance at Our Lady of the Sea Catholic Church, for the first time in her life she got onstage and jammed with a band.

Lady D (Diane Weatherall), Houston, Texas, 1995.

Following that exuberant initiation and other similar experiences as a guest rubboard player, she informed her mentor that what she really desired was to learn how to play the accordion. She also revealed her newly awakened and not-yet-confirmed aspiration to lead her own band:

I said, "You know, you ought to show me that accordion. Man, I like the accordion. But what I really like, I like the way you're so organized. You know, you're a leader, and I would like to be a leader. The rubboard is fine, but I would like to lead, you know."

He said, "Girl, you'd better stick with that rubboard." . . . I was dating him by then, but he would not show me. He just refused. . . . He said, "Accordion is not for a woman to play. It's for a man."

I say, "Why you know that? It's for anybody who want to play it." . . . And all these years later, with the success I've been blessed with, the CDs and everything, I realize something he was telling me back then. . . . The average man out there do not like the idea of me playing the accordion. It's not just the accordion. It's the business part, being the leader.

Following this rebuff by a male musician (as well as some mocking discouragement from certain family members back in Opelousas), Weatherall had little choice but to ask another man for instruction; as she points out, "There were no women I could turn to." But having learned a lesson, she intentionally sought out an older accordionist (whom she wishes also to remain anonymous); this elderly fellow had a reputation as a capable teacher to anyone who was willing to learn. She continues the story:

So I didn't know nothing. . . . Eventually I went around asking everybody to show me how to play the accordion, but nobody would really show me. . . . Then this older man who belonged to St. Francis Church—I can't reveal his name—I heard that he would probably help me because he had helped the other guys. So I got his number and I called him . . . and he agreed to help me. So every Wednesday I would leave work and go to his house and learn the accordion.

After a relatively short period of tutoring and rapid advancement in her instrumental skills, Weatherall consented when her trusted mentor arranged for her to perform at an upcoming dance at St. Nicholas Catholic Church. In fact, in advance publicity for that event, both the church sponsors and Weatherall herself promoted the occasion as a unique opportunity to witness a woman playing zydeco. An unusually large crowd showed up in response:

These people just wanted to see this female. I was going to be the first female over here in Texas to play this accordion, you know. . . .

And so we had this big dance at St. Nicholas, and I tell you, these people was amazed. And I was nervous. I had never played with a band before. . . . I was scared. But he had so much confidence in me when I did not. . . . And that gig we did at the church came out real nice. So from time to time I did other gigs with him.

Having learned to play the button-style accordion from this man, and then having performed with the band he had organized and at shows that he had booked and promoted, Weatherall obviously felt a sense of gratitude and debt to a friend she considered a sort of father figure. But suddenly the nature of their relationship changed in a way that would alienate her profoundly. It is a memory that she relates with palpable sadness, yet she now sees it as the key factor in her ultimate independence:

Then later on, he got flirty to the point that . . . well, I knew it was too good to be true that somebody would just take the time to show me something and wouldn't let me pay him. He didn't want the money. I knew it was too good to be true—that nothing was going to have to be offered, you know. . . . So after a while, he said it was time for me to pay him . . . and he tried to touch me in a certain way, you know . . . and I wouldn't let him do it. . . . So he said, "You know, you would have never learned that accordion except for me."
   I say, "Don't you know, when I got tired of you touching me, that I was going to have to tell you this, and you was going to stop?"

The man, of course, was angry, resentful, and as it turns out, spiteful too. Yet he somehow convinced Weatherall that she was still contractually obligated to appear with him at an upcoming church dance that was already being publicized as a "Lady D" show. However, when she kept her commitment by showing up to take the stage, she suffered yet another indignity, for the band members (at his urging, she assumes) deliberately sabotaged the music. "It sounded like crap," she asserts. "I had played these songs with these guys before, and they played it right, but now it was the wrong key!" Apart from being the target of this man's conspiracy of vengeance, Weatherall regretted immediately what such a fiasco might do to her budding reputation as a female zydeco player. "So the audience is looking at *me*. They don't know what's going on. They just know it don't sound right. . . . And they all seemed to figure it was somehow my fault. You know, 'That girl can't play worth a damn!' and all that."
   Publicly humiliated and forlorn, Weatherall left the church hall that night figuring that her short-lived music career might have come to a nasty end. In the aftermath of this sudden rift in what had once been, from her perspective, a wholesome student-teacher relationship and a mutually beneficial affiliation with his all-male group, she realized that as a musician and

singer, she had limited experience, no band, no sound equipment, and no knowledge of how to book a gig. "But I didn't give it up," she says. "I just fell in love with the music."

Within a few months, after more practicing and networking among musicians whom she trusted, Weatherall had organized the first version of the Zydeco Tornadoes. "I said, 'Look, I don't know nothing about putting a band together. But I want to show that old man [that] he taught me more than he think he taught me. . . . People want me to fail. But I'm not going to fail.'"

Originally she vowed to play for only one year, just to prove her detractors wrong. But the more she performed and developed a sense of camaraderie with her supporting players, the more she enjoyed it—both the music and, as leader, being in control of her own destiny. Reflecting on her zydeco career (which by her choice is limited to gigging that does not conflict with her full-time day job as a civilian employee of the Houston Police Department), she says,

I've learned so much. I mean, even my mother didn't have faith in me. Nobody had faith in me, you know. . . . But I'm focused, I'm strong, and I'm hardheaded. And that's what you've got to be, you know. You've got to be a woman one way, but in another way, you've got to be the boss and the leader. . . . Nobody runs my band for me but me. . . . I love the music, but I don't love it enough that I would quit my job. It gives me power to have my day job. I am not dependent on anyone else. . . .

And that's why I'm not really interested in going out there on the road too much and playing this music. There's just no way. I mean, I like it. I do it when I want to. And I'm doing a lot more than I expected to, because I was just going to play one year, and I did fall in love with it, you know. . . . But if I fell in love with some man, I still wouldn't quit my job. I understand what I need to do with my music—love it, play it whenever you want to, but don't depend on it as your only means of support.

If, as British writer Virginia Woolf argued in her famous 1929 essay, a creative woman must have "a room of one's own," Diane "Lady D" Weatherall's experience suggests a zydeco analogue. For as a Texas music trailblazer in the 1990s, she discovered, it seems, that the key for this woman is to have a band of her own. After all the gender prejudice and harassment that she has experienced, Weatherall is nonetheless content to have devoted a sizable portion of her life to zydeco. "Now it's almost ice cream and cake—almost," she says with a sigh.

The current lineup of Lady D and the Zydeco Tornadoes comprises musicians who, for the most part, have worked happily together now for many years (including Arthur "T-Put" Carter, the jovial rubboard man with whom she has collaborated the longest). As she has matured both musically and personally, Weatherall has never lost sight of the ultimate

Lewis Tezeno (of the Zydeco Tornadoes) and Lady D, Cosmos Café, Houston, Texas, 2003.

reward, the reason she has persisted as a professional musician. "It's a beautiful feeling when you're playing for people and they're *enjoying* it," she says. "And sometimes I think I might just keep doing that, you know, till I'm so old they won't let me do it no more."

THE FINAL TWO DECADES OF THE TWENTIETH CENTURY marked an era in which zydeco, a musical form that was born from social change, transformed itself in unprecedented ways. On the one hand, zydeco emerged to some degree as a more familiar presence in mainstream popular culture; on the other, it simultaneously (perhaps consequently) went through a process of radically redefining itself according to a multitude of contemporary realities and new possibilities. By the turn of the millennium, the z-word had become elastic enough to apply to a wide diversity of styles and players—from variations on the neotraditionalist theme to multifaceted offshoots of zydeco nouveau, from old-timers to Generation Xers, from an all-male performance context to one that became somewhat inclusive of women, and so on.

Perhaps the only absolute certainties in the ongoing evolution of this genre: accordions, rubboards, a rich heritage of dance rhythms, and ceaseless interchange along the east-west zydeco corridor. At the start of the twenty-first century, that back-and-forth movement of people and music remains as constant as the flow of tides.

Zydeco dancers, C. C.'s Hideout, Houston, Texas, 2004.

Five

LONE STAR LA-LA IN THE TWENTY-FIRST CENTURY

*I*t is just past nine o'clock on a Thursday evening, June 2004, in the downtown theatre district of Houston. Though most of the nearby office towers have been long emptied of workers for the day, a huge crowd congregates in an open-air performance venue that covers an entire city block. This attractively designed site, recently renovated by the municipal government, is called Jones Plaza, home to a local tradition of free weekly concerts that feature various forms of popular music. But during a special eight-week series this year, as well as at certain other times, these events are devoted solely to showcasing zydeco, a style that draws a diverse multitude of fans. Predominantly but not exclusively African Americans, those gathered here tonight include (to judge by appearance) many professionals, laborers, college and high school students, families with small children, retirees, tourists, and street people.

Located only a couple of blocks from the Buffalo Bayou landing where the city was founded in 1836, Jones Plaza is anchored by a large permanent stage situated near the intersection of Texas Avenue and Louisiana Street—a setting that seems appropriately symbolic, even though a mere coincidence, for the public presentation of black Creole music. Yet as the third and final band on the program commences to saturate these environs with its own sonic blend of amplified accordion, rubboard, guitar, bass, and drums, it suddenly strikes me as delightfully odd (and somehow subversive) for this lively production to be here of all places—literally across the street from the city's most prestigious venues: the Alley Theatre, the Jesse H. Jones Hall for the Performing Arts, and the grandiose Wortham Center. While these adjacent, elegant structures have hosted world-class drama, symphony, ballet, opera, and other forms of highbrow entertainment, they have never featured the kind of homegrown music that echoes off their stone facades tonight.

But most of the folks assembled here are probably oblivious of such contrasts, engrossed as they seem to be in the music, food, drink, and socializing that have attracted them to this spot. At five p.m., when the show started—and when rush hour and the late-afternoon heat were at their fiercest—Jones Plaza was sparsely occupied. But the numbers have increased steadily since then, going up as the sun goes down. Now masses of butt-shaking dancers and head-bobbing spectators are crammed onto the main floor, and others stroll or sit at bistro tables on the raised and artfully canopied concourse that encircles it.

Meanwhile, Brian Jack and the Zydeco Gamblers are in the middle of a spirited version of "Turn On Your Love Light," a classic R&B song that originated two generations earlier at Houston's Duke-Peacock Records and still is a favorite cover tune among many artists in the region. In addition to the five core members who regularly make up the band, there is an extra guest tonight: the leader's brother (and the former drummer for the group), Eugene Jack Jr., who passionately sings backup while banging a drumstick on a cowbell gripped in his left hand. At the microphone stand on the opposite flank of the stage, longtime rub-boardist Jody Lemelle bobs, weaves, and sings too—his hands pumping rhythmically all the while against the flashing metal plate.

Having reached the end of a stanza, Brian Jack now steps away from the center mic and spins around in a 360-degree rotation while guitarist Ben Black launches into a string-bending solo. Then as Jack continues to play his button accordion, he deftly passes it between and around his legs in a continuous figure-eight pattern—a move that brings to mind the cocky ball-handling wizardry of a Harlem Globetrotter.

At the conclusion of the song, the audience shouts, claps, whistles, and stomps its sweaty appreciation. In the brief lull that follows, while Jack straps on a new accordion and confers with Lemelle, the locus of the sound shifts momentarily out to the street. There seven fellows in leather vests and black T-shirts vociferously gun the engines on the idling Harley-Davidson motorbikes they straddle. Soon the traffic signal clicks to green, and they roar off into the urban nightscape. As their bombastic resonance fades away, Jack takes the mic and asks the crowd, "How many folks from H-Town, Texas, here tonight?" When the expected chorus of affirmation subsides, he then queries, "Do we have any Louisiana people here, people with Louisiana heritage in their background?" The response is equally loud, proud, and protracted. Finally as it slowly ebbs, Jack yells one request: "All the Creole people make some noise!" The band ignites the driving beat that punctuates another number, and

OPPOSITE PAGE: *Zydeco dancers (early arrivals) at Jones Plaza, Houston, Texas, 2004.*

the throng of bodies on the plaza floor seems to move like a multiform dance-crazed giant organism. Though many of the enthused participants cannot translate, and some probably don't even notice, the young Texas-born bandleader is singing this song entirely in French.

On the western periphery of the scene, across the thoroughfare in front of the sprawling Bayou Place entertainment complex, a fashionably dressed middle-aged white couple exits the Angelika Film Center. Upon stepping into the night, they stare in apparent wonder toward this climaxing outdoor concert. The parking valet takes a ticket from the man and shuffles off. The woman, her eyes still pointed toward the source of this distinctive music, gradually begins to smile and nod. Though she may not be sure of what she is hearing, she obviously is starting to enjoy it. By the time the valet returns with the BMW, her shoulders and pelvis are gently swiveling to the zydeco rhythms. Restrained though she may be, she is literally (who knows? perhaps for the first time in her life) dancing on a downtown street.

IN SOME RESPECTS BRIAN JACK might be understood to personify the status of much of Texas zydeco in the early twenty-first century. Youthful, and thus initially inclined mainly toward nouveau urban styles, he has gradually absorbed and synthesized more and more traditional Creole elements. Having played professionally for over a decade before reaching even his twenty-fourth birthday, Jack is already a veteran. But he is still growing and changing, and his ultimate identity has not yet been fully defined. And, his experience thus far parallels that of certain other black Creole musicians from his age group.

"Beau Jocque was mainly the person that was responsible for giving me the motivation to want to do this—because when I heard Beau Jocque play, I was not even into zydeco," Jack says, referring to his decision around the age of thirteen to embrace the funk-infused form of the music popularized by the late leader of the Zydeco Hi-Rollers. However, black Creole dance music was a genre with which Jack was already inherently familiar. "I just grew up around it," he adds. "The zydeco came from my mom's side, the Stoot family. Pierre Stoot [the accordionist best known for his 1990s stint with the Zydeco Dots] is my first cousin." After first gigging as a young guitar player in a Stoot-led zydeco band, Jack decided to take up the accordion himself, form his own group, and follow the path of the dynamic Beau Jocque. "I took the money that I was making playing guitar, and I saved about enough to buy me an accordion." Though mostly self-taught, Jack also picked up instructional tips during trips to his parents' home state. "I would go down to Louisiana every summer. That's where I would learn."

Like his early idol, and like most members of that post–Clifton Chenier generation of zydeco bandleaders that Beau Jocque directly inspired, Jack elected to play only the button accordion. "I really like the squeezebox, single-note accordions, over the piano-style because it has more of a grungy sound to it," he explains in the parlance of his time. "It just has a

OPPOSITE PAGE: *Jody Lemelle (of the Zydeco Gamblers), Crosby, Texas, 2004.*

kick-ass sound to it. The piano-note sound has a big sound, more like an orchestra sound or something, but it's really pretty. But a squeezebox, it just doesn't have a *pretty* sound. . . . It's raw."

Indeed when Brian Jack and the Zydeco Gamblers first emerged in nightclubs in Houston and then eastward along the zydeco corridor (and later at major festivals nationwide), they seemed to fall at least on the margin of that larger category of players who were specializing in the "grungy" style of hip-hop or contemporary R&B-influenced 1990s zydeco. It is a variation most commonly associated with Houston bands such as J. Paul Jr. and the Zydeco NuBreedz or Nooney and the Zydeco Floaters. And even though Brian Jack never really delved as much into rap-zydeco fusion as some of his peers did, Brian Jack and the Zydeco Gamblers were initially considered by many to be part of the same subcultural phenomenon.

Thus, Jack largely identified with the ultraprogressive approach that dominated the genre through the start of the new millennium. Visual signification of that urbanized self-image is readily apparent, for instance, in the cover photograph of the 2003 CD release by Brian Jack and the Zydeco Gamblers, *Getting Down to Business*. Decked out suavely in a tailored suit, dress shirt, and necktie, Jack stands pensively in a postmodern office space characterized by stylishly designed furniture and high-tech electronics. In another photograph inside the CD booklet, Jack, still sporting that first-class business attire, grips the handle of his closed Gabbanelli accordion in his left hand while holding a compact cellular telephone to his ear with his right. Whatever messages such imagery might be construed to communicate, none overtly imply any affiliation with zydeco traditionalism. Yet in a foreshadowing of things to come, this CD (Jack's third) includes a song rendered partially in Creole French ("Chere Bae Bae").

By the 2004 release of the next CD, called *Zydeco Time*, Brian Jack and the Zydeco Gamblers had expanded their repertoire of mostly original compositions to include one that is vocalized completely in French (despite its title appearing in the liner notes only in English translation, as "You Ran with My Heart"). But even more noteworthy for a band once deemed part of the new wave, on *Zydeco Time* Jack also elected to feature the instrumental talents of old-style Creole musician Ed Poullard of Beaumont, playing perhaps the ultimate anti-zydeco-nouveau instrument, the fiddle.

His incorporation of such traditionalist elements into his music clearly indicates that Jack is still evolving as a musician, one whose body of work defies overly simplistic classification based on a single phase of his career. "When I first started off, it was more of a progressive style. What some people started saying was 'nouveau zydeco' or whatever you want to call it," Jack says. "But I'm kind of crossing over a little bit into the traditional side, because that's our heritage."

OPPOSITE PAGE: *Brian Jack, Juneteenth Music Festival, Beaumont, Texas, 2003.*

When pressed to explain further his motivation for venturing into neotraditionalism (including his recent, self-initiated study of his ancestors' linguistic legacy), Jack asserts a preservationist ethos rarely encountered among most urban players of his generation:

This stuff needs to be passed down. . . . People just need to hear what it actually came from.
. . . I'm learning how to speak Creole. I always wanted to learn how to speak Creole, not even nothing to do with zydeco. It's just, you know, it's my heritage. And I just feel that it shouldn't be dying out. . . . I know a pretty good bit of older folks that actually speak it to this day. And they still use it amongst each other, right here in Texas and even more so back in Louisiana. And that's how I'm picking up on certain things.
And as for the music itself, it's because, you know, that's how zydeco started out. It was Creole. . . . It's best to give people, at least the best that I can, the real version of what zydeco should sound like. . . . But, you know, I venture out and still do something different every now and then. . . . The zydeco life for me has been a learning experience.

That willingness to learn from and about his ancestral past while still experimenting with new ideas is obviously the key factor in Brian Jack's ongoing evolution as an artist. He may have started by focusing primarily on certain exciting trends of the moment, but his work now also encompasses a grander sense of homage to the Creole culture and particular musical characteristics that defined early zydeco. As Jack and certain other younger Texas zydeco artists seem to be realizing, the future may well lie with those who appreciate and draw from their Creole heritage while still discovering ways to make the music anew.

IN SOUTHEAST TEXAS AT THE MIDPOINT of the first decade of the twenty-first century, there are still a significant number of older black Creole musicians who established their style of playing well before the zydeco nouveau craze of the 1990s. From Wilbert Thibodeaux, Chester Papillion, Willie Davis, Dan Rubit, Wilfred Chevis, Otha Sanchez, and others in the Houston area, to Billy Poullard and Ed Poullard in Beaumont, a sense of traditionalism that has nothing to do with the "neo-" prefix has survived.

However, just as former senior statesmen of Texas zydeco, such as L. C. Donatto or Lonnie Mitchell, have passed away, some elements of traditionalism are clearly on the wane. For example, the church-dance scene in Houston, long a key component of Texas zydeco culture, has in the last few years generally experienced diminished attendance. Why? Beyond the loss of many longtime participants from mortality or age-related infirmity, some of the previously regular attendees at such events may well have grown alienated by the trend toward zydeco nouveau by many of the younger bands. Accustomed to waltzes, blues, and at least the occasional song sung in French, many of the veteran church dancers have seen their fundamental

Billy Poullard, LaBelle, Texas, 2004.

Chester Papillion, Houston, Texas, 2004.

expectations go mostly unfulfilled since the passing away of the original zydeco patriarchy and the emergence of the post–Beau Jocque school of players.

Nevertheless, for those who have not abandoned the church dances, or for those who simply relish the sound of old-school zydeco, there is still hope. Exemplified by a growing phenomenon among bandleaders like Brian Jack, it is a reactionary form of neotraditionalism that is changing the course of Texas zydeco in the new millennium. Certainly not all, or even most, but some of the youngest and brightest players today are deliberately exploring a back-to-basics aesthetic. In addition to Jack, several young men (most of them still in their early twenties at the time of this writing) are earnestly initiating a whole new phase in the postmodern development of the music.

Though he is not widely known beyond Houston, and in fact has committed himself mainly to a career of service as a Christian pastor, Robert "Ra-Ra" Carter offers a case in point. Billing himself also as "The Minister of Zydeco," this charismatic singer, dancer, and accordionist possesses a self-confident verve that immediately appeals to youthful audiences, but he also is now deliberately reaching back to the sound of his elders. "I was born here in '83 and raised here, in the South Park area of Houston," he states. Although both of his parents came from Louisiana, it was his father's side of the family that provided the strongest link to his Creole heritage. "They were what we call 'the Frenchy folk.' Most of them are still Catholic, still speak French, you know."

After scraping some rubboard with Willie T. York's band as a youngster, Carter began to want to play accordion around age sixteen. With guidance from York, he first purchased what he calls "a little toy squeezebox" and experimented with it. "I was at Yates High School, walking down the hall, trying to figure that thing out," he claims. Making rapid progress, he soon acquired a real single-row accordion from his friend Thomas Henry, better known as "Mingo," another Houston zydeco player who also preaches in a local church. After his initial excitement at mastering an intermediate-level repertoire, Carter trusted his showman instincts and, with help from Mingo, daringly made his first stage appearance within a matter of months. "I couldn't play that awesome, but I made it work. Number one, it's more to it than just being a musician. It's also about being an entertainer. And that's what I did: I *entertained* folks, you know." The success of that bold debut was all it took to motivate Carter to form his own band. As he puts it, "Mind you, I'm sixteen years old, and I just booked a four-hundred-dollar gig! I was hooked."

As his group, Lil' Ra-Ra and the Zydeco Rebels, began playing occasionally around Houston, Carter also acquired and began to play a triple-note accordion, eager to explore new possibilities as a musician. But even before he had learned to exhaust those possibilities, he had gone on to adopt an even more versatile version of the instrument, a type rarely played by most members of his age group. As he tells it, "Dan Rubit and Wilfred Chevis, I got

Robert "Ra-Ra" Carter, Houston, Texas, 2004.

electrified when I saw them playing the piano accordion. Actually, that is what inspired me to play piano accordion. I played the triple-row accordion and the single-row accordion, but now I play the piano accordion too."

The evolution of Carter's instrumental choices ultimately led him to decide to expand his language skills too:

What really inspired me to go that way was that I was listening to Clifton Chenier. Mary Thomas, his sister, gave me an album, and all I could hear was those French songs in my head. . . . You know, "Cochon pour Toi" ["('I'm a) Hog for You"] and stuff like that. . . . Ever since then, I've been learning from my grandparents, who are both French, mixed French, and a lot of aunts and stuff. So I started getting more in-depth with trying to get closer to my heritage.

. . . It was something I was aware of growing up. I was like, "Why does my pa-pa speak different?" [laughs] . . . He was originally from Lafayette, and he had come here and worked on the waterfront. . . . But he never quit speaking that way. . . . So I heard it, even though I didn't learn it as a child. . . .

But eventually I learned some of those old songs from Clifton Chenier. . . . And one of the things which, you know, soon kind of brought me a lot of notoriety, especially from the older players, like Wilfred [Chevis] and them, was that I was one of the youngest guys that still sang in Creole French.

While Carter's responsibilities as a pastor at the Newfound Glory Christian Temple limit the time he can devote to performing, he continues to book his band for special events and club gigs whenever his schedule permits. With his piano-key accordion, he sometimes also plays renditions of favorite hymns at his church. He says he now has a sense of mission about the music and the need to cultivate awareness and appreciation of its roots. And though he has no plans to pursue a full-time career as a bandleader, this "Minister of Zydeco" is adamant in proclaiming the neotraditionalist gospel: "All the young black people in Houston who say they like zydeco, they need to get back in touch with what it's really all about."

ONE OF THE MOST IMPRESSIVE of the youthful neotraditionalists to emerge from Texas since the turn of the century is a full-time professional accordionist, singer, and bandleader who goes by the stage moniker of "Lil' Pop." He inherited that nickname as the son of C. J. Ledet, who is known to family and friends as "Big Pop." Corey Ledet was born in Houston in 1981, ten years after his parents had moved there from southwest Louisiana, and he grew up in nearby Sugar Land, on the southwestern edge of the metropolitan area. This upper-middle-class bedroom community might seem like an unlikely place to nurture new zydeco talent, but it was the boyhood home of one of the genre's most dynamic young musicians.

First around Houston, then in southwest Louisiana, and eventually as far away as France, Corey "Lil' Pop" Ledet has established himself in the early years of the new millennium as a potential major force in the future of zydeco. The now-elderly Creole guitarist Ashton Savoy, for example, describes Ledet as "hot stuff, the best there is among the youngsters, for sure." In fact, after witnessing an especially intense set by Ledet at an August 2004 jam at The Silver Slipper, Savoy stood (with the aid of a wooden crutch) and shouted his gleeful approval, then clutched my arm to cry, "This is how *Clif* used to do it!"

Though he is a native Texan, Ledet descends from a Creole family with deep roots in southwest Louisiana and the musical traditions of the zydeco corridor. His grandfather Buchanon "Tee Bu" Ledet, for instance, was a drummer who worked with major figures such as Clifton Chenier, Rockin' Dopsie, and Fernest Arceneaux. His cousin is Leon Sam, the former Houstonian who once fronted the Sam Brothers Five and, some years later, the Zydeco Dots. Moreover, C. J. Ledet says that when Corey was a baby, he often lulled him to sleep at night by softly playing "my favorite records by Clifton and Buckwheat." Zydeco is obviously in the young man's blood.

Like his grandfather, Corey Ledet launched his music career as a drummer. From age twelve through his late teens, he received formal training on the instrument, first in a middle-school band class and then as a member of both the Elkins High School marching band and the concert orchestra. But unlike most kids, Ledet was already working professionally on local zydeco stages by the time that scholarly instruction began. "I must have been about ten years old when I first started on drums," he recalls. As a child prodigy of sorts, and with his father's encouragement, oversight, and support, he began regularly gigging with the venerable Wilbert Thibodeaux "around the age of eleven." And while he says he enjoyed those experiences in the school bands, it is clear that Ledet's most valuable early music education occurred well off campus.

During his tenure with Wilbert Thibodeaux and the Zydeco Rascals, the juvenile musician made music with some of the most seasoned veterans of the Houston zydeco scene—in addition to his respected bandleader, players such as L. C. Donatto and Ashton Savoy, for instance. From them he absorbed a style of zydeco that was heavily influenced by the past. Unlike most players from his generation, Ledet enjoyed a lot of the old-timers' music, preferring it in some respects to the contemporary sounds of hip-hop and rap that captured the imaginations of so many of his Texas zydeco peers.

After a few years of listening and learning with the Thibodeaux band, Ledet eventually developed a craving to go beyond his drummer's role and to squeeze those timeless melodies from the accordion for himself. His ability to achieve that goal would ultimately be facilitated by his friendship with another Houston musician who, though a generation older than he, was still a relative newcomer to the accordion at the time.

Corey "Lil' Pop" Ledet, The Big Easy Social and Pleasure Club, Houston, Texas, 2003.

That man, Houston native James B. Adams Jr. (b. 1956), had grown up attending local church dances that instilled in him a strong sense of pride in the black Creole culture of his Louisiana grandparents. His Beaumont-born father had made a point of introducing him to such gatherings, so years later when Adams had a son of his own, they continued the family tradition. "I would always go to dances with my dad. And my oldest son, Ricky, he would go with us. And he was just fascinated with the accordion," Adams explains. "So when my oldest son decided he wanted an accordion, I bought him one for his birthday." However, when the boy's mother (Adams's ex-wife) objected, that gift was promptly returned to the giver. "So I was stuck with an eight-hundred-dollar accordion, and didn't know what to do with it. This was in 1989," Adams relates. "So I said, 'Well, I might as well try it.'"

Over the next few years Adams toyed with that instrument during time off from his full-time employment at the ExxonMobil chemical plant in Baytown. He would scrutinize the fingering techniques of accordionists performing on local stages, but did not make much progress when he tried to play on his own. Then on his way back to Texas from a visit to see family members in southwest Louisiana, Adams happened to stop at the Prairie Acadian Culture Center in Eunice, and there he purchased an instructional-book-and-cassette-tape package produced by noted Cajun accordion builder Larry Miller. Gradually, by working through the exercises in that book, listening repeatedly to the songs on the tape, and practicing in the privacy of his home, Adams developed basic accordion skills and some measure of self-confidence. Eventually he started going out to zydeco clubs to play with other musicians at weekly jam sessions around the city. It was in such a context that he would fall into his unique role as Corey Ledet's mentor and colearner.

"I met James when I was playing drums with Wilbert Thibodeaux. I was like thirteen or fourteen, and James would come to the jams, at The Silver Slipper and at Pe-Te's," Ledet recalls. Adams had once previously appeared onstage at the invitation of Lonnie Mitchell, an incident that had culminated in a disorienting case of nervousness. So now he was gravitating toward Thibodeaux's gigs for a particular reason. "Back then I was dating Wilbert's niece," he explains. "So Wilbert Thibodeaux, he started letting me sit in with him, just to try to get some of the stage fright out. When he'd come to Pe-Te's, he'd let me sit in and do three or four songs." It was on such occasions that Adams and Ledet initiated their friendship. "Corey would say, 'Could you teach me to play accordion? I just want to learn how to play,'" reports Adams. So though still a fledgling student of the instrument himself, he began to invite Ledet to visit him (during his days off from the shift work at the chemical plant), and he commenced to explain and demonstrate the limited accordion knowledge and repertoire that he had accumulated to date.

It was not long, however, before those sessions evolved from a tutoring relationship into

James B. Adams, University of Chicago Folk Festival, Chicago, 2005.

the spirited interaction of two musical peers who were learning together. Adams continues the explanation:

I kind of just listened to the records on my own—and would try to just take a song and section it off, in three sections. Get the first part, the middle, and then the end. That's how Corey and I both learned together, at my house sitting in the living room. . . . That's how we would piece the songs together. If he'd get a piece of it, then I'd get the other piece, and then we'd combine all the elements together and make one song.

For his part, Ledet adds, "When I started playing the accordion, James was really, really helping me figure it out, like the technique and the songs, and stuff like that."

After this early period of mutually beneficial consultation, another road trip by Adams to see kinfolk in Louisiana opened new, unexpected doors leading to the next phase in their development. He narrates the fortunate sequence of events:

So I stopped back by the cultural center in Eunice. And I saw that book. It was still there, two years later. . . . And I asked the lady [at the checkout counter], "I wonder if this guy's still living?" She say, "Who?" I say, "Larry Miller." I say, "I want to go and tell the man that his selling that book really helped, that it got me in the ballpark." She say, "Just a minute." She got on the telephone and called him, and I didn't know what she was doing. So she called him and say, "Here," and handed me the phone. And that's how I met Larry Miller. And I told him, "Hey man, your book works. It helped me a lot." And he said, "Well, you're the first person who ever called and told me that." . . .

And he told me how to get to his house. Went to his house, met the man, and he made me play a song. I think I played "J'ai Passé devant Ta Porte" or something like that. . . .

He said, "Well, have you ever been to any workshops or anything?" I didn't even know what a workshop was. . . . And he gave me a brochure and said, "Why don't you consider coming to one of these camps? I think they'll help you out a lot." And this was in February of 2000. And I said, "OK, let me think about it."

So I come back to Houston and told Corey about it. So then I took Corey to meet Larry Miller. And by then, I had started doing a little [acoustic] guitar on my own. We both went. I let Corey meet Larry, and we just kind of did like a duet type of thing for him. And he said, "Why don't you guys go back home and put what you've just done on a videotape, about fifteen minutes, and mail it to this address up in West Virginia. . . . We'll see if we can get you guys a scholarship to get in the workshop."

Lo and behold, two weeks later, we got a scholarship. So we end up in Elkins, West Virginia . . . and it changed my life.

The workshop experience that Adams refers to was part of the annual Cajun/Creole Week sponsored by the Augusta Heritage Center at Davis and Elkins College. Adams and Ledet made their first trip there in July 2000, and it immediately yielded important results—for their musicianship as well as their ability to network with other enthusiasts. Ironically, for instance, Adams and Ledet had to travel all the way to West Virginia to meet Ed Poullard of Beaumont (where many of Adams' relatives lived, a city he had visited throughout his life). Poullard would become a significant mentor to them both, but especially to Adams, who now performs with him at folk festivals and other workshops. But during that week at the Augusta Heritage Center, the most important influence would come from Poullard's West Coast–based older brother, Danny.

Through interactive videoconferencing technology, Danny Poullard taught the workshop class, live, via satellite, from California. Although he was not physically present on the West Virginia campus, Poullard nonetheless made a dramatic impact on his students, as Adams attests:

We took an intermediate-accordion class from Danny Poullard. . . . And that's when the door just opened up. You know, it just opened up right there on the spot—because we knew we were missing something. And he showed us the way. I had always tended to stick to the really traditional style of music, but Corey he didn't like it so much at first. But you can sure hear it now in his music. . . . It made a huge difference for him, me too. We were in the class with Danny, and he said, "Don't let me down. Don't forget this music."

The instruction and inspiration imparted by Poullard proved immediately invaluable to the two, so his death the following year refocused Adams's sense of motivation:

And it was like the very next year, that's when he died. And it kind of broke my heart a little bit because I never actually met the guy in person. But for him to embrace us the way he did, I knew it was something I needed to keep doing. . . . I knew he meant it, and I felt like I had to do it. . . . It became my mission. It kind of grasps your soul.

In the two years following that first visit to the Augusta Heritage Center workshops, Adams and Ledet continued to collaborate as fellow students of the music and fellow per-formers on stage. Then in 2002, Ledet decided to move from his parents' house in Texas and live with an aunt in Parks, Louisiana—the small town in St. Martin Parish where his father had been born and raised. "It's something I always wanted to do, like just to be around the culture and the heritage and the language and music and everything. So, when I got the chance, I just went on ahead and did it," he explains, adding reflectively, "Something about it—I just couldn't be away from it."

Once he was based in southwest Louisiana, he formed Corey Ledet and His Zydeco Band, a group that includes veteran Creole musician Joseph "Black" Rossyion on guitar. Traveling back and forth along the zydeco corridor, the band soon was working the main venues between Breaux Bridge and Houston, impressing audiences with their authentic grasp of the classic zydeco sound, as well as their originality and versatility.

By 2003 Ledet had released *3 Years 2 Late*, an excellent debut recording of mostly original compositions. Featuring members of his regular band as well as a few special guests (including James Adams), it highlights Ledet's ability to play a broad range of zydeco—from hard-driving two-steps and shuffles to down-home blues to harmony-laced ballads to poignant waltzes and more. It also demonstrates his maturation into an effective singer who compellingly articulates lyrics in both English and French. The steady gigging and the positive response to the CD have combined to raise the level of general awareness (in zydeco circles, at least) of Ledet's considerable talents, leading to higher-profile bookings at the 2005 New Orleans Jazz and Heritage Festival and other festivals beyond the region and overseas.

In an unsigned 2004 article on the Contemporary Cajun, Creole, and Zydeco Musicians Web site, a CD reviewer notes Ledet's multifaceted stylistic nuances, saying he "excels at both the urban Zydeco sounds of his home town, the Creole music played in days past by his relatives in rural Louisiana, and the contemporary Zydeco beat that draws crowds to dance halls across the region and beyond." Writing for *Dirty Linen* magazine, Dan Willging observes in 2005, "Whereas most purveyors of the z-stuff specialize in a single idiom . . . [he] covers it all. . . . Admittedly, his heart lies within the Clifton Chenier old-school realm, but the crafty Ledet . . . stratifies his original music with attributes from various eras."

Ledet's versatility extends to (indeed, is made possible by) his command of various types of the main instrument. In addition to the single-row and triple-row button types favored by most of the younger players, he also regularly incorporates the piano-keyboard accordion. "I didn't want to be limited to one style of zydeco. I wanted to do it all," he says. "I always had a piano-note, but I never really fully learned it at first. I was kind of messing with it. And then I got a single-note and started going back and forth to different kinds of accordions, triple-row too. And now I just like to play them all."

In addition to his multifaceted work on accordion, Ledet also performs on organ, rub-board, and drums on selected tracks of *3 Years 2 Late*. But there is one particular featured instrument that he does not play, and its presence profoundly informs several of the songs (none more so than "Tante Eun Waltz," an eerily beautiful gem evoking the sonic legacy of Creole music pioneers such as Amédé Ardoin). That instrument's presence also makes *3 Years 2 Late* the recording debut of another remarkable newcomer who already seems

Cedric Watson and Corey Ledet, Pe-Te's Cajun Barbeque House, Houston, Texas, 2003.

destined for greatness. For apart from the dazzling musicianship of Ledet and his regular bandmates, this self-produced CD incorporates some exquisite old-style Creole fiddling, compliments of another young Texan from just west of Houston, Cedric Watson.

THE RISE OF FIDDLER CEDRIC WATSON (B. 1983) from almost complete obscurity to nationally recognized Creole-music phenomenon has caught most observers off guard. As Dan Willging notes, "there had never been an abundance of Creole fiddlers" in the first place, and with the deaths of the seventy-two-year-old Canray Fontenot in 1995, the ninety-two-year-old Bébé Carrière in 2001, and the eighty-year-old Calvin Carrière in 2003, "things looked bleak" for the future of this fine instrumental tradition. With the exception of a very few middle-aged practitioners of the form (mainly Beaumont's Ed Poullard and the Louisiana-based D'Jalma Garnier), there seemed to be nobody poised to carry on, particularly among the younger generation of black Creoles. That fact punctuated for some a sense of loss on a larger scale—as yet another element of a distinctive culture appeared to be on the verge of disappearing.

Then, during the April 2003 Cajun-Creole Heritage Week sponsored by Louisiana Folk Roots, things changed. Many of the participating folk musicians and fans who had gathered for the workshops at Lake Chicot State Park (near Ville Platte) witnessed the key moment: an initially tentative yet nonetheless moving performance by a tall, polite, and somewhat shy young man from Texas. That occasion marked the start of a significant shift in perspective among followers of the music. In the course of one weekend, the tone of thought about the future of Creole fiddling changed from elegiac to hopeful. As the executive director of Louisiana Folk Roots, Jody Hebert, told Willging about that day, "everybody realized the importance of what was happening."

Over subsequent months Watson traveled back and forth along the zydeco corridor, playing discretely at jam sessions around Houston and making a few well-received appearances in southwest Louisiana. On the east side of the Sabine River, the public embraced this fiddle prodigy as if he were almost some kind of savior. As Andrea D. Rubinstein observes in her "Notes from Acadiana—Early Spring 2004":

A few weeks ago, after showing up playing fiddle with Zydeco Force over Mardi Gras, with Corey Ledet on the Creole heritage workshop at Festival Acadiens, and as one of the dinner bands at Balfa weekend with James Adams . . . Cedric (along with Corey and James) . . . [appeared on] a live Saturday morning radio broadcast on KRVS–FM, the local University of Louisiana NPR affiliate. He played and sang old Canray Fontenot tunes, among other things, and the phone started ringing off the hook his entire set, and for weeks afterwards. The DJs are still talking about his visit on the air, imploring him to come back.

Cedric Watson, University of Chicago Folk Festival, Chicago, 2005.

In a similar vein, David Simpson describes and comments upon Watson's April 2004 appearance at the Dewey Balfa Cajun and Creole Heritage Weekend alluded to above:

During lunch at the Conference Center on Saturday, Cedric Watson, a remarkable young fiddler from the town of San Felipe, Texas . . . performed with James Adams on guitar and Christine Powell on triangle. . . . Watson has not only learned the fiddle style of the late Canray Fontenot, but he is also a gifted vocalist who does an excellent job performing Canray's songs like "Les Barres de la Prison" and "Bee de la Manche." In addition, he sang "Valse de Balfa" and, with Christine's encouragement, performed the tongue twister "T'en a eu tu n'auras plus" ("Step It Fast"). Creole fiddlers are now a rarity, so it is especially heartening to see a young musician embrace this style with such commitment.

As Simpson's comments illustrate, not only did Watson immediately impress Louisiana audiences with his heart-stirring renditions on the fiddle, but also with his ability to sing in and speak authentic Creole French. For one so young, who until recently had never lived east of Houston, his facility with the language at first seemed incredible. Laraine Bridges, in her report for *Cajun Life and Times* on meeting Watson before his performance on the music stage at the 2004 Breaux Bridge Crawfish Festival, echoes that observation:

Cedric[,] who hails from Texas but has Louisiana grandparents . . . told us that he wants to be able to speak French fluently but he thought he wasn't very good. However, on speaking to him in French we found he replied extremely competently. If he applies the same dedication to learning the language as he has to Creole fiddle (he has been playing for three years), he will be fluent by the next festival!

As Watson later explained to Nick Pittman, "The language, to me, is more important than anything. The language, because without the language you don't have the music." Pittman's December 2004 feature article in the *Times of Acadiana* describes not only Watson's prodigious talent for speaking French and making music but also his late-2004 decision to move from Texas to Louisiana, where he has now settled in the small community of Duralde, near Eunice. There is a deeper pool of mentors and potential collaborators to be found there, as well as a better job market for the performance of old-style Creole music. However, like Corey Ledet before him, Watson has relocated mainly because he feels a special bond with both the people and the place from which his ancestry originated.

That fascination with Louisiana struck Watson early in his young life. As Pittman points out, in his childhood Watson noticed and was intrigued by the occasional French expression that surfaced in the conversations of older members of his family in Texas. But when he began to make regular summer visits to an uncle in the southern Louisiana town of Kinder, "he was struck by the culture and the French language's presence on the radio." Before long he began taping radio broadcasts and taking them back to Texas, where he would practice his listening comprehension and pronunciation. Then when he turned thirteen, his Creole grandmother gave him a compilation recording of traditional French music from southern Louisiana and an acoustic guitar. As he repeatedly listened to and played along with that tape, he grew increasingly aware of and interested in the fiddle sounds that graced several tracks. At the age of seventeen, as a gift from the same grandmother, he acquired his first fiddle and proceeded to teach himself how to play.

Over the next year or so Watson worked diligently in relative isolation, studying old recordings and practicing on his instrument. As a teenager living in a small Texas town, he did not know anyone who could teach him or who was even much interested in the style of fiddle music that now obsessed him. But he discovered a kindred spirit through a weekly radio program, *Zydeco Pas Salé*, on KPFT, a nonprofit Pacifica Foundation–affiliated FM station broadcasting from the nearby city of Houston. That volunteer DJ, once only a disembodied voice in the night, soon became a close friend—the man, in fact, who ultimately introduced Cedric Watson to the Creole music aficionados of Acadiana and beyond.

James B. Adams, the same fellow who had helped Corey Ledet get started on the accordion, had been a reluctant recruit to serve as occasional program cohost on the late-Sunday-night *Zydeco Pas Salé* show that Mary Thomas had anchored for years. Because of the demands of his work schedule at the ExxonMobil plant plus his live-music activities (including regular participation in the Sunday-evening jam sessions at The Big Easy), the amount of time he had available for contributing to the radio show was limited. But after Thomas repeatedly implored him to do so, he eventually agreed, starting in the summer of 2002.

Adams viewed this opportunity to influence radio programming as perhaps another way of fulfilling that sense of personal mission that the late Danny Poullard had inspired. As he explains,

Corey [Ledet], Mingo [Thomas Henry], and I used to sit up and talk about doing radio work. . . . We wanted to see if we could change the course of the music and kind of lean it more towards the traditional sound. Because we saw so much of the old sound leaving the music—you know, as far as the style of playing the accordion, some of the singing, the acoustic guitar, and especially the fiddle. It just seemed like it was gone from the music we were hearing, like it just went away.

Thus, whenever his schedule permitted, Adams began selecting CDs from his collection of classic Creole music (Amédé Ardoin, Canray Fontenot, the Lawtell Playboys, and such) and carrying them down to the radio station to play on Thomas's show. Not only did he gladly spin such discs, but he also talked between songs about the legacy of the legendary Creole artists he featured and about Creole heritage in general, adding a deeper historical perspective to the long-running program.

Late one Sunday night at KPFT, while taking song requests over the telephone, Adams had his first encounter with Cedric Watson:

Then the second month I was there on the radio show, Cedric called, but I didn't know him. He just called out of the blue one night, and he started requesting certain songs. So I started playing them. He called about eight times in an hour—and kept requesting these songs. . . . So I played every one of them.

Then I announced the weekly jam session at The Big Easy every Sunday night. He called again. . . . I told him where it was at and everything. . . . He was living out there around Sealy, San Felipe, you know, on the far, far west side of the area.

Curious about this unknown radio listener who had requested all those old-timey songs, Adams wondered what instrument and style of music the guy might play and hoped he would show up the next week at The Big Easy.

The following Sunday night, while onstage making music with Corey Ledet, Adams spotted a fresh-faced stranger in the crowd—a teenager who looked (and was in fact) too young to gain legal entrance to such an establishment (fortunately, nobody was checking IDs that night). But apart from the underage appearance of this newcomer, Adams was struck immediately by what the youngster held in his hand:

He showed up, and I saw this little case he was carrying. And I looked and I say to myself, "This guy has got to be Cedric, but don't tell me this young guy has got a fiddle!" He had never told me what he played or anything. So I say, on the mic, "Is Cedric Watson in the house? If so, come up to the bandstand and sign the book" [to reserve a set in the rotation of musicians on stage]. And he turned around, and I just looked at him.

So we got off the stage, and they came up, and I just stood there, and I just watched him and thought, "Well, I'll be damned. That is a fiddle!" And he was eighteen then. . . .

When his little band cranked up, they were so together. They were so tight. . . . I could not believe it, this kid on the fiddle, you know. And everybody just stood there and watched.

Following Watson's startling debut set at the Big Easy jam, Adams promptly pulled the upstart fiddler to the side to talk:

I said, "You do good on that fiddle. I know some people who might be interested in what you're doing. So you like the old music?" He said, "Yeah I like it, but I've never really been around people

that were doing it." Because, he said, where he was living, nobody really cared for that old-timey music. I told Cedric, "I want to meet your folks. And I want to see if I can take you to Louisiana to meet some people that I know."

Unknown to Watson, Adams had developed a special friendship with an elderly Louisiana Creole accordionist named Goldman Thibodeaux (b. 1932), the only surviving member of the Lawtell Playboys. During some of their field trips back to Acadiana, Adams and Ledet had visited in Thibodeaux's Lawtell home and casually demonstrated some of the traditional repertoire they were learning. To their delight, he seemed to enjoy their duets, and encouraged their efforts, and they heard "a lot of stories about the old Creole music" from the revered figure in return. In fact, at the conclusion of their most recent visit to Thibodeaux's house, something dramatic occurred when the older musician made a personal request that had haunted Adams ever since:

And he asked me, on the way out, he said, "J. B., why our young people don't play fiddle anymore?" I told him that I didn't know. He walked outside . . . and he put his hands on my shoulder . . . and looked me dead in my eyes and he say, "You find me a Creole fiddler before I die." . . . I said, "Mr. Goldman, I'll do what I can."

That commitment had been troubling Adams deeply, for common knowledge suggested that there simply were no young black Creoles—in Louisiana or in Texas—engaged in fiddle playing anymore. Adams therefore briefly considered contacting high-school orchestra directors back in Houston, hoping to find at least one African American youth who might already be studying violin and who might be persuaded to investigate the Creole fiddle tradition as a sideline. But before ever acting on that strategy, and only a few months after Thibodeaux's request, Adams discovered Cedric Watson at The Big Easy and immediately realized he had received a previously unimaginable answer to his prayers:

So I took Cedric to Goldman. I told him, "It's going to be a whole other world. You're going to be under the microscope when you get there." He didn't know what I was talking about.

Before we went, I let him watch every documentary [videotape] I had on Cajun and Creole music. The first night he come to my house, he didn't sleep. He stayed up all night, watched two or three of them two or three times, got the fiddle out, and he played so much. He learned so many songs in just one night, just from listening to records and watching documentaries. He went to sleep finally with the fiddle in his hands, sitting in a chair.

We got up the next day and went straight to Mr. Goldman's in Lawtell. I introduced Cedric to him, but we didn't bring any instruments into the house, and we didn't say anything about a fiddle.

. . . So then I say, "I've got something for you." I say, "Cedric, go get your toy." And he went out to the car and came back in. Mr. Goldman was kind of fidgeting, like he was kind of tired. But when Cedric come in with that little case and opened it up, Mr. Goldman's eyes got big. And then they started filling up with water. And Cedric started playing "Bluerunner" for him. It was just beautiful. Mr. Goldman stood up, and he looked at me, and he say, "You did it."

Within a few months of that meeting, Adams and Watson, often accompanied by Corey Ledet, were regularly driving from Houston to southwest Louisiana for appearances at special workshops and such. Word of this young Creole fiddle player had begun to spread throughout the folk-music community of southwest Louisiana, but Watson at that time had yet to take the stage at any major event. Then over the course of one weekend in August 2003, all that would change—first with a guest appearance at a legendary zydeco venue and then the following day at a regional festival. Both of these breakthrough performances came as a result of invitations from one of Watson's neotraditionalist Texas peers, Brian Jack.

It all started at the historic Lawtell nightclub called Richard's, where Brian Jack and the Zydeco Gamblers were headlining one Friday night, and Adams and Watson just happened to be in town. At Adams's suggestion, Jack agreed to let Watson join him onstage for a couple of songs. For most people in the audience, seeing a fiddle player with a young zydeco band was an absolutely unprecedented experience. "He let Cedric sit in, and Richard's went berserk. Everybody in there lost it. They were so happy," Adams says. "There were people standing in this club and crying. A lady come up to me with tears in her eyes, and she say, 'I wish my daddy was alive to see this.'" As Adams would later relate to Dan Willging about that scene, "I think they were more amazed because they saw somebody young, black—that looked like the crowd—playing the fiddle. . . . They probably heard of the older musicians that have passed on, but to see somebody almost their same age doing what he is doing, they were in shock."

Following that momentous introduction to the zydeco public of southwest Louisiana, Watson appeared the very next day, again as a guest of bandleader Brian Jack, during the Zydeco Gamblers' set at the Southwest Louisiana Zydeco Festival in the nearby town of Plaisance. Playing for a larger and equally receptive crowd, Watson gained even more exposure and awestruck acclaim. As Adams sums up the result, "And that's when everybody in Louisiana knew it, knew about Cedric on that fiddle, from that point on."

Since then, the young fiddle sensation from Texas has toured the East Coast with the band Zydeco Force as well as with Dexter Ardoin and the Creole Ramblers, has played with Ed Poullard and James B. Adams (in the trio called Les Amis Creole) at folk festivals as far away as Chicago, and has performed with his own band at the New Orleans Jazz and Heritage Festival. Additional touring opportunities and recording projects are said to be in the

Les Amis Creole (left to right: Cedric Watson, Ed Poullard, James B. Adams),
University of Chicago Folk Festival, Chicago, 2005.

works, including one with D'Jalma Garnier and Jeffrey Broussard in a supergroup side project called the Creole Cowboys. Most observers believe that the intensely positive exposure that Cedric Watson has received thus far marks only the beginning of what could be a significant career in the twenty-first-century history of black Creole music.

In fact, some insiders have recently begun to speak of the possibility of a larger renaissance of interest in the traditional songs and styles that form the roots of zydeco, a vibrant renewal led by members of the younger generation of black Creoles. Back during the heyday of the zydeco nouveau trends of the late 1990s, such a phenomenon had seemed highly unlikely, even impossible. But now, the emergence and creative evolution of artists such as Cedric Watson, James Adams, Corey Ledet, and Brian Jack makes it no longer seem quite so far-fetched. And for those who truly understand social history, neither should the fact that this hoped-for renaissance might be inspired, in part at least, by Creoles born in Texas.

SINCE THE DEATH OF CANRAY FONTENOT IN 1995, one of the most widely recognized caretakers and practitioners of the Creole fiddle tradition has been Ed Poullard, a native of Eunice but a resident of Beaumont since his early infancy. "I was the last child of eleven children born in Louisiana, and my family came to Texas when I was only nine months old," he says. "My father came here to find work." That patriarch, John Poullard, naturally brought with him the French language, folk music, food customs, and religion of his upbringing. Living in a boomtown community heavily populated by fellow Creole and Cajun transplants or their descendants, he remained directly connected to these essential elements of his cultural heritage, as did the family he raised in Texas. And for the Poullards, music was always an integral part of life.

"My dad was playing dances when he was twelve, house dances," Ed Poullard says. Though his father did put aside the accordion for a while during several years of necessary concentration on earning wages and raising a family, he eventually returned to the instrument when Ed was still a boy. "And he started *jamming* on that thing, man. And it was unbelievable. It was pretty cool," he adds with a laugh, "pretty cool to see your old man play an instrument like that." Before long, the youngest son had acquired an acoustic guitar and begun to provide occasional accompaniment. As a loosely structured Poullard family band evolved, including various cousins and uncles, Ed filled in on guitar throughout his teenage years whenever his services were needed—not even realizing at the time how much of the old music he was absorbing.

Even after graduating from Kelly High School, Poullard never entertained the notion of being a fiddler. The guitar was his instrument, or so he thought. Within a few years, however, he was eagerly learning to play the diatonic accordion in the traditional style, and ultimately that experience laid the foundation for his fascination with the fiddle. But first he had to travel to the West Coast and be inspired.

His brother Danny, fourteen years his senior, had long ago settled in California, where he was active in the small but vital Creole-Cajun folk-music scene near San Francisco. Ed explains how Danny's early struggle to master the squeezebox triggered his own music epiphany:

One year I went out to meet Danny, when he was living in San Francisco. . . . At that time he was first learning the accordion. He was playing bass with Queen Ida and Lil' John Simien and a bunch of different people in that area. . . . I had never really realized that I had learned so much about the music until he started learning how to play. . . . Although I couldn't play either, on the accordion, when he would try to learn how to play a song, I could tell him, "No, that's not right. I've been playing with Daddy, and I know how it's supposed to sound." [laughs] . . . You know, he was on the West Coast, and I was on the Gulf Coast. . . . I was there at home. When my dad played the accordion, I was right there watching him, or listening or playing the guitar with him. . . . When I realized I could do that—that I had absorbed those old songs from Daddy—from talking with Danny, I said, "Hell, I ought to try to learn play too." So before that visit was over, I was hunting and pecking on the thing and almost working something out, before I even left from visiting with him.

And when I came home, I got my dad to kind of sit with me and try to play slower, so I could kind of see what he was doing. But that was out of the question: he didn't play slow! [laughs]

. . . I learned pretty quick, though, because of the fact I was sitting right in front of my dad. And I got some really good coaching from my mother too. . . . She knew the music just as good as he did.

Encouraged by a good-natured rivalry with his brother in California (with whom he would spend "hours at a time" discussing and playing accordions over the long-distance telephone line) as well as by the direct influence of his parents' musicianship and cultural knowledge, Ed Poullard became a serious disciple of the Creole squeezebox, and a human repository of many of its traditional songs. However, he would soon give up that instrument, at least for a good while—and not by choice.

While an employee of the United Parcel Service, Poullard suffered a work-related injury that left the ring finger of his right hand seriously damaged. During his recuperation from that accident, he grew increasingly frustrated by his inability to make any music—not on his beloved accordion and not even on his first instrument, the guitar. This undesirable situation, however, established part of the context that would lead him to become a fiddler:

It was during that time that my grandfather passed away . . . and my dad being the oldest child, he got his fiddle. . . . So he brought it home and kind of fixed it up . . . but nobody was playing it. It was just sitting in the case, doing nothing. Every now and then he'd take it out and scratch on it just a little, just to amuse himself . . . and then he'd put it back. And I was so accustomed to playing—something, you know. But I couldn't play guitar because I had this big old splint on my finger. And I couldn't play accordion. And one day my dad said, "Well, why don't you try to learn how to play that thing. It's just sitting there doing nothing." I said, "You know, that's a good idea, but I don't have anybody here that can teach me."

After experimenting for a while with the inherited instrument, Poullard developed a new-found passion. He had never heard his grandfather play the fiddle, to his regret. But he began to pay special attention to fiddle work on old recordings, and he self-reliantly practiced as much as he could. Eventually he decided to seek out some of the few surviving older musicians who had mastered the tradition, for there were none that he knew of around Beaumont.

"There wasn't a whole lot of fiddle players anywhere, to begin with. They were pretty few and far between," says Poullard. "So I started taking some trips to Louisiana to see Canray [Fontenot] and another guy named Calvin Carrière."

While Canray Fontenot would in many respects become his ultimate role model (and both Ed and Danny Poullard would eventually tour and record with him), Calvin Carrière's ready availability facilitated his role as one of Ed's first important mentors. Poullard elaborates:

Canray was playing a lot back then. He was playing with Bois Sec [Ardoin] a lot, and they traveled a lot too, Europe and everywhere else.

So while the family band was still playing together, we started getting Calvin to play with us. So I kind of got a little advantage there. We spent more time together, and he started teaching me more. And it wasn't long! I was catching on pretty quick.

During this same time, Poullard was still regularly traveling to visit and make music with his brother Danny in California, where he also received important instruction on fiddle from Ben Guillory and Edgar Ledet. "I got help from a whole lot of people," he says. "They were available when I needed them."

By the 1980s, however, Poullard was primarily apprenticing under the legendary Canray Fontenot, appearing with him (along with Danny) on festival stages all over the nation. It was in such a context that Ed began to realize, albeit reluctantly, some of his potential as a singer of the old French songs. "At first I was concentrating just on playing the instruments. The singing really didn't come along until . . . *having* to sing, when Canray and Danny and I were doing the festival circuit," he attests. He claims that the other two men would sometimes (in the case of Danny, perhaps frequently) decline to vocalize when they got onstage, often claiming to have forgotten the words. So it fell to him, the youngest member of the group, to sing.

Ed Poullard at home, Beaumont, Texas, 2004.

"The vocals carry the song. . . . So if I didn't remember them, I learned them. And I sang them," he says with a smile. "And that's how that got started."

In the first few years of the twenty-first century, Ed Poullard's musicianship, both as fiddler and singer, has been well documented on several CDs, most notably the 2001 release *Poullard, Poullard & Garnier* on Louisiana Radio Records (which was also the last appearance on record by his late brother Danny). On the Arhoolie label, in addition to being featured on various tracks with Canray Fontenot, Poullard shares equal billing with Cajun accordionist Jesse Legé on the 2002 release *Live at the Ilseton Crawdad Festival*. And when the record producer, Louisiana French music historian, and performing musician Ann Savoy assembled a large cast of all-star supporting talent for the 2004 Vanguard Records disc *Creole Bred: A Tribute to Creole & Zydeco*, the only fiddler of Creole descent in the group was Poullard.

Since the mid-1990s he has also been fairly regularly involved as a teacher (of fiddle, accordion, and guitar) during the annual Cajun/Creole Week at the Augusta Heritage Center in Elkins, West Virginia, as well as at other folk-music workshops around the nation. However, although he thoroughly enjoys that role, he has limited time available to pursue it. Poullard is an accomplished woodworker who does some custom cabinet building and remodeling work, but his primary employment since around 1980 has been as an electrical mechanic at the DuPont plant in Beaumont. Like his father before him, he plays music whenever he can, but would never depend on it to make a living.

For the son, though, the mastery of ancestral music traditions has provided opportunities to travel, perform, and teach all over North America. "I am glad to do it. I wish I could do more. I'm limited because I work full-time," he says. Yet in recent years Poullard has been able to do some important mentoring and tutoring without leaving southeast Texas. In particular, he has provided guidance, musical instruction, and moral support to several of the most noteworthy young Creole neotraditionalists from the western region of the zydeco corridor. Thus, he is also a personal conduit of cultural memory and insight, an invaluable resource for those—such as Cedric Watson, James Adams, and Brian Jack—who never played with the likes of Canray Fontenot but surely wish they had.

Since zydeco struck its first major chord in the consciousness of pop culture back in the 1980s, it has become increasingly common for the general public to encounter live performance of the music. In southeast Texas, beyond the traditional venues of nightclubs and the church dances, it is now regularly part of large-scale gatherings such as the Houston International Festival or the Mardi Gras festivities in Galveston and Port Arthur. It has also, of course, become the focus of its own marathon concert productions such as the Original Zydeco Jamm Festival in Crosby and the Creole Heritage Zydeco and Crawfish Jambalaya in downtown Houston. Occasionally, there are even special four-day "Zydeco

Cruise" tours from the Port of Galveston, promoted by the Carnival line. On a less grandiose scale, the music is often featured at trail rides, wedding receptions, and corporate parties. But beyond special occasions such as these, restaurants provide one of the most ubiquitous and popular showcases for much of Texas zydeco today.

In a 1999 interview, Wilfred Chevis, a veteran bandleader on the Houston scene for over thirty years, offers his perspective on the evolution of this phenomenon:

Zydeco wasn't very popular in Texas in '69, you know. Very few places, outside the black community, were playing it then. You had, like, the Continental Ballroom Lounge, a place in South Park, The Silver Slipper, and the Catholic halls. That was about it, doing zydeco then. And that went on for maybe ten years, and then the restaurants started doing zydeco here. Don's Seafood and a place called Gaido's was the two first places that started with the zydeco in the restaurants, and then it just spread from then on. All the Cajun seafood restaurants [are] doing zydeco now, all the Pappadeaux, Atchafalaya's, Landry's—all of them doing zydeco now.

Indeed, certain large restaurant chains, such as the Houston-based Pappadeaux Seafood Kitchen, have cultivated much casual appreciation of zydeco among people who initially sought only culinary delights.

While the most prominent touring and recording bands generally do not perform in dining establishments, for many of the other groups, such gigs are often a crucial source of steady income and exposure. In fact, over recent decades some Texas-based Creole blues-guitar players—such as Ashton Savoy and Joe James—have elected to work as supporting players in zydeco combos (as opposed to continuing to front their own blues bands) simply because the job opportunities are more frequent and the pay is better—primarily because of the many restaurants that hire zydeco players to perform. As Savoy once told me, "Those restaurant jobs are all right . . . because you get done early, you always get paid, and they bring you back next week." That principle is echoed by Chevis, who says, "Working in the restaurants isn't glamorous or anything, but it helps pay the bills, you know. And the people are nice. Some of them have never really listened to zydeco before, and they like it when they hear it in the restaurant."

Across southeast Texas there are certain zydeco musicians who seem to have settled almost exclusively into the restaurant niche. Joseph Gillum (b. 1959), bandleader of Zydeco Joseph and the H-Town Players, is one such example. Because he has a full-time career as a research technician for the Halliburton Corporation, Gillum performs mainly only on weekends, and then mostly at the Pappadeaux Seafood Kitchen located in the popular waterfront district in Kemah (a coastal community on upper Galveston Bay, southeast of Houston). In fact, this Houston native credits Wilbert Thibodeaux with helping him get over his initial

Joe James, The Silver Slipper, Houston, Texas, 1997.

Zydeco Joseph (Joseph Gillum), Houston, Texas, 2004.

Big Red (Josef Arline), Pappadeaux Seafood Kitchen, Beaumont, Texas, 2004.

stage fright, back when he first started performing in public in the 1990s, by letting him in sit in on a restaurant gig. "Thibodeaux was playing at a restaurant, and me and Ra-Ra [Robert Carter] went there," he recalls. "And I had brought my accordion, and I guess he knew that I was just starting off. So he told me, 'Just stand right there on the side.' He say, 'Just play with me.' . . . So I actually got my start playing zydeco in a restaurant."

In the Beaumont area, Billy Poullard, one of the more experienced and traditional bandleaders in the region, often appears with his Zydeco Combo at down-home eateries such as the Pine Tree Lodge or Fat Mac's Bar-B-Q. Meanwhile, at the sprawling Pappadeaux Seafood Kitchen on the west side of the city, relative newcomer Josef Arline (b. 1970, also known as "Big Red") regularly performs with his group, Big Red and the Zydeco Playmakers.

A resident of Hillister, a small town about fifty miles north of Beaumont, Arline says, "I'm a Texas boy, but I have lineage from Louisiana." Like Joseph Gillum, he took up the accordion in his adulthood, but Arline has been singing in church or in various bands for much of his life. Using button accordions built by Port Arthur native Jude Moreau, Arline draws from his background in reggae, soul, and rock to flavor his presentation of zydeco, and his diversity of stylistic references surely appeals to the Pappadeaux customer base.

In metropolitan Houston alone there are currently ten Pappadeaux restaurants (any of which might feature live zydeco music on a given weekend), as well as other chains, such as Boudreaux's Cajun Kitchen and Landry's Seafood House, that often book zydeco bands. And so do various independent restaurants such as Cosmos Café, Crawdaddy's Bayou Grill, Creole Shack Café, and Drexler's World Famous BBQ and Grill. In many cases, and especially at the larger establishments, the live music is a secondary complement to the food and drink—not usually the primary draw for the majority of patrons.

But two unusual and spacious Houston restaurants stand out as exceptions to that pattern of business. Though they both are known for selling good food at reasonable prices, they have also evolved into special gathering places with long-standing music traditions. In short, at certain times each week, the free presentation of live zydeco (as well as the dancing that naturally accompanies it) takes priority over the sale or consumption of edibles, and hundreds of people show up to participate in the proceedings.

Founded, owned, and operated since 1979 by Les "Pe-Te" Johnson, Pe-Te's Cajun Barbeque House was—until its closing in 2005—one of the most well-known venues in all of southeast Texas for regular Saturday-afternoon dancing to zydeco or Cajun music. Created on the site of an old gas station located southeast of Houston, across Galveston Road from the Ellington Field air base, this rustic establishment featured a cafeteria-style kitchen up front and a large dance hall adjoining in the rear. The total floor area measured about 7,000 square feet, and for most of the 1980s, '90s, and halfway into the first decade of the twenty-first century, it was packed every Saturday afternoon with dancers and fans of the music.

OPPOSITE PAGE: *Lester "Pe-Te" Johnson, Pe-Te's Cajun Barbeque House, Houston, Texas, 2004.*

Zydeco dancers (with members of the band Bourbon Street),
Pe-Te's Cajun Barbeque House, Houston, Texas, 2004.

Paul "Cowboy" Citizen, Pe-Te's Cajun Barbeque House, Houston, Texas, 2003.

Every Saturday morning Johnson (a native of Eunice, Louisiana, who moved to Texas in 1960) also hosts a three-hour KPFT radio program called *Pe-Te's Cajun Bandstand*. Thus, he easily maintained an electronic grapevine of sorts for providing dance updates concerning which band had been booked to play at his restaurant, the hours (typically two to six p.m.), and any special events (such as the birthday of one of the regular patrons) to be celebrated that afternoon. Though Johnson is Cajun, most often the live music at his club was performed by black Creoles playing zydeco (and that style continues to be prominently featured on *Pe-Te's Cajun Bandstand* each week).

The diverse clientele at Pe-Te's traditionally included large numbers of immigrant Cajuns and Creoles along with their descendants, plus a racially and generationally mixed cross section of urban and suburban Houstonians—including many workers from the nearby headquarters of the National Aeronautics and Space Administration. In fact, Pe-Te's was so popular with NASA personnel that an entire wall section was covered with autographed publicity photos and posters of astronauts who had dined or danced there. Moreover, as Carol Rust points out in a *Houston Press* article, "Several of NASA's finest have played tapes of Lester 'Pe-Te' Johnson's Saturday-morning Cajun radio program on KPFT while in outer space," and the restaurant recently "was among the first stops for several Russian astronauts after an extended, Spartan stay aboard the space station Mir."

Throughout the week and even on dance days, folks devoured plenty of Pe-Te's locally famous brisket barbeque, jambalaya, gumbo, and such, but the food was not the primary motivation for squeezing into the memorabilia-covered confines when a band was playing. As an unsigned article from the Night and Day archives of the *Houston Press* puts it, "It's on Saturday afternoons . . . that the place really comes to life" as "dancers of every race and age fill the large darkened dance floor and waltz, two-step and boogaloo to their hearts' content."

However, to the dismay of thousands of area fans of the Saturday-afternoon dances, that tradition abruptly ended in March 2005. Having officially retired from the proprietorship in 2004 and transferred operation of Pe-Te's Cajun Barbeque House to his forty-two-year-old son Johnnie, Johnson regretted the actions, but could not dissuade his son from, first, eliminating the weekly dances and then closing the restaurant. Thus, after a run of almost twenty-four years, the Saturday dance events—good-natured gatherings at which countless Houstonians and their visitors celebrated zydeco and Cajun music—have now ceased, presumably forever.

Nevertheless, at another large, equally casual, and family-friendly dining establishment, this one in central Houston, regularly scheduled zydeco dances continue to draw huge crowds every Friday night (and sometimes for specially scheduled events on Saturdays too). In fact, on Friday evenings from six to ten, Jax Grill on Shepherd Street is arguably the best zydeco venue in the entire city, maybe the state.

Zydeco dancers, Jax Grill, Houston, Texas, 2004.

Weasel (Ronald W. Lewis Jr.), Houston, Texas, 2004.

Cedric Powell, Jax Grill, Houston, Texas, 2004.

Located slightly north and west of downtown, and just a few blocks south of Interstate 10 between Durham and Shepherd Streets, Jax consistently draws overflow crowds of hundreds of patrons who come to listen and dance to live zydeco. The participants represent all age ranges and various races (though African Americans tend to predominate). The stage space along the east wall of the main room mainly features top-notch Houston bands: from the better-known groups (led by figures such as Step Rideau, Leroy Thomas, Brian Jack, or Wilfred Chevis, to name only a few) to up-and-coming bands (such as Weasel and the Zydeco Clan, Lil' Porter and the Zydeco Hustlers, J. D. and the Zydeco Lawbreakers, or the group known simply as the Zydeco Players, led by Cedric Powell, b. 1984). Jax provides a large, comfortable, after-work site that each Friday highlights the deep pool of zydeco talent in the area (sometimes including southwest Louisiana bands led by the likes of Roy Carrier, Chris Ardoin, and others). At the same time it nurtures much local appreciation of the music form—as well as the vigorous dancing that it can incite.

Another element of the popular appeal is that Jax, like Pe-Te's (and unlike most clubs or church dances), has never instituted a cover charge for attending the zydeco events. As Bon Ton Mickey Guillory once shouted into my ear while gently elbowing his way through the crowd, "If it's free, the dancers *all* come out."

This self-service restaurant's interior is roomy, but on Friday nights is usually so crowded that it can indeed be a challenge to navigate smoothly through the joyful throng. In addition to the people claiming every chair and table, scores more stand around the rectangular-shaped island bar in the center of the room, as well as along the walls and in the aisles. On the west wall to the rear is the kitchen, where numerous customers cluster in line at the counter to place their food orders or to pay for the bottled drinks they have pulled from the ice-packed reach-in cooler. In the most distant corners on the north side of the restaurant, the floor space is cluttered here and there with sacks of corn, cases of beer, and other staples. But the closer one gets to the source of the live music, the more intensely congested the hardwood floor becomes. Anyone who ventures to squeeze beyond the bar area and toward the bandstand is almost immediately caught up in a current of dance moves that proliferate despite the limited maneuverability.

Much of that mass of bouncing bodies conveniently spills through the large openings afforded by two raised garage-style doors along the southern boundary of the room. That convertible wall opens onto an enormous attached wooden deck, completely covered by a sloping tin roof and crammed with additional tables and chairs. During the Friday-evening dances, that open-air deck holds almost as many people as the primary space indoors. Whether inside or out, many of the folks who gather each week for live music at Jax seem to embrace a collective spirit of joie de vivre. Though they appear to come from every

Onlookers and zydeco dancers, Jax Grill, Houston, Texas, 2004.

Zydeco dancers (Gay Ann Gustafson and Willie Bushnell), Jax Grill, Houston, Texas, 2004.

stratum of society, and though some are Creoles who have always known zydeco and others are recent converts, a sense of family reunion pervades each event.

And in some cases, the family reunion is literal. For example, one musician who has regularly performed at Jax since relocating to Houston is the California-born accordion sensation Andre Thierry (b. 1979), leader of the band Zydeco Magic. At his July 2004 appearance at Jax, Thierry's band included his cousin Steve Nash, who played the rubboard while his own young son, Timothy, toddled in front of the stage inaudibly pumping a toy accordion. Meanwhile, that precocious child's proud grandmother (Nash's mother and Thierry's aunt), danced happily a few feet away, shouting her fervent encouragement to each one of her relatives on the bandstand.

Thierry's invigorating presence on the Houston zydeco scene during the early twenty-first century is due in part to Nash's influence. For over a year, the longtime Houstonian opened his home to Thierry so that the richly talented young musician could more readily work the venues of the zydeco corridor from a southeast Texas base. As he did so, Thierry earned a well-deserved reputation as one of the most exciting and versatile of the neotraditionalists from west of Louisiana. As Wilfred Chevis says about him, "He's a young guy, but he's playing like Clifton Chenier, man. Oh yeah, he plays on the piano key, and he plays the button accordion too. . . . And he can sing in French. . . . He is good!"

Thierry's uncanny grasp of the music began early. Though born in Richmond, California, he descends from Creoles originally from the area near Eunice, Louisiana—including his grandmother, the matron of the West Coast church-dance phenomenon, Lena Pitre. As the soft-spoken Thierry tells it, "My grandmother used to throw dances in California. She's been throwing dances like that since the '60s, in Richmond, zydeco dances. Clifton even did a live album there, on the Arhoolie label." That 1971 Clifton Chenier album, *Live at St. Mark's*, was one of the first productions to call national attention to the French Creole community that had put down roots in the Bay Area in the decades following World War II. Thus, born into one of the major zydeco families of the region (the same area where Chenier's longtime record label, Arhoolie, is based), Thierry grew up in the occasional presence of the king. "They say Clifton used to hold me in his lap, when I was a child," he says, before reeling off a list of the most famous names in the recent history of zydeco and adding casually, "I knew all of them."

To date, Thierry's remarkable dexterity on any type of accordion and his supple, maturing singing voice have been documented mainly on two Andre Thierry and Zydeco Magic CDs—the 2000 debut *It's About Time!* (no label), and the 2004 release called *A Whole Lotta Something* (La Louisianne Records). Additionally, Thierry's instrumental skills grace one of the tracks on the Ann Savoy celebrity tribute production called *Creole Bred* (2004, Vanguard Records); he contributes accordion to accompany Michelle Shocked's singing on the zydeco

classic "Paper in My Shoe." Given all this, zydeco observers nationwide expect to hear much more from this young man in the new century.

Though he has moved back and forth between Houston and Richmond in recent years, Thierry remains (especially since the death of Danny Poullard) one of the best known of the zydeco players associated with California. Of his reasons for living in Houston at least part-time since 2002, he says, "It was a combination of factors. But mainly I just wanted more chances to play." After explaining that he devotes himself full-time to making music, he adds, "And there are lots of gigs to be had in this area. . . . Right now southeast Texas is bigger than the Louisiana scene." Whatever the case, many of the folks at Jax seem now to consider Andre Thierry one of their own. Along with many of his Houston-based relatives, they look forward to his always-well-received appearances there (and at various other venues around the metropolitan area).

However, whether Thierry is the featured talent or not, the Jax faithful will surely congregate in large numbers at the appointed time to hear the music, dance, drink, eat, and socialize heartily. For many of them, it is an end-of-the-week ritual that has fostered much goodwill and a special sense of belonging, a feeling of membership in a unique zydeco community. And as the diversity of those who gather at Jax each Friday demonstrates, it is a bond that transcends many of the categories that so often divide people (such as age, race, and class). The fact that Jax is a casual public restaurant open to anyone who wants to participate in the dances, free of charge, imbues the zydeco dances there with the atmosphere of a multicultural house party. And in the nation's fourth-largest city at the start of the twenty-first century, that is a rare and precious phenomenon—a presence that stokes the vitality of Texas zydeco today.

WITHOUT THE DISTINCTIVE CULTURAL LEGACY of black Creoles from southwest Louisiana, this music called zydeco would not exist. As this book has endeavored to show, those people and their descendants—wherever they might have resided, in state or out—have been the primary inheritors and key translators of this rich musical tradition. But this music as we know it today is also the product of movement and change. Its development beyond its rural folk origins has depended in large part on the steady interchange of social and musical influences along the complete range of the Louisiana-Texas zydeco corridor. Moreover, the fertile back-and-forth flow of people, talent, tradition, and innovation continues today.

Whether a twenty-first-century Creole musician happens to live in Louisiana or Texas, his or her primary identity likely has less to do with a mailing address than with personal upbringing and values. "The people that have the same fundamentals, same beliefs, same ideals, same everything . . . they don't just drop it on the other side of the bridge," says Ed

OPPOSITE PAGE: *Andre Thierry, Houston, Texas, 2004.*

Cedric Powell and dancers, Jax Grill, Houston, Texas, 2004.

Poullard. "They bring it over here, and they try to influence their family with the same ideals, the same beliefs that they had, coming up. There is no difference. . . . It did not just stay in the state where it began."

Over the past century or more, because so many of those southwest Louisiana folks have chosen to cross that bridge and settle in Texas, the sociocultural history of both states has been significantly enriched. As Port Arthur native C. J. Chenier puts it, "From Houston all the way to Lafayette, man, is just one big zydeco family." Both the eastern and the western branches of that lineage have contributed in crucial ways to defining the whole. As such, it has been—and likely will continue to be—a mutually beneficial kinship.

Since 2004, for instance, a black Creole craftsman has been making history by building his own brand of accordion. Though his people have skillfully played the instrument for generations, none among them ever actually *made* one till now. Although there has long been a tradition of Cajun accordion-makers in the region, this development represents a new and significant phase in the social history of *la musique française* on the upper Gulf Coast. And this chapter, like certain other key moments in that history, is being scripted west of the lower Sabine, in southeast Texas.

From his home shop in Beaumont, Ed Poullard takes great pride in what he has recently been learning and laboring to produce (with his own hands, tools, machinery, and musical instincts): a traditional diatonic squeezebox bearing the family name—the Poullard Accordion. Showing off one of his early prototypes, he points to the trademark and softly says, "It's got my name on it. I am the first. . . . There's never been a Creole guy who built accordions before. . . . Several have been able to tune them, or repair them, but nobody who is a Creole has ever built them before."

Reflecting on his nascent achievement, Poullard adds, "Everybody that knows me always knew I did woodwork; they just didn't figure me for anything like this." His recent decision to devote himself to such an undertaking came about, like his music, because of the influence of family, starting with his older brother. "Danny had been trying to get me to build accordions for twenty-five years. He kept telling me, 'You can do it,'" he says. But following some tentative inquiries with established Cajun accordion builders in Louisiana, the younger Poullard gave up the idea—believing it was too challenging and time-consuming for him to pursue.

However, many years later, when his own daughter started learning to play the accordion, Poullard asserts, "It kind of blew me away." Inspired by her fervor, he soon approached his Cajun friend and master accordion-builder, the Port Arthur–based Jude Moreau, to commission him to custom-build one for his daughter. "Jude said, 'No, I am not going to build her one. The only way I am going to build one is if you help me,'" he relates. "So he sucker-punched me into that [laughs], and we built one together."

Ed Poullard at home (in his accordion-building shop), Beaumont, Texas, 2004.

Encouraged by that experience with Moreau and the satisfaction of providing his daughter with the gift of a traditional accordion created with his own hands, Poullard eventually made a new commitment—one that has been supported in part by a grant from Texas Folklife Resources. Though he maintains his full-time job in local industry and continues to perform nationwide as a musician, he now also makes time to master the craft of accordion building.

"I've been doing this totally unassisted," he says. "But when I need help, I get on the phone and say, 'Hey, I'm stuck.' And Jude's only fifteen minutes away." Since 2004 Poullard has personally manufactured several of the instruments, receiving "some pretty good reviews from some of the other accordion builders" along the way. In addition to the mentorship provided by Moreau, Poullard credits a large part of his success to his musicians' intuition:

Somebody that's been playing accordion for years knows what an accordion is supposed to feel like—the action, the keyboard, the feel of it. I've got a slight advantage because I already play. I've been playing for years. I know what I want those things to feel like in my hands. I know what they want to sound like. And I'm not going to stop until I achieve it.

Like his devotion to preserving the old-style music he learned from his father, Poullard sees this undertaking as a personal mission for the sake of a culture he loves. "This is a whole new experience for me," he says, "but it's for the Creole people too. . . . It's a start, a new tradition."

Ultimately, in some respects the story of the Poullard Accordion parallels that of Texas zydeco at large. For both encompass the necessary balancing of a strong connection to the ancestral past with a self-reliant willingness to engage with change and redefine the future.

Both remind us too that a living culture, like a dance, is never really static, but always on the move.

NEXT PAGE: *Zydeco dancers, C. C.'s Hideout, Houston, Texas, 2004.*

Appendix: Catalogue of Interviews

Adams, James B., Jr. Interview by author. Tape recording. Houston, TX, January 15, 2005.
———. E-mail interviews by author. Responses received March 16, 2005; March 28, 2005.
Anderson, Guy Michael. Interview by author and James Fraher. Tape recording. Humble, TX, August 12, 2004.
Ardoin, Chris. Interview by author. Tape recording. Crosby, TX, March 13, 2004.
Arline, Josef ("Big Red"). Interview by author and James Fraher. Tape recording. Beaumont, TX, November 20, 2004.
Ballou, Cedric. Interview by author. Tape recording. Crosby, TX, March 13, 2004.
Ballou, Cedryl. Interview by author. Tape recording. Crosby, TX, March 13, 2004.
Ballou, Classie. Interview by author. Tape recording. Crosby, TX, March 13, 2004.
Batiste, Jerome. Interviews by author. Notes. Beaumont, TX, June 21, 2003; Crosby, TX, March 13, 2004.
———. Interview by author and James Fraher. Tape recording. Houston, TX, July 24, 2004.
Bradley, Cedric. Interview by author. Tape recording. Houston, TX, August 29, 1999.
Broussard, Dalton. Interview by author and James Fraher. Tape recording. Houston, TX, June 3, 2005.
Broussard, John ("Tee Bruce"). Interview by author. Notes. LaBelle, TX, July 24, 2004.
Carter, Arthur ("T-Put"). Interview by author. Tape recording. Houston, TX, June 17, 2004.
Carter, Robert ("Ra-Ra"). Interview by author. Notes. Houston, TX, July 25, 2004.
———. Interview by author. Tape recording. Houston, TX, August 13, 2004.
Charles, Joseph ("Tee June"). Interview by author. Tape recording. Houston, TX, July 25, 2004.
Charles, Montanya ("Me-Me"). Interview by author. Tape recording. Houston, TX, August 13, 2004.
Chavis, Raymond. Interview by author. Tape recording. Houston, TX, March 16, 2004.
———. Telephone interview by author. Notes. March 11, 2005.
Chenier, C. J. Interview by author and James Fraher. Tape recording. Houston, TX, March 18, 2004.
Chenier, Walter. Interview by author. Tape recording. Houston, TX, June 16, 2004.
Chevis, Martin. Interview by author and James Fraher. Tape recording. Houston, TX, March 16, 2004.
Chevis, Wilfred. Telephone interviews by author. Tape Recording. January 15, 1998; August 18, 1999.
———. Interviews by author and James Fraher. Tape recording. Houston, TX, December 15, 2003; March 16, 2004.
Cometta, Jon. Interview by author. Notes. Beaumont, TX, June 21, 2003.
Cormier, Curley. Interview (presumed to be by Robert Damora). Tape recording; transcribed by author. Houston, TX, June 5, 1993. From the Big Easy archives, used by permission.
———. Interview by author and James Fraher. Tape recording. Houston, TX, January 8, 1998.
Davis, Willie. Interview by author and James Fraher. Tape recording. Houston, TX, November 19, 2004.
Delasbour, Steve. Telephone interview by author. Tape recording. February 28, 2000.
———. Interviews by author. Notes. Beaumont, TX, June 21, 2003; Crosby, TX, March 13, 2004.
Donatto, L. C. (Alcide). Interview by author. Notes. Galveston, TX, January 8, 2000.
Donatto, L. C. (Alcide), Jr. Interview by author and James Fraher. Tape recording. Houston, TX, July 25, 2004.
Doucet, Joseph ("Little Joe"). Interviews by author. Tape recording. Houston, TX, November 19, 2004; January 27, 2005.

Francois, L. J. Interview by author. Notes. Houston, TX, July 11, 2004.

Gabbanelli, Mike. Interview by author and James Fraher. Tape recording. Houston, TX, March 17, 2004.

Gallien, Clarence, Jr. Interview (presumed to be by Robert Damora). Tape recording; transcribed by author. Houston, TX, 1993. From the Big Easy archives, used by permission.

Gillum, Joseph ("Zydeco Joseph"). Interview by author and James Fraher. Tape recording. Houston, TX, August 13, 2004.

Glenn, Donald ("Jabo"). Interviews by author. Tape recording. Houston, TX, July 9, 2004; July 25, 2004.

Gonzalez, Edward. Interview by author and James Fraher. Tape recording. Houston, TX, March 18, 2004.

Goodwin, Emmit. Interview by author. Notes. Houston, TX, March 13, 2004.

Grant, (John) Paul (J. Paul Jr.). Interview by author. Notes. Crosby, TX, March 13, 2004.

Harris, Stephen. Interview by author. Tape recording. Houston, TX, January 7, 1998.

Hawkins, Jeremy. Interview by author. Notes. Beaumont, TX, August 15, 2004.

Hunter, Jerri. Interview by author and James Fraher. Tape recording. Barrett, TX, August 14, 2004.

Jack, Brian. Interview by author. Notes. Crosby, TX, March 13, 2004.

———. Telephone interview by author. Tape recording. July 8, 2004.

Jackson, Tiffany. Interview by author. Notes. Houston, TX, July 31, 2005.

James, Joe. Interview by author and James Fraher. Tape recording. Houston, TX, April 20, 1997.

Jasper, Pat. E-mail interview by author. Response received February 21, 2005.

Jenkins, Dora. Interview by author and James Fraher. Tape recording. Houston, TX, August 13, 2004.

Johnson, Lester Peter ("Pe-Te"). Interview by author. Tape recording. Houston, TX, August 14, 2004.

Jolivette, Jean-Paul. Interview by author. Tape recording. Houston, TX, July 11, 2004.

Joseph, Gerald Wayne. Interview by Ray Gomez. Videotape recording; transcribed by Carl Lindahl. Galena Park, TX, February 13, 1998. From the University of Houston Folklore Archive, used by permission.

Ledet, C. J. Interview by author. Notes. Houston, TX, November 7, 2004.

Ledet, Corey ("Lil' Pop"). Interview by author. Tape recording. Houston, TX, January 15, 2005.

———. Telephone interview by author. Notes. March 25, 2005.

Ludd, Robert, Jr. ("Beefcake"). Interview by author. Tape recording. Houston, TX, July 25, 2004.

Manuel, Peter. Interview by author and James Fraher. Notes. Port Arthur, TX, June 22, 2003.

Manuel, Rita. Interview by author and James Fraher. Notes. Port Arthur, TX, June 22, 2003.

Mayhon, John. Interview by author. Tape recording. Houston, TX, August 24, 2004.

McClendon, Doris. Interview (presumed to be by Robert Damora). Tape recording; transcribed by author. Houston, TX, 1993. From the Big Easy archives, used by permission.

———. Interview by author. Tape recording. Houston, TX, September 29, 1996.

McCormick, Mack. Interview by author. Notes. Houston, TX, May 2, 2002.

———. Interview by author and James Fraher. Tape recording. Houston, TX, November 16, 2003.

———. Interviews by author. Tape recording. Houston, TX, December 22, 2003; July 21, 2004.

McLendon, Tom. Telephone interview by author. Tape recording. June 24, 2002.

Miller, Norma. Interview by author. Notes. LaBelle, TX, July 24, 2004.

Mitchell, Lonnie. Interview (presumed to be by Robert Damora). Tape recording; transcribed by author. Houston, TX, 1993. From the Big Easy archives, used by permission.

Murphy, Robert. Interviews by author and James Fraher. Tape recording. Houston, TX, October 3, 1997; July 25, 2004.

Nash, Steve. Interview by author and James Fraher. Tape recording. Houston, TX, March 19, 2004.

Norman, Joe. Interview by author. Notes. Houston, TX, July 24, 2004.

———. Interview by author. Tape recording. Houston, TX, August 14, 2004.

Papillion, Chester. Interview by author. Tape recording. Houston, TX, June 17, 2004.

Potter, Tom. Telephone interviews by author. Tape recording. July 21, 1999, July 10, 2002. Notes. March 16, 2005.

Poullard, Billy. Interviews by author. Notes. LaBelle, TX, July 24, 2004; Beaumont, TX, August 15, 2004.

———. Telephone interview by author. Notes. August 18, 2005.

Poullard, Ed. Telephone interview by author. Notes. August 11, 2004.

———. Interview by author and James Fraher. Tape recording. Beaumont, TX, November 20, 2004.

Powell, Cedric. Interview by author. Tape recording. Houston, TX, June 16, 2004.

Rideau, Gene. Interview by author. Notes. Houston, TX, March 12, 2004.

———. Interview by author. Tape recording. Crosby, TX, March 13, 2004.

Rideau, Step. Telephone interview by author. Tape recording. September 28, 1999.

———. Interview by author. Tape recording. Beaumont, TX, June 21, 2003.

Robertson, Sherman. Interview by author and James Fraher. Tape recording. Houston, TX, April 17, 1997.

———. Interviews by author. Tape recording. Houston, TX, August 22, 1997; June 10, 1998; January 19, 2000.

———. Telephone interview by author. Tape recording. September 21, 1998.

Rossyion, Joseph, Jr. Interview by author. Tape recording. Houston, TX, January 15, 2005.

Rubit, Dan. Telephone interview by author. Notes. July 22, 2004.

———. Interview by author. Tape recording. Missouri City, TX, July 25, 2004.

St. Julien, Robert Peter. Telephone interview by author. Notes. July 23, 2004.

Sanchez, Otha. Telephone interview by author. Notes. June 6, 2005.

Savoy, Ashton. Interviews by author. Tape recording. Houston, TX, November 11, 1995; August 22, 2004.

———. Telephone interview by author. Tape recording. January 14, 1998.

Stoot, Pierre. Interview by author. Tape recording. Houston, TX, August 14, 2004.

Stout, Willie. Interview (presumed to be by Robert Damora). Tape recording; transcribed by author. Houston, TX, 1993. From the Big Easy archives, used by permission.

Strachwitz, Chris. Interviews by author. Tape recording. Jonesboro, AR, April 16, 1998; April 17, 1998.

———. Interview by author. Notes. Houston, TX, October 20, 2004.

———. Telephone interview by author. Notes. February 23, 2005.

Terry, Brian. Telephone interviews by author. Tape Recording. September 9, 1999; July 8, 2004.

———. Interview by author. Notes. Beaumont, TX, June 21, 2003.

Thibodeaux, Wilbert. Interview (presumed to be by Robert Damora). Tape recording; transcribed by author. Houston, TX, 1993. From the Big Easy archives, used by permission.

———. Telephone interview by author. Notes. November 14, 2003.

Thierry, Andre. Interview by author and James Fraher. Tape recording. Houston, TX, March 19, 2004.

Thomas, Leo. Interview by author and James Fraher. Notes. Crosby, TX, March 13, 2004.

Thomas, Leroy. Interviews by author. Notes. Beaumont, TX, June 21, 2003; Crosby, TX, March 13, 2004.

Thomas, Mary. Interview by author. Tape recording. Houston, TX, September 13, 1998.

———. Telephone interview by author. Tape recording. July 8, 2004.

Toups, Wayne. Telephone interview by author. Tape recording. July 8, 2004.

Vowell, Mike ("Vee"). Telephone interview by author. Notes. March 13, 2005.

Weatherall, Diane ("Lady D"). Telephone interview by author. Notes. July 30, 2001.

———. Interview by author. Notes. Houston, TX, December 12, 2003.

———. Interview by author. Tape recording. Houston, TX, July 7, 2004.

Wills, Thomas. Interview by author and James Fraher. Tape recording. Houston, TX, July 25, 2004.

Wilson, Charles ("Lil' Reb"). Interview by author. Notes. Houston, TX, July 25, 2004.

———. Interview by author and James Fraher. Tape recording. Barrett, TX, August 14, 2004.

York, Rita. Interview by author and James Fraher. Tape recording. Houston, TX, August 13, 2004.

York, Willie T. Interview by author and James Fraher. Tape recording. Houston, TX, August 13, 2004.

Young, Frank, Jr. ("Nooney"). Interview by author. Tape recording. Houston, TX, August 4, 2004.

BIBLIOGRAPHY

Ancelet, Barry Jean. *Cajun and Creole Music Makers*. Jackson: Univ. Press of Mississippi, 1999.

———. "Cajuns and Creoles." In *Encyclopedia of Southern Culture*, Vol. 2, ed. Charles Reagan Wilson and William Ferris, 38–41. New York: Anchor Books, 1991.

———. Introduction to *Cajun Music and Zydeco*, ix–xxi. Baton Rouge: Louisiana State Univ. Press, 1992.

———. "Zydeco/Zarico: The Term and the Tradition." In *Creoles of Color of the Gulf South*, ed. James H. Dormon, 126–143. Knoxville: Univ. of Tennessee Press, 1996.

Beeth, Howard, and Cary D. Wintz, eds. *Black Dixie: Afro-Texan History and Culture in Houston*. College Station: Texas A&M Univ. Press, 1992.

Brasseaux, Carl A., Keith P. Fontenot, and Claude F. Oubre. *Creoles of Color in the Bayou Country*. Jackson: Univ. Press of Mississippi, 1994.

Bridges, Laraine. "Breaux Bridge Crawfish Festival Report." *Cajun Life and Times* 2004, http://www.cajunlifeandtimes.com/breaux_bridge_crawfish_festival_2004.htm (accessed October 17, 2005).

Clark, Michael D. "Lil' Brian Terry Gets His Z-funk On." *Houston Chronicle*, August 12, 2001, Preview sec.

"Corey 'Lil Pop' Ledet and His Zydeco Band." *Contemporary Cajun, Creole, and Zydeco Musicians*. http://www.lsue.edu/acadgate/music/coreyledet.htm (accessed October 17, 2005).

Damora, Robert. "Houston Zydeco: From Churches to Clubs." *Living Blues* 116 (Aug. 1994): 44–47.

"Donatto: Mr. Alcide Donatto SR." Obituary. *Houston Chronicle*, July 12, 2002, sec. A.

Dormon, James H. "Ethnicity and Identity: Creoles of Color in Twentieth-Century South Louisiana." In *Creoles of Color of the Gulf South*, ed. James H. Dormon, 166–179. Knoxville: Univ. of Tennessee Press, 1996.

———. Preface to *Creoles of Color of the Gulf South*, ix–xv.

Douglass, Frederick. *Life and Times of Frederick Douglass*. Hartford, Conn.: Park, 1881; rev. ed., Boston: DeWolfe, Fiske, 1892; reprint, New York: Macmillan, 1962.

Evans, Roxanne J. "Black Catholics." In *The New Handbook of Texas*, 1:561–562. Austin: Texas State Historical Association, 1996. Also available at http://www.tsha.utexas.edu/handbook/online/articles/view/BB/icb3.html (accessed October 17, 2005).

Fox, Ted. Liner notes to *Funky Nation*. Tomorrow Recordings (TMR 70003–2), 2000.

———. Liner notes to *On a Night Like This*. Island Records (90622–1), 1987.

Fuselier, Herman. "Zydeco Is Not Cajun Music." http://www.zydecoevents.com/History2.html (accessed October 17, 2005).

"Gabbanelli: Gianfranco 'John' Gabbanelli." Obituary. *Houston Chronicle*, December 19, 2003, sec. A.

Govenar, Alan. *Meeting the Blues: The Rise of the Texas Sound*. Dallas: Taylor, 1988.

Graves, John. *Texas Rivers*. Austin: Univ. of Texas Press, 2002.

Hall, Gwendolyn Midlo. *Africans in Colonial Louisiana*. Baton Rouge: Louisiana State Univ. Press, 1992.

Harris, Sheldon. *Blues Who's Who*. New Rochelle, N.Y.: Arlington House, 1979.

Hartman, Gary. "French Music." In *The Handbook of Texas Music*, ed. Roy R. Barkley, Douglas E. Barnett, Cathy Brigham, Gary Hartman, Casey Monahan, Dave Oliphant, and George B. Ward, 110–112. Austin: Texas State Historical Association, 2003.

Hatano, Jiro. "Goldman Thibodeaux and Creole Music." *Southwest Louisiana Express*. http://www.ucs.Louisiana.edu/~yxs8143/goldman.htm (accessed October 17, 2005).

Howard, Aaron. Review of *Tribute to Clif* by Leon Sam and the Zydeco Dots. *Houston Press*, May 18–24, 2000. http://www.houstonpress.com/issues/2000-05-18/music/localrotation.html (accessed October 17, 2005).

———. "Zydeco Connection." *Houston Public News*, April 5, 1995.

Isaac, Paul E. "Beaumont, Texas." In *The New Handbook of Texas*, 1:447–448. Also available at http://www.tsha.utexas.edu/handbook/online/articles/view/BB/hdb2.html (accessed October 17, 2005).

Kaplan, David. "Houston's Creole Quarter." *Houston Post*, March 19, 1989, sec. F.

Kever, Jeannie. "Note of Sorrow: Late Accordion Maker Recalled as Master." *Houston Chronicle*, December 20, 2003, sec. A.

Key of Z Rubboards. http://www.keyofzrubboards.com (accessed October 17, 2005).

Kleiner, Diana J. "Barrett, Texas." In *The New Handbook of Texas*, 1:393. Also available at http://www.tsha.utexas.edu/handbook/online/articles/ BB/hgb3/html (accessed October 17, 2005).

———. "Fifth Ward, Houston." In *The New Handbook of Texas*, 2:996–997. Also available at http://www.tsha.utexas.edu/handbook/online/articles/FF/hpfhk.html (accessed October 17, 2005).

———. "Frenchtown, Texas." In *The New Handbook of Texas*, 2:1177. Also available at http://www.tsha.utexas.edu/handbook/online/articles/FF/hrfvg.html (accessed October 17, 2005).

———. "Liberty County." In *The New Handbook of Texas*, 4:188–190. Also available at http://www.tsha.utexas.edu/handbook/online/articles/LL/hcl8.html (accessed October 17, 2005).

Lichtenstein, Grace, and Laura Dankner. *Musical Gumbo: The Music of New Orleans*. New York: Norton, 1993.

Lindahl, Carl. "Accordions and Community: The Zydeco Tradition." A paper presented at the First international Accordion Festival, San Antonio, September 2001.

———. "What Is Texas Cajun Music?" In *The Accordion as King: Essays on Diverse Accordion Traditions*. Austin: Texas Folklife Resources, n.d.

Lucko, Paul M. "Choates, Harry H." In *The Handbook of Texas Music*, 49–50.

"A Map of New Spain" (1804). In *Contours of Discovery: Printed Maps Delineating the Texas and Southwestern Chapters in the Cartographic History of North America, 1513–1930*. Austin: Texas State Historical Association, 1981.

McComb, David G. "Houston, Texas." In *The Portable Handbook of Texas*, ed. Roy R. Barkley and Mark F. Odintz, 437–441. Austin: Texas State Historical Association, 2000.

Minton, John. "Creole Community and 'Mass' Communication: Houston Zydeco as a Mediated Tradition." *Journal of Folklore Research* 32, no. 1 (1995): 1–19.

———. "Houston Creoles and Zydeco: The Emergence of an African-American Urban Popular Style." *American Music* 14, no. 4 (Winter 1996): 480–526.

Mitchell, Rick. "Continental Ballroom Celebrating 50 Years." *Houston Chronicle*, November 3, 1994, sec. D.

———. "History Comes to Life at Fest." *Houston Chronicle*, July 31, 1986, Preview sec.

———. "King of Squeeze: Music Legends Celebrate the Accordion." *Houston Chronicle*, June 7, 1993, Houston sec.

———. "Persistence Pays Off for Lil' Brian." *Houston Chronicle*, April 13, 1995, sec. D.

———. "Pushing All the Right Buttons." *Houston Chronicle*, May 6, 1999, Preview sec.

———. Review of *The Kingdom of Zydeco*, directed by Robert Mugge. *Houston Chronicle*, December 16, 1994, sec. E.

———. "Zydeco: A Spicy Blend Made in Louisiana and Bottled in Texas." *Houston Chronicle*, February 23, 1992, Zest sec.

———. "Zydeco's Past, Future Fused in Chenier-Simien Rhythm Frenzy." *Houston Chronicle*, December 31, 1990, sec. D.

Ogilvie, Mary H. "Gallagher, Nicholas Aloysius." In *The New Handbook of Texas*, 3:49. Also available at http://www.tsha.utexas.edu/handbook/online/articles/GG/fga7.html (accessed October 17, 2005).

Olien, Roger M. "Oil and Gas Industry." In *The New Handbook of Texas*, 4:1119–1128. Also available at http://www.tsha.utexas.edu/handbook/online/articles/OO/doogz.html (accessed October 17, 2005).

"Pe-Te's Cajun BBQ House." *Houston Press*, Night and Day Archives, http://listings.houstonpress.com/gyrobase/Events/Results?location=oid%3A22021 (accessed January 14, 2005; listing now unavailable).

Phelps, Marie Lee. "Visit to Frenchtown." *Houston Post*, May 22, 1955.

Pittman, Nick. "Non-Native Son: It May Be Smaller than the State of Texas, but for Cedric Watson, Acadiana Is the Place to Be." *Times of Acadiana*, December 8, 2004, http://www.timesofacadiana.com/html/A3DB8F5D-7C65–41D3–9946–17DB91A42B31.shtml (accessed December 30, 2004; article now unavailable).

Racine, Marty. "Suddenly, the Accordion Is Everywhere." *Houston Chronicle*, June 17, 1990, Zest sec.

———. "Zydeco: Fans Call It 'Happy Music.'" *Houston Chronicle*, Feb. 5, 1989, Zest sec.

Rubinstein, Andrea D. "I Have Seen the Future of Zydeco: The Original Zydeco Jamm Festival, March 16–17, 2001, Crosby, TX." http://www.sfbayou.com/journal12.htm (accessed October 17, 2005).

———. "Notes from Acadiana—Early Spring 2004." http://www.sfbayou.com/b2b_0404_1.htm (accessed October 17, 2005).

Rust, Carol. "Continental Lounge Owner, Zydeco Promoter Dies After Stroke." *Houston Chronicle*, November 27, 1997, sec. D.

———. "End of a Cajun Era: Rustic Pe-Te's Closes after Decades of Keeping Gulf Coast Music Traditions Alive." *Houston Press*, March 17–23, 2005, 11–12.

———. "Frenchtown: Snatches of French, Whiff of Boudin, and the Joyous Zydeco Beat Still Define this Refuge of Houston's Creoles." *Houston Chronicle*, February 23, 1992, Lifestyle sec.

Ryan, Steven P., S.J. "Beaumont, Catholic Diocese of." In *The New Handbook of Texas*, 1:446–448. Also available at http://www.tsha.utexas.edu/handbook/online/articles/BB/icb1.html (accessed October 17, 2005).

Sandmel, Ben. *Zydeco!* Jackson: Univ. Press of Mississippi, 1999.

Savoy, Ann Allen. *Cajun Music: A Reflection of a People*, Vol. I. Eunice, La.: Bluebird Press, 1984.

Savoy, Mark. "Accordions in Louisiana." http://www.savoymusiccenter.com/ (under "Writings"; accessed October 17, 2005).

Simpson, David. "Dewey Balfa Cajun and Creole Heritage Weekend." www.lsue.edu/acadgate/Music2/balfaspo4/balfaweekendo4-2.htm (accessed October 17, 2005).

Snyder, Jared. "Amédé's Recordings." In the liner notes to *Amédé Ardoin: The Roots of Zydeco*. Arhoolie (CD 7007), 1995.

Spitzer, Nicholas R. "Zydeco." In *The Encyclopedia of Southern Culture*, Vol. 3, ed. Charles Reagan Wilson and William Ferris, 346–350. New York: Anchor Books, 1991.

Stewart, Richard. "Homemade Squeeze Boxes Hold Cajun to His Heritage." *Houston Chronicle*, February 6, 1994, sec. B.

Storey, John W. "Port Arthur, Texas." In *The New Handbook of Texas*, 5:271–272. Also available at http://www.tsha.utexas.edu/handbook/online/articles/PP/hdp5.html (accessed October 17, 2005).

Strachwitz, Chris, dir. *Clifton Chenier: The King of Zydeco*. Videocassette. Arhoolie (ARV 401), 1987.

———. Liner notes to *The Best of Clifton Chenier*. Arhoolie (CD 474), 2003.

———. Liner notes to *Lightning Hopkins: The Gold Star Sessions, Vol. 1*. Arhoolie (CD 330), 1990.

———. Liner notes to *SAM (Get Down)*. Arhoolie (CD 9044), 1979 and 2004.

———. Liner notes to *Zydeco: Volume One, the Early Years, 1949–62*. Arhoolie (CD 307), 1989.

Supplee, Joan E. "Criollo." In *The New Handbook of Texas*, 2:405–406. Also available at http://www.tsha.utexas.edu/handbook/online/articles/CC/pfc4.html (accessed October 17, 2005).

Theis, David. "Zydeco Blues." *Houston Press*, September 8–14, 1994, 6.

Thomas, Lorenzo. "From Gumbo to Grammys: The Development of Zydeco Music in Houston." In *Juneteenth Texas: Essays in African-American Folklore*, ed. Francis E. Abernethy, Patrick B. Mullen, and Alan B. Govenar, 139–150. Denton: Univ. of North Texas Press, 1996.

Tisserand, Michael. *The Kingdom of Zydeco*. New York: Arcade, 1998.

Walker, Phillip. "One Ear in Zydeco, One Ear in Texas Blues." Interview by John Anthony Brisbin. *Living Blues* 131 (Jan.–Feb. 1997): 50–61.

Wheat, John. "Lightnin' Hopkins: Blues Bard of the Third Ward." In *Juneteenth Texas: Essays in African-American Folklore*, ed. Francis E. Abernethy, Patrick B. Mullen, and Alan B. Govenar, 254–271. Denton: Univ. of North Texas Press, 1996.

Willging, Dan. "Louisiana's Prodigal Son: Creole Fiddling." *Dirty Linen* 117 (Apr.–May 2005): 44–48.

———. Review of *3 Years 2 Late* by Corey "Lil' Pop" Ledet. *Dirty Linen* 117 (Apr.–May 2005): 50.

Wood, Roger. "Black Creoles and the Evolution of Zydeco in Southeast Texas." In *The Roots of Texas Music*, ed. Lawrence Clayton and Joe W. Specht, 192–216. College Station: Texas A&M Univ. Press, 2003.

———. *Down in Houston: Bayou City Blues*. Austin: Univ. of Texas Press, 2003.

———. "Eldorado Ballroom." In *The Handbook of Texas Music*, 93.

———. "Gare-on-teed Phat: Lil' Brian Terry Drags Zydeco into the Hip-Hop Era by Mixing It with Rap." *Houston Press*, November 18–24, 1999, 98.

———. "Houston's Blues Teachers." *Living Blues* 140 (July–Aug. 1998): 40–45.

———. "H-Town Get Down: Crosby, Texas, Hosts Some of Zydeco's Finest." *Houston Press*, March 16–22, 2000, 87.

———. "Sherman Robertson: The In-Between Blues." *Living Blues*, 152 (July–Aug. 2000): 21–31.

———. "Southeast Texas: Hot House of Zydeco." *Journal of Texas Music History* 1, no. 2 (Fall 2001): 23–44.

———. "Zydeco." In *The Handbook of Texas Music*, 365–366.

———. "Zydeco Rap? Houston's Step Rideau Drags Creole Music into the '00s." *Houston Press*, October 14–20, 1999, 89.

———. "Zydeco's Birthplace." *Houston Press*, September 2–8, 1999, 79.

Wooster, Robert. "LaBelle, Texas." In *The New Handbook of Texas*, 3:1180. Also available at http://www.tsha.utexas.edu/handbook/online/articles/LL/hrl4.html (accessed October 17, 2005).

"'Zydeco King' Clifton Chenier Dies at Age 62." *Houston Chronicle*, December 14, 1987, Sec. 1.